VIRAGO
MODERN CLASSICS
503

Daphne du Maurier

DAPHNE DU MAURIER (1907–89) was born in London, the daughter of the famous actor-manager Sir Gerald du Maurier and granddaughter of George du Maurier, the author and artist. A voracious reader, she was from an early age fascinated by imaginary worlds and even created a male alter ego for herself. Educated at home with her sisters and later in Paris, she began writing short stories and articles in 1928, and in 1931 her first novel, *The Loving Spirit*, was published. A biography of her father and three other novels followed, but it was the novel *Rebecca* that launched her into the literary stratosphere and made her one of the most popular authors of her day. In 1932, du Maurier married Major Frederick Browning, with whom she had three children.

Besides novels, du Maurier published short stories, plays and biographies. Many of her bestselling novels became award-winning films, and in 1969 du Maurier was herself awarded a DBE. She lived most of her life in Cornwall, the setting for many of her books, and when she died in 1989, Margaret Forster wrote in tribute: 'No other popular writer has so triumphantly defied classification . . . She satisfied all the questionable criteria of popular fiction, and yet satisfied too the exacting requirements of "real literature", something very few novelists ever do'.

THE
DU MAURIERS

Daphne du Maurier

with an Introduction
by Michael Holroyd

Virago

VIRAGO

Published by Virago Press 2004
Reprinted 2009

First published in Great Britain in 1937
by Victor Gollancz Ltd

A CIP catalogue record for this book is available
from the British Library

ISBN 978-1-84408-064-9

Typeset in Bembo by Palimpsest Book Production Limited,
Polmont, Stirlingshire
Printed and bound in Great Britain by Clays Ltd, St Ives plc

Papers used by Virago are natural, renewable and recyclable
products sourced from well-managed forests and certified
in accordance with the rules of the Forest Stewardship Council.

Mixed Sources
Product group from well-managed
forests and other controlled sources
www.fsc.org Cert no. SGS-COC-004081
© 1996 Forest Stewardship Council
FSC

Virago Press
An imprint of
Little, Brown Book Group
100 Victoria Embankment
London EC4Y 0DY

An Hachette UK Company
www.hachette.co.uk

www.virago.co.uk

Introduction

Daphne du Maurier published her family history, *The du Mauriers*, in 1937 when she was aged thirty. She had already in her twenties written a remarkable biography of her father, the famous actor-manager Gerald du Maurier, and four novels, the last of which, *Jamaica Inn*, was a spectacular success.

But if her literary career seemed effortless and happy, her childhood and adolescence had been unusually complex. Her mother was an actress and had met her husband during a production of J. M. Barrie's comedy *The Admirable Crichton*. Barrie seems to have been Gerald du Maurier's favourite dramatist – St John Ervine calculated that 'his tally of Barrie pieces was eight, including *Peter Pan* (in which he "created" the parts of Captain Hook and Mr Darling)'. He was something of a Peter Pan himself, a man who would not grow up – at least not gracefully or with generosity. As the younger son and youngest child of a family of five, he was his mother's favourite and, made secure by her love, continued to feel happy during his schooldays at Harrow and confident of his success in the theatre. His nonchalant, easygoing style of acting, which concealed a fine technique, made it appear as if his great triumphs on stage came without any special exertion – indeed with the same inevitability as his daughter was to win her popularity as a novelist. 'He did not know what it was to wait at stage doors to interview managers,' she wrote of him, 'and to beg for parts in a new production.'

Everything began to change after his marriage. 'Muriel, I love you,' he wrote to his wife shortly after they married in

1903. 'It is a splendid thing that has happened to us both, dearest, and I hope the Great Spirit will bless us. It's by our truth, loyalty and devotion to each other that we shall accomplish a beautiful life . . . I seem to love you in all ways, as a child, as a boy, as a grown man.'

But the Great Spirit which blessed his first thirty-five years and granted him 'a beautiful life' was about to take away what he called his 'sweet sense of security'. The painful death from cancer of his brother-in-law Arthur Llewelyn Davies in 1907, followed by his sister Sylvia's death three years later and, at the beginning of the First World War, those of his mother and his brother Guy, destabilised what had appeared to be Gerald's naturally buoyant and optimistic nature. The joker who was always such good company, the charmer who became everyone's favourite and who had been spared adult responsibilities was 'more than normally overwhelmed' by these tragedies. Daphne du Maurier's perceptive biographer Margaret Forster tells us also that he grew dissatisfied with his acting career, became subject to a strange 'moodiness' and eventually to periods of alcoholic depression which he inflicted on his wife. 'Mo', as she was called, 'worked hard at ensuring Gerald's "boredom" was kept at bay,' Margaret Forster writes.

> [She] gave Gerald what he needed: stability, adoration, the comforts of a well-run home. But as he became more dissatisfied with himself Gerald began to grow restless . . . What Mo could not respond to was the mercurial side of Gerald's character, the side of him which was quick, a touch wicked, even a little crazy . . . She was the centre of Gerald's life, but increasingly he liked to travel away from it.

She also gave him three daughters, but not the son for whom he longed to carry on the name and history of the du Mauriers. Daphne, the middle sister, was born on 12 May 1907. During her early years she worshipped her father. He was funny, companionable, attentive – almost like another child. In temperament they were very similar. But he could not conceal his wish that she had been born a boy, and so, to please him, she imagined herself to be one – and he encouraged this. 'My tender one,' he wrote to her,

> Who seems to live in Kingdoms all her own
> In realms of joy
> Where heroes young and old
> In climates hot and cold
> Do deeds of daring and much fame
> And she knows she could do the same
> If only she'd been born a boy.
> And sometimes in the silence of the night
> I wake and think perhaps my darling's right
> And that she should have been,
> And, if I'd had my way,
> She would have been, a boy.

The onset of menstruation put an abrupt halt to Daphne's fantasies of being a boy. But the more she observed and experienced adult sexuality, the more bewildered and unhappy she grew. Though her father complained that he could not get to sleep without Muriel beside him, he had no difficulty in going to bed with a series of young actresses. Why did her mother put up with such philandering? Daphne could not understand it. But mother and daughter had never been close, largely because Gerald came so awkwardly between them.

Daphne was educated by governesses at home and then, at the age of eighteen, sent to a school outside Paris to complete her education. Here she formed an emotional attachment with one of the teachers. 'She has a fatal attraction . . . and now I'm coiled in the net,' Daphne wrote. '. . . She pops up to the bedroom at odd moments . . . it gives one an extraordinary thrill.' So perhaps, she reasoned, she really was a boy after all. 'I like women much better than men,' she confessed. But the knowledge that she was partly lesbian – or had 'Venetian tendencies' as she described it – further complicated her emotional life because she knew how much her father abhorred the 'filth' of homosexuality.

Daphne's flirtations with men, and her first, rather lukewarm *affaire* with the actor-manager Beerbohm Tree's illegitimate son, the future film director Carol Reed, provoked many scenes of possessive jealousy and anger from her father. Gerald seemed increasingly dependent: sometimes clinging to her, at other times accusing her of blatant immorality – to all of which was added her mother's disapproval for causing him such misery.

It was to find emotional and financial independence that Daphne took up writing. Her first short stories, apparently influenced by Katherine Mansfield and Guy de Maupassant, but nearer in mood, as Margaret Forster suggests, to Somerset Maugham, were bleak exposés of the hypocrisy and unhappiness of sexual relations between men and women. But though she would intermittently return to the contemporary world in her fiction and explore problems she herself experienced, her main strength as a novelist arose from the longing she felt to be someone other than herself and her need to escape the problems of contemporary life. Her passionate interest in other people, and the intensity of her desire to travel into their lives, gave her novels their extraordinary narrative power and a pervasive atmosphere that held her there, and holds the reader too.

These thrilling adventure stories and engrossing family sagas provided the entertaining fantasies and sense of security that were so desperately needed in an age of devastating world wars. The spirit of the age was with her and she was to lead a flourishing revival in romantic fiction. Her own needs and those of the country seemed to coincide, and she achieved a similar feat of popular escapism to that of her father, whose natural style of acting had led many audiences to think of highly dissimilar roles as being merely aspects of himself. Gerald believed that Daphne was furthering the du Maurier destiny by following the example of his father, George du Maurier, the famous author of *Trilby*. For this reason he supported her writing career even though it was to make her an independent woman.

More surprising was his approval of his daughter's husband, 'Tommy' Browning, whom she met in the spring of 1932 and married that summer. He looked like someone who might have stepped from one of her romances: a tall, athletic Old Etonian and 'the best-looking thing I have ever seen'. A much-decorated officer in the Grenadier Guards, Browning had a commanding air of authority which reassured Daphne that he would never become emotionally dependent on her like her father, and which also impressed Gerald himself as being beyond bullying.

Gerald was to die suddenly, following an operation, in April 1934. Daphne did not go to his funeral partly because, in her grief, she did not wish to admit he was dead. Almost immediately afterwards she began writing his biography, *Gerald: A Portrait*, bringing him back to life on the page. It is an extraordinary book, part biography and part autobiography, though written in the style of a novel. It gives a vivid evocation of her father's charm and engaging humour and, though not charting all his philandering escapades, it conveys something of the more difficult aspects of his character and their effect on her ('I wish I were your brother instead of your father'). The book was written at top speed, completed within four months and published before the end of the year.

The du Mauriers, published three years later, is a companion volume going further back in time. It was written under unusually vexing circumstances. Her husband, now in command of the second battalion, the Grenadier Guards, had been posted to Egypt where Daphne and their daughter Tess, with her nanny, accompanied him. While he busied himself happily with troop manoeuvres in the desert, his family settled down in the heat and dust of Alexandria. Daphne hated her life there. She hated the natives who were all 'dirty', often blind or covered with sores, and who 'don't speak English'; and she hated the English themselves who filled their empty days with gossip and cocktail parties.

'I never realised I liked England so much,' Daphne wrote. It was to England, and also to France, in more glamorous times, that she escaped in *The du Mauriers*. She cut herself off from everyone and sat sweating over her typewriter in temperatures of 100°F, 'writing it like *Gerald*, so that it reads like a novel', though fearing that it might develop into 'a sort of Forsyte Saga'. By September 1936 it was finished. 'I feel it is something of a *tour de force* to have written it in an Egyptian summer,' she wrote to her publisher, Victor Gollancz. Such was her success at immersing herself in nineteenth-century Europe and obliterating contemporary Egypt from her mind while re-creating the lives of her great-great grandmother, mistress of the Duke of York, and of her own grandfather, the sensational novelist and artist George du Maurier, that it was only after she had dispatched the book to England that she became aware she was pregnant.

Gerald: A Portrait and *The du Mauriers* belong to a vintage period of Daphne du Maurier's writing, a period that produced two of her best-loved novels: her Gothic thriller *Jamaica Inn* and the melodramatic novel of suspense, *Rebecca*. *Gerald: A Portrait* was composed in the imaginative genre of biography made fashionable by *Ariel*, André Maurois's life of Shelley. But *The du Mauriers* goes further than this. Though there are a few biographical bones to be seen lying around, they have been exhumed and reassembled not by any systematic research or pretence of scholarship, but by pure dramatic instinct. The story is full of terrible events – prison, penury, a missing husband here, a court case there – all arranged as romantic comedy and marvellous entertainment (it would make a fine basis for a musical). The pain of life has been eradicated. Daphne du

Maurier describes her great-grandfather, the mercurial Louis Mathurin's fruitless search for an astronomical 'invention [that] will change the face of the world'. In this engaging book, his great-granddaughter has come up with a fictional equivalent of that magical device.

By the 1960s, following the publication of George D. Painter's *Marcel Proust* and Richard Ellmann's *James Joyce*, Daphne du Maurier's inventive essays in biography appeared terminally dated. But today, when Peter Ackroyd, Julia Blackburn, Andrew Motion and others are experimenting with hybrids of fiction and non-fiction, her two volumes of family biography find a new place in the history of the genre, reminding us of the need we all have in our lives for the consolations of romance and adventure.

Michael Holroyd
2004

In the belief that there are thirty-one descendants of Louis-Mathurin Busson du Maurier and his wife Ellen Jocelyn Clarke alive to-day, this story of the past is dedicated to all of them, with affection.

DAPHNE DU MAURIER

October 1936

Contents

FAMILY TREE OF THE DU MAURIERS

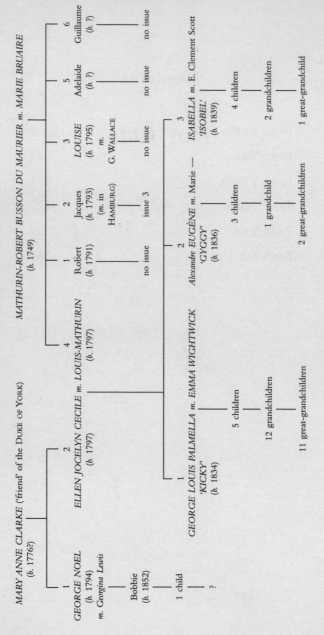

Thirty-one descendants of Ellen Jocelyn and Louis-Mathurin alive today.

Part One

1

On a cold spring day in 1810 a little sallow-faced girl of twelve leant with her nose pressed against the windowpane of a tall house in Westbourne Place. She was in the servants' bedroom because the other rooms in the house were being stripped of their furniture, and strange men she had never seen before were strolling backwards and forwards through the two drawing-rooms pointing to the chairs and tables, feeling the legs of the little gilt boudoir couch with coarse dirty hands, running inquisitive fingers up the rich brocaded curtains. She had watched them for a time earlier in the day, and no one had noticed her; she had been free to wander through the rooms and passages and see the severe-looking gentleman in the dark coat put numbered tickets on the dining-room chairs. Then he went away, and in a few minutes came back again with two workmen who wore aprons and had their shirt sleeves rolled above their elbows, and he told the men to take the chairs away.

The room held an air of odd surprise when the chairs had gone. Then another man came and laid out all the best glass and china on a side-table, and, when he had arranged them to his satisfaction, he carried them through to the drawing-room and put the table against the wall. The chairs had been placed back to back in a long row, and the pictures had been taken down from their hanging-rails and stacked in a pile on the floor.

The callous indifference of these men towards her mother's possessions was, to the child, like a little stab of pain. She had known for some time that Westbourne Place was to be sold, and she and her mother would move to another home, but she

3

had not understood that the chairs and the tables, the glass and china, the very plate off which they ate, would be theirs no longer. One by one the familiar things were touched and tested by unfamiliar hands, and a dreary procession formed itself like a line of mourners at a funeral, bearing from the house a succession of little corpses that could not say farewell. When the gold timepiece was lifted from his place above the stairs the child could stand no more, and she turned away with tears in her eyes and crept upstairs to the servants' bedroom at the top of the house.

That clock had been a friend to her in the many lonely hours. He had a singing chime every quarter that she would listen for when she lay awake in bed, and that note of reassurance had never failed her yet. Now she would never hear him again. And he would go perhaps to people who would care nothing for him, who would forget to dust his smiling face, and let his chime rust and ring false. As she knelt with her nose and chin smudged against the window, she felt for the first time a little sting of bitterness against her mother, who permitted these things to happen.

Ever since last year her world had been changed and insecure, and that daily life that every child imagines will continue into eternity had suddenly ceased to be. No longer did she ride in the phaeton every morning, with her mother at her side, up and down Hyde Park in a procession of carriages, or sometimes out to Richmond to drink porter with Lord Folkestone, who used to measure her with his riding-crop to see if she had grown. And, while her mother laughed and chatted, teasing Lord Folkestone in her own inimitable way, whispering oddities to him behind her hand that made him shout with laughter, the child Ellen sat silent, like a little sallow mouse, watching the play between them with a strange inborn sense of disapproval. If this was how grown-up people spent their time, she had little use for them; for herself she preferred books and music, having a thirst for knowledge of all kinds that her mother declared to be positively wearisome in a child not yet thirteen.

'You see,' she would say to her friends, with a tiny shrug of her shoulders and a shadow of mock despair in her eyes, 'my children have outgrown me already. It is monstrous. I am too young for them; they consider me irresponsible and giddy. Master George must lecture me from school like an old professor, and Ellen here, clasping solemn hands, asks "May I learn Italian, m'am, as well as French?"' At this there would be much laughter at Ellen's expense, and the child would flush uncomfortably until they had forgotten her again.

Yet driving in the Park or at Richmond was a pleasure, for there were so many things to see, and so many people to watch, and even at ten or twelve Ellen must consider herself a student of human nature.

She was old beyond her years because she had never had the companionship of other children. George, her only brother, and an idol, had been sent early to school, and was now so much taken up by his new companions, the horses he had learnt to ride, and the talk of his future military career, that the conversation of a small sister was something to be heard with impatience.

Ellen had to depend upon herself. Books became her friends then, and music, when her mother had money enough for a master; but she must understand, her mother would say, that living as they did amongst such elegance, keeping the table they did, and with the carriage and horses, there was little over for such fads as music-lessons and an Italian master. 'I will see if it can be arranged,' she would say vaguely, waving her hand in the air; and, smiling that brilliant smile that meant she was thinking of something else, would pull the bell for the servant to discuss the dinner-party for the evening.

There was such profusion of good things, such abundance of fruit and cake and wine, such glitter of glass upon the table, such smooth white napery, that it seemed hard the pound or two necessary for the music-master had to be given over to that extra bunch of grapes. A child's nature is such that she accepted it as inevitable, and later in the day would hear from the privacy of her own room the clatter of the party below — that peculiar parrot sound, strained and shrill, that distorts the human voice when men and women come together.

Such was her home, and she was contented with it, having known nothing else but this funny superficial brilliance as far back as she could remember. A season or two at Weymouth and Brighton, and then London — Park Lane, Gloucester Place, Bedford Place, Westbourne Place, a succession of town houses following one upon the other; and all was froth, and entertainment, and show; her mother coming in with a new ring on her second finger as pleased as a kitten with a ball of string, laughing over her shoulder to the puppy-faced officer in his scarlet tunic who followed at her heels, his slow mind stumbling awkwardly in pursuit of her swift brain.

'This is my babe, Captain Venning, my little Ellen, so shy and solemn, so unlike her silly mother.' And with a trill of laughter she had passed into the drawing-room, having first signalled with her eyes to her daughter that she might run away to her own room. And Ellen, climbing the stairs sedately with her mouth pursed, caught sight of herself in the tall mirror and hovered an instant, staring at her own reflection, struck by her mother's words.

She wondered whether it mattered very much to be born without beauty. The contour of her face was lean and angular, in contrast to her mother's rounded cheeks and dimpled chin. Her chin was sharp and the prominent nose curved to her narrow mouth, adding severity to the solemnity that was already there — for all the world, the child told herself, like a pair of German nut-crackers; and she stroked the high bridge of her nose with her fingers, thinking of the tip-tilted, provocative feature that was perhaps one of her mother's greatest charms. Their eyes and their hair were alike in colour — a soft warm brown – but there all resemblance ended; for the child's eyes were deep set, lacking lustre, and the crimped hair had difficulty in curling.

Her mother's eyes would change with every mood. One moment they would sparkle with gaiety, bright and clear like cut amber turned to the light, and the next moment they would be swimmy, clouded, more alluring even than before, full of that lovely blindness peculiar only to near-sighted persons.

Her hair, too, curled softly round her forehead, dressed as it was in the new style with her ears showing, drawn away from the white column of her neck, leaving this white and free and sloping without shadow to the superb shoulders. Ellen's hand wandered slowly from her nose to her pale sallow cheeks, and thence to her own small rounded shoulders – so rounded, in fact, that a servant once, in an ill-tempered mood, had called her 'Hunch-back'. The child had never forgotten this, and she flushed now at the memory. Then, with a shrug of these same despised shoulders, she turned from the mirror towards her room, the sound of her mother's voice, quick and eager, coming up to her from the drawing-rooms below.

Well, those days were over now. There had been no parties for more than a year. The officers in their bright tunics came no more; even Lord Folkestone had gone abroad, and of course His Royal Highness, who used to visit them so often when they had lived in Park Lane, had not been near them now for four years. Ellen had almost forgotten him. Other people began coming to the house – tradespeople; she recognised them, dressed as for Sunday in their dark clothes, and, when her mother refused to see them, they would shout rudely at the servant, as though it was his fault.

One day there had been quite a crowd of them at the front door, and they had pushed their way in and forced themselves into her mother's presence. They had not remained for long. Her mother had listened to their complaints, shaking her head gently at them, letting them exhaust themselves with talk, and

7

then, when the ringleader, an upholsterer from Lamb Street, near by, drew breath, expecting her to eat out of his hand, she left fly at him with a string of gutter-words, well chosen, that struck him and his companions in such confusion that they were left without weapons of retaliation.

They had stared at her, open-mouthed, and she had swept them from the room before they could recover, and she was left then, her cheeks scarlet and her eyes flashing, mistress of the field.

That day was followed by days and weeks of insecurity, when her mother was never at home, or when she was she would have no time for Ellen but an impatient hug, and 'Run away to the servants, child; I have not a moment,' closeting herself at once with a strange visitor; and the two would talk away in the boudoir for hours, the low murmur of their voices going on and on. There was a tense atmosphere about the house, sinister and disturbing to a child who was used to the normal conti- nuity of things, and she longed for an explanation that was never given. If she found her way to the kitchen, the servants stopped talking when she approached, and the silly footman giggled behind his hand, thrusting a pamphlet into his breeches pocket. George remained at school for Easter and did not come home. When Ellen wrote to him, he did not reply. The child was tortured by the fear he might be ill, or that this was to be a permanent separation. Her mother gave her half-answers to her repeated questions. One morning, before she left the house she found Ellen hovering behind her like a shadow. 'Be finished, child,' she said impatiently, 'plaguing me as you do. I have told you a hundred times your brother is well.'

'Then why does he not return home?' said Ellen, setting her narrow mouth.

'Because it is better for him to stay there for the moment,' came the reply.

'What is the reason, then, for all these changes? Surely I am old enough to know? I am not a baby, to be pacified with fairy tales. The servants gossip in corners. People come to the street and stare up at the house. Yesterday some boys threw a stone at me when I looked from the window. You can see where the stone has shattered the pane. Why was I followed when I took my walk in the Square, and pointed at, like a monkey in a cage, and why did a strange gentleman, winking to his friend, stop me on the step and say, "And who was your father, little maid, the duke or the dustman?"'

She spoke with passion, her eyes blazing, her small face white and tense.

The mother looked at her uncertainly, her hand fidgeting with her kid glove, her poise shaken momentarily by these questions flung at her by a little girl of twelve.

'Listen, Ellen,' she said swiftly. 'Your mamma has enemies – never mind why. People who would see us all flung penniless on the streets like dogs. They would like to have me crawl to them for bread, beg for it in the gutter. They were pleased enough to dine at my table once, but that's over now. I've got to fight 'em for our future, yours and mine and George's. I've no money and no friends. Only my wits. They have served me before and they will serve me now. Whatever happens, and however much dirt they fling at me, remember one thing – that I am doing it for your sake, for you and for George, and so to hell with 'em.' She waited a moment, as though she would say more; and then, thinking better of it, she laid one finger on the child's cheek, smiling an instant, and was gone, leaving behind her the little trail of perfume that was part of her. On the parquet was a piece of paper, torn in two. It must have fallen from her hand unwittingly. Ellen stooped to pick it up that she might put it with the waste letters. She saw that it was a lampoon, vulgar and splodged, sold by some hawker in the street. Her mother had torn it right across, but Ellen could see the four last lines smirking up at her like a leer.

And when I strove to chaunt my Mrs Clarke
With rhyme, confused, I knew not which was which,

But, as I went on fumbling in the dark,
I set down bitch for Clarke and Clarke for bitch.

The child threw the paper away so that she could see no more, and went quickly to the door; but, seeing the footman there with his foolish, vacant face, she went back again, and kneeling beside the paper-basket, she took from it the discarded paper, and tore it piece by piece until it was in shreds.

2

A year had come and gone now since Ellen Clarke had found the lampoon against her mother. She had seen many more during the twelve months that had followed. Old copies of the *Gazette*, left open by the servants, taught her in bold black print what she had not known before. Loyal and passionate, she would have defended her mother against the world that blackened her, but she was only a child, a powerless, ridiculous figure, shut away at the top of a house like a small bird in a cage. There had been a great trial – so much she understood – and her mother had been chief witness in this trial, bringing charges against His Highness the Duke of York, who only a few years ago had been their dearest friend. What these charges were Ellen did not know, but because of the trial the world had turned against her mother. All the scurrilous gossip of the day came to her ears and turned to poison. At twelve years of age her eyes were opened to all that was base and ignoble in a sordid world. She began to understand how they had lived during the years that had passed.

A hint here, a word there, a pamphlet thrust under the door, servants talking behind a screen, and the string of her own little recollections going back to babyhood, totalled a sum that could not be ignored. She remembered how they had never lived long in one house, and how the circle of her mother's friends had changed with her position. Snatches of forgotten scenes swam home to her memory once more. She saw herself a toddling baby again, with George a few years older, peering through railings to a dirty pavement in Flask Walk at Hampstead, and how they had left in the middle of the night and gone to

Worthing to stay with Sir Charles Milner, and Sir Charles had given George a spaniel puppy and herself a china doll. There were gaps then in her memory, and a forgetting of Sir Charles, and suddenly they were living in a big house in Tavistock Place, and a gentleman called Uncle Harry came to see them every day. Her mother must have quarrelled with him, for one evening Ellen heard him shouting at her in the drawing-room, and, peeping through the crack in the door, the child had seen her mother, cool and sweet, listening to him with her chin in her hand and yawning in his face as though fatigued.

They went from Tavistock Place a week later, and spent the summer in Brighton, and Ellen and George drove up and down in a little carriage with two grey ponies. The following winter they had a fine house in Park Lane, and their mother gave dinner-parties four times a week. Ellen remembered coming to the drawing-room hand in hand with George, and seeing His Highness standing on the rug before the fire. A giant of a man he seemed, with great bluff red face and bulging eyes, and he bent down to them and swung them on his shoulder. 'So you'd be a soldier, eh, would you?' he said to George, pulling his ear, 'and go to France to fight Boney? Well, a soldier you shall be.' And he laughed, turning to their mother, and, flourishing an enormous handkerchief, he made rabbit's ears for Ellen.

During the three years that followed, His Highness came every evening to the house, when he was in Town, and he chose the school for George and bought him a pony too. Ellen, shutting her eyes, could see him now, striding into the house and bellowing for her mother, swinging his ponderous belly before him, thrusting snuff with finger and thumb up the left nostril of his prominent nose. And now the Duke was fallen and disgraced, because Ellen's mother had spoken against him at the trial.

'Whatever I do, I do for you and George,' she had said; and, with a sting of shame at her own disloyalty, Ellen wondered what man or woman had ever known her mother or had guessed what lay behind those changeable brown eyes. In November of that year the street-boys had burnt her effigy instead of Guy Fawkes's. From her bedroom window Ellen had heard them singing at the corner of the street:

'Mary Anne, Mary Anne,
Cook the slut in a frying-pan,'

and they had run with flares through the foggy night, with a fat turnip, in a lace night-cap and pink ribbon, perched sideways on a pike.

Now it was spring again, and these vile memories behind them, but the old continuity of life had been broken and nothing could ever be the same again. Her face smudged against the window, Ellen saw a carriage drive to the door of the house, and out of it stepped her mother, and her mother's friend, Lord Chichester. She supposed that they had come to see how the sale of the furniture progressed. A curiosity almost morbid in its intensity came over the child to watch how her mother would behave. Once again she crept downstairs to the reception-rooms, and she found that the crowd of inquisitive strangers had gone now, the floors and the walls were stripped, and in the centre of the little bare room stood her mother and Lord Chichester, ticking off prices with a sour-faced clerk.

'A hundred and four guineas for the drawing-room suite!' she was saying. 'But when I tell you that those chairs were fifty pounds apiece—'

'Yes, but you never paid for them,' observed his lordship drily.

'That is neither here nor there. My boudoir couch, forty-nine guineas – a monstrous bargain they have gained indeed! Ninety guineas I gave for that couch, scarcely four years ago, and they now fling bare fifty in my face.'

'A good price, in its condition, madam,' said the clerk. 'The surface was badly worn and stained, and one leg cracked.'

'That couch had seen some service,' murmured Lord Chichester.

She looked at him, her tongue in her cheek, and fluttering her lashes.

'The sort of service which should make it of double value to the purchaser,' she said. 'A glass of wine, a little imagination, a room discreetly lit – my dear Chichester, you should have bought the couch yourself! It might have fanned the flame that burns so seldom in you nowadays.'

'Ah, we are none of us as young as we were, Mary Anne.'

'Precisely. That's why you would have found the couch so useful. A hundred and eighteen guineas for my glass. That is not badly done. The best I have kept. Fifty pounds for the clock with the silver chimes! How often he has brought me to my senses when it was too late! I am not sorry to see him go; he had an inquisitive note. Five guineas for a miniature of the Duke! Five fiddlesticks and they'd be right. . . . Why, Ellen, what are you doing at the door? The child becomes more like a gnome every day.'

'How old are you, Ellen?' said Lord Chichester.

'Barely eight,' said her mother.

'Twelve and a half,' said the child.

His lordship laughed. 'You can't make a fool of your own daughter, Mary Anne,' he said, and he remembered the expression she had used during the trial. 'My babies,' she had said: 'my little girl, scarcely out of the cradle'; and he saw again the pitiful tremor of her mouth, the tear beneath her lashes, the rather helpless shrug of her lovely shoulders. What an actress the woman was, and how completely unscrupulous in every way! She would sell her best friend for money, and her own soul too; but she did not desert her children. But neither does a vixen in her burrow desert her cubs. . . . The boy's future was secure; she had seen to that; the remainder of his schooling would be paid and a commission bought for him in a regiment of the line. As for this child, the annuity would come to her when her mother died. Lord Chichester wondered what use she would make of it; with those sharp features and those round shoulders she would hardly follow in the footsteps of Mary Anne. She had no charm at the moment, none of her mother's gutter loveliness, impudent, provocative, the more alluring because it was ill bred.

But Mary Anne, who, rakish and disgraceful, faced life like an urchin in the street, her finger to her nose, had not fared too badly since her separation from the Duke, for all her pretended poverty. Folkestone had seen to that. And paid her debts into the bargain. That was her trouble, of course; money trickled through her hands. She would have to reduce her scale of living if she proposed existing on the Duke's settlement. A thousand pounds would be nothing to her.

He followed her now into the boudoir, bare of its furniture, the walls stained and blackened where her pictures had hung. The room had a dissolute, untidy air; boxes half packed with her belongings were piled on top of one another on the floor. A case of trinkets sprawled on a one-legged stool, partly covered by an embroidered shawl, and here and there were scattered beads that had broken loose from their knotted silk, a book or two, a miniature, a sheet of music; and, amidst them all, panting, a gold collar encircling his gross pleated throat, a ridiculous lap-dog, like an over-fed toy, who yapped and spluttered at their approach. The room smelt heavily of dog and stale perfume. The windows were tightly closed. Lord Chichester raised an eyebrow, and put his cambric handkerchief to his nose. The room was a betrayal of its mistress, and, smiling drily, he pictured the origins whence she had sprung – the coarse lodging-houses of her youth, ill kept and dirty; beds that were never made; half-eaten breakfast rotting on an unwashed plate, and bawling from the street below a drunken father with shrill gutter cry. He saw Mary Anne as she must have been at twelve – the same age as this little microbe here – full-bosomed, impudent, and

15

curly-haired, full of a premature vulgarity. Red-lipped and calculating, she would watch men from the corners of her eyes, making a note of their stupidities, and, fully aware of her pernicious charm, she had flung herself, with deliberate abandon, into that walk of life that suited her.

No word of that early life escaped her now. Actress and prostitute she may have been; wife, too, at seventeen of some wretched tradesman at Hoxton, so rumour ran; but in her present position as late mistress of the Duke of York she did not welcome enquiries into the past.

Lord Chichester smiled again, thinking of her sharp tongue and ready wit, and how she had set the court into fits of laughter at the trial by her quick answer to the learned judge. As she played now with her trinkets in the boudoir, and fondled her fat dog, he narrowed his eyes and conjured again the memory he had of her in the witness-stand, a vision in a blue silk gown, dressed as though for an evening party, a white veil on her head, her small hand playing carelessly with her ermine muff. He watched again the demure expression on her face, belied by that pert tip-tilted nose, her head a little on one side, as the judge bent down to her with infinite condescension, pausing a moment, a half-look to his audience as though to warn them he would make her writhe, and saying, 'Under whose protection are you now, Mrs Clarke?' And quick as a rapier-thrust came the reply: 'I thought, m'lord, that I was under yours.' What a titter had escaped the court; turning to broad laughter at his lordship's flush, and, while he fumbled stupidly with his pen and groped for his papers, she had waited for his next question, cool and unmoved, the point of her tongue just showing between her teeth!

He would be sharp indeed who bettered Mary Anne! She had all the low cunning of her sex, all the base qualities. Greedy, avaricious, faithless, and a liar, she had passed from petty triumph to petty triumph, using her lovers as a purse to prosperity, and yet – and yet – Lord Chichester looked at her again – the

16

white throat, the curve of her chin, the loose, rather petulant mouth – and he shrugged his shoulders and forgave her everything.

'What are your plans?' he said abruptly.

She turned to him with vague, untroubled eyes, fingering the bracelet on her wrist. 'Plans?' she echoed. 'I never make any plans beyond to-morrow. Have you ever known me live otherwise? I have taken your advice about quitting the country. Ellen and I leave for France on Saturday. Beyond that – who knows? The future can take care of itself.'

The child, who had been watching her intently, seized upon her words.

'Are we to go from England?'

Her mother made a pretence of emotion, and, drawing her towards her, covered her with kisses. 'My poor baby, they are hounding you from home. We must be outlaws in a foreign land; friendless and unwanted. We shall wander from country to country, seeking a shelter for our weary heads, no one to—'

'With a thousand pounds in the bank, beside your nest-egg from Folkestone, and all your jewels and your plate intact,' interrupted Chichester, 'you will live like a queen if you can keep from gambling. You have not forgotten the terms of the contract?'

'Am I likely to?'

'You are capable of committing any atrocity, Mary Anne, if you should think it worth your while. Give me the contract and I will read it to you again.'

'Then Ellen must leave the room.'

'Nonsense. Ellen shall stay. Her future is concerned in this.'

The mother made a gesture of indifference, and, rising to her feet, she went to one of the boxes in the corner of the room and fumbled in it for a moment, returning presently with a sheet of parchment.

Lord Chichester took it from her. 'You understand,' he said, 'that this is only a copy. The original is in the possession of the Duke.'

She nodded, watching him with amusement, her tongue in her cheek.

He frowned, seeing no occasion for levity, and began to read:

'*In consideration of the terms proposed and agreed to, I, Mary Anne Clarke, promise to deliver up every Letter, Paper, Memorandum, and Writing, in my power or custody respecting the Duke of York, or any of the Royal Family, and particularly all Letters, Memorandums, and other writings written or signed by the Duke. I also promise to procure all the Letters not in my custody, entrusted by me to others, and deliver them to the Duke's friend.*

'*I also agree that I will, when required, make a solemn declaration on oath that I have delivered up All the letters and writings from the Duke to me, and that I know of no others. I further promise not to write, print, or publish any Article respecting the connection between me and the Duke, or any Anecdote, either written or verbal, that may have come to my knowledge from the Duke. I further consent that in failure of my complying with the several stipulations above stated, the Annuity agreed to be paid to myself for my Life, and to my Daughter after my decease, shall become absolutely forfeited. I will deliver up all Letters, but the Manuscripts and all that is printed thereof shall be burnt before any Person appointed for that purpose. I also promise to keep no copy or copies of the Duke of York's Letters, or of any Manuscripts. Dated this first day of April, 1809.*

'(*Signed*) MARY ANNE CLARKE.'

'So you see, my dear Ellen,' continued Lord Chichester, folding the paper and returning it to her mother, 'that your entire future depends upon your mother keeping her bond. Do you understand?'

The child nodded her head gravely. Her mouth was set hard,

and her eyes were cold. She looked tired, and old beyond her years.

'If my mother has quarrelled with the Duke, why does he pay us money?' she asked. 'How are we of any interest to him? Why does he keep George at school? Surely it is very generous of him to concern himself at all?'

Lord Chichester considered her, a ghost of a smile on his lips. An imp of malice stole into his brain, and brewed mischief.

'Go and look at yourself in the mirror,' he said.

The child obeyed him without humour, stung with curiosity, and, walking to the one cracked mirror that had not been sold, she considered her small person with interest.

'Do you see no resemblance?' said Lord Chichester, fluttering an eyelid at her mother.

Ellen observed once again her high cheek-bones, her prominent beak of a nose, her firm narrow mouth, and a sudden understanding of Lord Chichester's words came to her in a flash. She was stunned for a moment, doubtful and perplexed, and then a little seed of excitement took root in her childish, unformed mind. She hovered an instant in a world of fantasy, her thoughts broody with historical tales. A giddy procession of the Kings and Queens of England swam past her in a riot of silver and gold.

Then she straightened her round shoulders, lifted her pointed chin, and without another word walked proudly from the room.

Lord Chichester tapped his snuff-box and sighed.

'How disgraceful of me!' he said. 'She will wander through life believing she has royal blood in her veins, and it will poison her existence. The germ will linger until the third or fourth generation. . . . Did you see the expression in her eyes? Heigho! Pride is the besetting sin of mankind! Indulge my curiosity for once. Who was her father?'

Mary Anne yawned prodigiously, and, stretching her arms above her head, she ran her fingers through her loose brown curls. For a moment she looked supremely innocent, like a

19

tousled, sleepy child. Then she wrinkled up her nose and laughed – that soft, intimate, rather vulgar laugh that was infectious and irresistible because it was part of her.

'So many people at Brighton,' she murmured. 'Such a poor memory for faces.'

3

The sea at Dover was whipped with a white foam, and the packet-boat rocked uneasily at her berth beside the wharf. The little knot of passengers stood huddled together on the quay, postponing as long as possible the moment of departure. The chalk cliffs of England leant with supreme security against the grey menace of the sky. Gulls darted to the sleek harbour water with fretful cries. Already in the wet air there was a flavour of fish, and stale food, and that indescribable boat smell, pitchy and sour, that assails the sensitive nostrils of those who must embark against their will.

Outside the harbour the green Channel seas lurched tipsily, racing one another and tumbling in horrible confusion to the far horizon. Even the most confident of travellers knew what to expect when the ship, straining from the wharf, made her first curtsy to the sea. She would lift for an instant, slowly and with dignity, hovering for a fraction in time on the crest of a hill; then sink, fearfully and crookedly, with an immense shudder from stem to stern, groaning and hissing like a breathless dame. Farewells were being said; hands were clasped, and final messages screamed into heedless ears.

Ellen, in her best pelisse and fur-trimmed bonnet, leaned over the rail to watch the confusion on the lower deck. The poorer passengers, like animals in a pen, turned this way and that in wretched endeavour to stake claims for space. Some, resigned to the inevitable, were hunched already against the bulwarks, handkerchief to mouth, with loose eyes turned in pale anguish to the heaving seas. Children were crying, and women yapped hysterically to quieten them, pressing fruit and

21

cake in their unwilling mouths. Men shouted for no reason, packages were lost, and the very tumult of chatter and discussion added to the disorder. The deck where Ellen stood was comparatively quiet, and the few better-class passengers were seated, well muffled and veiled, smelling-salts or books in hand according to the strength of their stomachs.

Ellen's mother, with her usual audacity, had taken possession of a small cabin, either by smiles or bribery, and this compartment was now littered with her possessions – capes, furs, packages, and trunks – and the lap-dog thrown in among them all, groomed and scented, the saliva running from his jaws.

Fladgate, the lawyer, who had journeyed from London to see them safely embarked, glanced at the packages with disapproving eye. Such style of travelling made unnecessary expense, and augured ill for the future. It was obvious to him that his client had no intention of living within her income. For the last time he began a little lecture on the need for caution, urging economy, figures in proof of his argument tripping off his tongue, while Mary Anne listened to him patiently, a smile on her lips, her eyes wandering over his shoulder towards a fellow-passenger who stood near by, complacent and conscious of her gaze, his curly-brimmed hat pulled low over his eyes.

She looked very lovely, and ridiculously over-dressed, while the spot of rouge on her cheek just matched in tone the satin bow on her cape and the tinted feather that curled upwards from her bonnet.

What a contrast she made, thought Ellen, to the drab, sober-clad Frenchwoman on the lower deck, with her tired, lined face and her worn hands, the black stuff gown, the grey woollen shawl. This woman, with a brood of children, had at last succeeded in making a place for herself in a corner of the deck, and, having settled a small boy and a little wailing girl on the lap of their elder sister, turned now to her eldest son, and with tears in her eyes prepared to say farewell. Catching a broken word or two in French, Ellen could gather that the son would remain behind, sending word as often as he could of his health and prospects, while his mother – a widow perhaps, and alone – returned to make a place for him in France. Seeing her tears, the boy also lost his courage, and, great fellow that he was – of eighteen perhaps, or more – he blubbered and hung his head like a little child, crying, '*Maman, maman*,' and reaching for her hands. As Ellen watched them, she felt a pang of discomfort for their sorrow, and a sting of envy, too, at their affection; for here was this lad in the arms of his mother, and George was at school, careless and indifferent, having sent a laconic message of farewell which Mary Anne had kissed in a frenzy of emotion and then laid aside.

'As soon as we are settled you shall come to us, Robert,' said the woman, and these were the words that her mother should have given George, and had not, thought Ellen; and, because she was without brothers and sisters, she lingered still by the rail, sharing the trouble of this poor French family on the lower deck. The woman smiled now through her tears, and straightened her shawl. 'We're going home, Robert, you must remember that. Home after nineteen years. Back where we belong. Back to our own people.' And the boy smiled pitifully at this, spreading out his hands. 'Your home, *maman*, not ours. How can it be ours when we have never seen it?' At which she shook her head, her mouth a thin line of obstinacy. 'When you come, you will understand. It will be so simple and natural to be French again. You can't go against your blood, Robert. I know what I mean. I have lived too long now in an alien land. It becomes a poison.'

She kissed him again, and then pushed him from her, and he turned away, his mouth working. He reached out his hands to his brothers and sisters, blabbing last messages that had no meaning in words. 'Good-bye, Jacques. You are the eldest now. You must take care of them all': this to his brother, younger by a year or so, pale-faced and anxious, who glanced over his shoulder to the lifting sea, and whose thin boyish shoulders looked inadequate to bear responsibility.

'Louise, dearest sister, you will write often, very often?'; and the girl promised him, throwing her arms round his neck, her long, fair hair brushing his cheek. What a gentle, lovely face, thought Ellen, and how good, how tender; she would never be angry. Then Robert bent to the little boy on her lap, and the small girl. 'Be good, Guillaume. Remember your prayers, Adelaide.' And the children set up a wail at this, rubbing their eyes with their fists, unnerving him again, so that he must slip away from them now, unobserved, and make his way to the quayside.

'But where is Louis-Mathurin? He is not with us,' cried the mother suddenly, a note of panic in her voice, and at once there was a disturbance, and confusion, and heads turning this way and that, and above the mother's voice the sharp, anxious tones of the girl Louise: 'Louis-Mathurin, where have you gone?'

Ellen leant forward on the rail, at one with this anxiety for the lost child. As she did so she heard a little laugh behind her – that particular laugh of her mother when she was gratified – and, turning her head, she saw her standing there, a faint smile on her lips, and a tall, dark stranger by her side. 'What are you doing, Ellen, watching these common people? You will catch fleas on your pelisse, leaning so close to the dirty rail. Come and make your curtsy to this gentleman, who has so kindly asked us to dine with him.'

The stranger fawned down at her, and patted her head with a large jewelled hand. 'How are you, little maid?'

Ellen regarded him sullenly, and, turning her back, caught at her mother's sleeve. 'Those poor French people – look, they have lost one of their children. Perhaps he has fallen from the ship.'

The stranger laughed, and pressed forward with her to the rail.

'Such confusion always on the lower deck, and nowadays, with these *émigrés* returning home, it is worse than ever. Such a crowd of them this winter; month by month they flutter back, hoping to pick up the lost threads of their property. That woman below is a Breton, I should say, by her accent. Look at her flat features and her chestnut hair. They are all the same.'

'And you, sir, what part of France has a claim upon you?'

Mary Anne's tone was provocative; her voice had a certain challenge.

The stranger smiled down at her. 'I come from the Midi,' he murmured, 'where feelings are strong and warm, and men and women have large appetites for pleasure.'

Ellen turned away from them impatiently, and went to the rail once again. Her mother's friends were all the same – affected and insincere, their conversation a continual mockery of people and things. The poor family on the lower deck had no claim upon their sympathy.

And then suddenly she saw him – the lost boy for whom they had been looking – standing precariously on the ship's side, one foot dangling in the air, his right hand clasping a rope. He was a boy of about her own age, scarcely taller than herself, with round face and snub nose, and curling chestnut hair. His face was upturned to the sky, his light blue eyes followed a darting gull; and as he swung between sea and sky, oblivious of the crowd below, he sang to himself, his boy's voice, sweet and true, rising in the air effortless and free like the flight of the bird he was watching.

'Louis, come down at once, you will fall,' called his mother; but he continued swaying on his one foot, searching the wind-swept sky, losing himself in song. Ellen watched him, fascinated, and even her mother paused an instant in her flirtation with the stranger, and listened, her mouth curling in a smile. 'That boy sings like an angel . . .' she said, and then suddenly he stopped, conscious of the gaze of the crowd, and, flushing all over his face, he slid to the deck below. The charm was broken. He was no more than a little snub-nosed boy with impudent blue eyes.

'Come, Ellen,' said her mother, 'we are going below to dine.

Let us leave the *émigrés* to their bread and cheese.'

The ship plunged heavily in the short Channel seas, and a stinging rain mingled with the spray, irritating and cold, chilling the hands and feet.

Dinner was not a success. Faces paled perceptibly, the chatter of voices dwindled, and the dark stranger, who had offered wine so gallantly, fell to abrupt silence when he had emptied his glass. His very smile was strained, and he coughed uneasily. Finally he murmured an excuse and disappeared. Mary Anne wrinkled up her nose and laughed. The motion of the ship worried her not at all. She carved at her steak with relish, the blood running upon the plate, and, piercing a lob of fat with her fork, she offered it to her dog, who licked his chops and swallowed the fat in one. Ellen tossed in her berth, her knees tucked to her chin, and pictured her poor, deserted bedroom in Westbourne Place. When Mary Anne had dined, she wrapped herself in her cloak and stepped out upon the deck. The rain and the wind found the stray curls beneath her bonnet and blew them about her face. She walked to the rail where her daughter had stood before dinner and looked down upon the *émigrés*.

The French family were seasick. The woman, her hands folded in prayer, rocked sideways with the ship, a rosary strung between her fingers. Now and again she moaned, as the ship rose to its dizzy height and sank again.

The fair-haired daughter held the younger children on her lap, and the lanky Jacques lay prostrate on the deck. Even the singing angel had lost his voice, and watched the seas with a look of anguish in his pale eyes.

'Poor fellow,' laughed Mary Anne, 'you had not known there was such a gulf between England and France'; and, opening her purse, she threw a coin down to him on the deck.

The boy stared up at her in surprise; and, when she nodded and smiled at him, pointing to the coin, he flushed in pride and shame, and turned away his head. Mary Anne laughed again, and would have called to him, but a sailor, shouting above her head, caused her to look beyond – and away there yonder, over the bows of the vessel, she saw the first dark smudge of France.

The boy watched her under cover of his arm, and, when he saw she had forgotten him, and looked on the horizon, he glanced stealthily at his seasick family and, seeing himself unobserved, stretched out his hand, and in a flash the coin was in his pocket. He leant back again, feigning sleep, while his sister – disturbed by his first movement – bent over him in consolation, running her hand through his curling chestnut hair.

Mary Anne hummed a tune under her breath, and tapped her ridiculously small foot upon the deck. She was thinking of the life of vagabondage ended, and how she could at last afford to please herself instead of pleasing men. These last years had been insufferable, and the position of discarded mistress an intolerable one. There was no greater degradation. To be courted and flattered and welcomed in every house, servants and friends at her command, possessing power in no common degree, and then to be neglected and thrust aside, yawned at openly, insulted by menials, badgered by shopkeepers, disdained by the very friends who kissed her hand before . . . no, that could never be forgiven. Never, never more, as long as she should live. She had made him suffer already, and he should suffer again. How she loathed him now, his red blotched face, his great paunch, his purple bulbous nose! How she loathed him, and his brothers, and the whole family; the thickness of their speech, their gross habits, the very manner of their eating, drinking, sleeping . . .

Oh, God in Heaven, what she had endured! But it was over now, and behind her, and beyond lay a new country, a new world in which to travel.

She would amuse herself, and relax for the first time in her life. She had got what she wanted: the annuity for herself and Ellen; a commission in a regiment of the line for George. Her debts were all paid, her furniture sold. The agreement was drawn

27

up, signed, and witnessed. Cox and Greenwood would see to her affairs. Chichester had stood by her to the end.

And, whatever happened, she had the trump card still. She smiled, and patted the lining of her muff. Yes, there they were, most cunningly and successfully hidden; it was surprising that such a bulky package could be so well concealed. And how revealing were the contents, how damning to the reputation of the writer! She caressed them almost lovingly through the lining of her muff, knowing by heart the tinted paper, the crest upon the envelope, the ugly sprawling hand. They would represent another little income the day she needed it, those dozen letters of the Duke of York that had by some freak of fortune escaped the incurious fire.

Part Two

4

L a Maison d'Éducation in the rue Neuve St Étienne was a grim, sober building sandwiched amongst old houses that had once been gay, but were now untenanted, the original owners having fled during the Revolution, never to return.

Once the *salons* had rung with laughter, and the passages echoed with music and song; the rustle of silk gowns and the pretty tap-tap of high heels had sounded from room to room, and long after midnight link-boys had run about the cobbled street below bearing torches and flares to light Madame la Comtesse home. There had been gaiety then, in those days before the storm; a tinkle of viola and spinet, the trill of compliments charming if insincere, a flow of conversation that meant everything and nothing, an intriguing atmosphere of powder, patch, and mask, of laughter behind the hand.

The bubble burst with the Revolution, and all the froth and superficial sweetness vanished as though it had never been; even the walls of the old houses darkened with suspicion, the windows staring and unlit as though some spy crouched there, his ear against the wall, afraid of his own shadow.

There was a stain upon the houses, and a blood trail in the street, and the anguish and suffering of the Terror blew its cold panic breath into the stones of the buildings, freezing the poor bewildered ghosts who wandered there.

When the drums rolled for Napoleon, and the flags became banners in the air, there was a movement in the houses as though they would wake again; a window opened to receive the sound, and a new draught, borne by a new wind, hummed into the passages. The alarm was false, though, and the houses sank back into decay. The old gaiety could never return again; the eighteenth century had gone for ever. The Bourbons who followed the Emperor were like puppet monarchs with dummy crowns upon their heads, and there was something ridiculous, almost shameful, in the attempt to rekindle the trodden fires, to resurrect the dead, to drag the follies of the Trianon and the glories of Versailles into the sober bourgeois eighteen-twenties. It was striking the wrong note at a party, forcing the unwilling guests to act charades. The costumes were worn and out of date, and no one had the talent or the *flair*, no one wished to play.

So the houses in the rue St Etienne remained shabby and forlorn, and some became offices, and some were pulled down, and one became a warehouse, and No. 8 became a Maison d'Éducation under the able supervision of a Madame Pousard.

Here the daughters of the new society studied German and Italian and English, dabbled in water-colours, and strung embroidered silks, hammered or tinkled upon the piano according to their nimble fingers, and in the privacy of their own rooms chatted and giggled as young girls have always done.

Madame la Directrice considered herself lucky when she obtained the services of Mademoiselle Louise Busson du Maurier as English teacher. She spoke the language fluently, having spent her childhood in London. She had returned to France at the age of fifteen, and though, like all the returned *émigrés*, she was a little proud, a little inclined to consider herself a member of the departed *noblesse*, it did not matter very much; it was easily forgiven. She was so gentle, so tender-hearted, and such a favourite with the pupils. She had a tremendous sense of decorum, most appropriate to her position as governess, and was deeply religious into the bargain.

'If it had been possible, madame,' she had explained to the Directrice on entering the *pension*, 'I would have taken vows and entered the Convent of the Sacré Cœur. I know that the only true happiness is to be found in a life devoted to the Seigneur. Perhaps, in the years to come, I shall be able to do so. For the present I must earn my living and help to support my family. I must confess that I was not brought up to work, and never for a moment believed it would be necessary.'

'May I enquire your circumstances, mademoiselle?'

Mademoiselle Busson du Maurier (the tag du Maurier surely a little ridiculous in these days when property meant nothing at all, thought the Directrice) sighed and shook her head.

'We were greatly disappointed when we returned to France,' she admitted. 'My father had expected much more would be done for him. The glass factory founded by my grandfather was destroyed and our château in ruins. No one wished to see us, or even remembered us. It broke my father's heart.'

'Twenty years is a long time to remain in exile, mademoiselle,' said the Directrice coldly. Her husband had been commissar at St Denis, and she was a staunch Republican at heart. She had little sympathy with these returned *émigrés* who fled from their country in moments of danger and then expected to be welcomed home with open arms.

'So you received no reparation?' she added.

The English teacher produced a sheet of parchment.

'Nothing but this,' she said bitterly, 'and we are supposed to smile and be grateful. There are six of us, Madame Pousard, besides my mother, and this is all we have in the world, now my father is dead.'

The Directrice took the paper from her and read:

'J'ai l'honneur de vous prévenir, mademoiselle, que le Roi, voulant vous donner une preuve de sa bienveillance et récompenser en vous le dévouement et les services de votre famille, a daigné vous accorder une pension annuelle de deux cents francs. Cette pension, qui courra du premier janvier mil huit cent seize, sera payée au Trésor de la liste civile (aux Tuileries), de trois mois en trois

mois, après que la présente lettre y aura été enregistrée, sur la présentation de votre certificat de vie.

'*J'ai l'honneur d'être, mademoiselle, votre très humble et très obeissant serviteur,*

'*Le Directeur-général, ayant le Porte-feuille,*

'COMTE DE PRADELY.

'*Paris, le* 10 *mai*, 1816.'

'Two hundred francs is two hundred francs,' said the Directrice, handing back the paper. 'Better that than to have lost your head under the guillotine. It seems to me that the *émigrés* do not do so badly.'

Mademoiselle Busson was silent. She thought of her father, exiled in England with his heart in Sarthe, returning at last to his home and finding all destroyed; then pinching and scraping that his children might live, and dying at last, a broken schoolmaster, at Tours.

'And the rest of your family, how do they employ themselves?'

'My eldest brother, Robert, is in London, madame; a clerk in the City. Jacques works at Hamburg in a bank. The two youngest live here in Paris with my mother, in the rue de la Lune, and it is for their sake that I wish to teach English here at your *pension*.'

'And the sixth? Did you not mention another brother?'

A shadow crossed the English teacher's face. 'Yes. I have another brother. Louis-Mathurin. Unfortunately, he has gone against all our wishes and is studying to become a professional singer.'

'Perhaps he will make his fortune.'

'Hardly likely, madame. He is careless, inconsequent, always in debt. You can understand that it is very hard for us, his family, seeing him waste himself in a career that can lead nowhere. He has made an impossible choice. . . . A Busson du Maurier singing for his bread. . . .'

34

Madame la Directrice gazed thoughtfully at the young governess. Monsieur Perét was getting rather old and deaf. She knew she would have to make a change in the near future. If she could obtain the services of the English teacher's brother . . . a few francs for every lesson; doubtless he would be glad of the money. She herself would be in pocket over the affair.

'Naturally you could not bear to have a brother upon the stage,' she said complacently. 'Brought up as you appear to have been, and a strict Catholic too, the disgrace would be irredeemable. However, there is nothing dishonourable in teaching, as you realise yourself. If you would care to mention to your brother that I am looking for a singing master – the pay is small, of course . . .'

Mademoiselle Busson flushed all over her face.

'You are very kind, madame,' she said. 'When I see Louis next I will suggest it to him. But I am a little doubtful – he is so independent.'

The Directrice shrugged her shoulders. 'As he wishes, of course. I can get the services of a hundred masters. It was merely the idea of doing you a kindness. Good morning, mademoiselle. I hope you will find your pupils well behaved.' The English teacher was dismissed with a wave of the hand.

'It is a little hard,' reflected Mademoiselle Louise, as she opened page nine of the English grammar before a row of shining faces, 'that here I am obliged to give lessons in order not to starve in the streets, when other women, of my birth and position, are leading a life of leisure in their own châteaux, preparing for marriage with a marquis or a duke. And Louis-Mathurin, who should be director of his own glass factory, has sunk to painting his face and prostituting his talent for a handful of silver. I must learn to be humble; I must conquer my pride. *Père pardonnez-les, ils ne savent pas ce qu'ils font*. Open your books, mesdemoiselles, if you please. "*Je ferme la porte* – I shut the door. *Tu fermes la porte* – thou shuttest the door."' She pronounced the words firmly, correctly, her prim, rather childish mouth pursing over her words, her soft, fair hair drawn severely from her face. Heiress to two hundred francs, Mademoiselle Busson du Maurier, whose only legacy from the past was a dusty glass tumbler blown by her own grandfather in the factory that no longer existed, had started her career as governess in a Maison d'Éducation.

She was successful; not because she was particularly well versed in English grammar or especially qualified in the mysteries of verbs and gerunds, but because she possessed the happy faculty of making herself beloved by her pupils. She had a gift of understanding, a knack of sympathy, that made an instant appeal to those who learnt from her, and, even if she was a little too religious, a little too severe, why, they forgave her for it, because of her sweet expression, her fair hair, her mild blue eyes.

If you were in trouble, then Mademoiselle Busson must be told of it. Had you a pain, a distress, a shadow on your conscience – why, dearest Mademoiselle Louise would take your hand in hers, murmur a prayer upon your head, shed perhaps a tear or two, and lo! you were absolved, even as the angels.

Little Eugénie St Just made a pact of eternal friendship with her and a genuine interest and affection grew up between them; they shared one another's books, exchanged ideas, discussed the problematical future, their hopes and their ideals. It was so great a pleasure to inspire affection in somebody, and life at home was rather shaky, rather strained, with no money and the two younger members of the family to keep, and Louis-Mathurin behaving like a mountebank.

'It's not so much his singing that we mind,' explained the sister to her new friend. 'He should give thanks to God for such a voice; it is a gift from heaven; but to mix with the company he does – people from the opera, actors and actresses. My mother is nearly in despair. Robert has written to him from London, and Jacques from Hamburg – all to no purpose.

And, Eugénie, there is something even worse to tell you, something that even my mother does not know.'

The little pupil opened her large dark eyes. 'Oh, mademoiselle!'

'If I tell you, you must promise never to breathe a word to anyone. Eugénie – my brother has become an atheist!'

They stared at one another in horror, the younger girl bereft of speech, and slowly the English teacher nodded her head again.

'Yes,' she said slowly, 'it is true. Louis–Mathurin does not believe in God.'

She gazed from the window to the white-clouded sky and wondered how it were possible that her brother, who had learnt his prayers at her knee, made his *première communion* at her side, could have so lost himself as to deny the faith that cradled him. She shuddered as she thought of the inferno that awaited those miserable wretches who forsook their faith. . . .

A knock at the door disturbed the two girls, and the English teacher put aside her embroidery. 'What is it?' she called.

'Mademoiselle Busson is required in the *salon*.'

Louise smoothed her ringlets and pattered downstairs in the train of the servant.

Madame la Directrice met her at the door of the *salon*. 'We have the prospect of a new pupil,' she said swiftly, 'a young English lady of about your own age. She wishes to take a course in French literature for two or three months. I have told her you were free for private lessons on Tuesday afternoons. She speaks the language fluently enough, but the mother, who is here as well, insists on interrupting. Her accent is atrocious. . . .'

As Louise went into the room she was assailed at once with the pungent odour of strong scent, and she heard a voice saying in loud, definite tones:

'Tea? No, thank'y, I never touch the stuff. A glass of porter if you have it.'

37

A murmur of apology from the Directrice, and the offer of a mild *apéritif*. Louise prepared herself for the worst.

The owner of the voice was seated on the one comfortable chair in Madame Pousard's *salon* and was leaning back as though the place belonged to her. She was *petite*, middle-aged, and incredibly over-dressed. An enormous poke bonnet, suitable for a girl of seventeen, crowned her curled, dyed hair, and a white satin dress showed beneath her fur cape.

She wore evening shoes with scarlet heels, and she sat crossed-legged, like a man, swinging her small foot in the air. Her face was heavily painted and powdered, which, instead of concealing the crows'-feet as it was meant to do, only served to accentuate the lines. A pair of fine, rather ribald brown eyes looked out from beneath false lashes. She had rings on every finger, and wore them over her gloves; and she toyed with a monstrous little hairless dog, scented and beribboned like herself, that shivered upon her lap.

'May I present our English teacher to you, Mrs Clarke?' said the Directrice.

And as Louise advanced nervously to the proffered hand, the English stranger had the ill-breeding to hiccup, spilling her *apéritif*, and then – horror upon horror – winked at her, her tongue in her cheek.

'Wind under the heart,' she murmured. 'Can't avoid it when you get to my age. My doctors tell me I must not drink with my food. Drink with my fiddlesticks, I say! How d' do, then, Mamzelle Buss? Know what it means in English?' She broke into a trilling laugh, and, winking again, she poked Louise in the ribs.

'Mother,' came a low, warning voice at her side.

'Damme, Ellen, what have I said now?' The creature turned round in her chair, flushed and aggrieved, her large bonnet already a trifle crooked.

'*Bonjour, mademoiselle, J'espère que vous vous trouvez en bonne santé.*'

The daughter – for this was she, supposed the bewildered Louise – spoke rapidly in rather stilted French, ignoring her mother, who shrugged her shoulders and fell to feeding her dog with lollipops from a box. The daughter was a complete contrast to her mother – very plainly dressed in quiet tones, her sallow complexion unrelieved by colour, and, instead of greeting Louise with a broad smile, as her mother had done, she looked her up and down critically, taking her in from top to toe, reserving her judgment for later.

'We have been in Italy for several years,' she said, 'and in the south of France. Now that we are to settle in Paris for a while, I intend to see all I can, and study as much as possible. Perhaps we could read literature together, mademoiselle – the plays of Corneille and Racine – Molière I know already – and some of the earlier poets – Ronsard, Villon, for choice – so that I can compare them with the early Italians. Would it be possible for you to show me something of the picture galleries? When we were in Rome and Pisa I studied the primitives. I am rather ignorant of French art, and wish to correct this failing. Do you paint yourself, by any chance?'

'A little. More to amuse myself than anything else. I am rather fond of painting flowers. My brothers used to tell me I had quite a little talent that way.'

'That will be delightful. It is a great pleasure to meet anyone cultured. My mother and I live rather quietly nowadays. I fall back upon books and music for company.'

'You are musical?'

'Yes, I play the harp. I had a very good master in Italy. At the present we are making certain economies, so I must go without.'

She flinched as the tail end of a sentence fell upon her ears: 'I tell you what it is, madame, the girls are all hypocrites these days,' her mother was saying. 'Go red under the ears if they meet a pair of breeches, and turn the other way. No curiosity to see what's inside 'em. What are breeches for, I say? Let 'em marry young and find out. . . .'

The Directrice, too stunned to reply, sat expressionless, her tea-cup poised in mid-air.

Louise, flushing in sympathy for the daughter, looked down upon the polished floor to avoid her eyes. 'There are many excellent masters in Paris,' she heard herself pronouncing, 'students at the Conservatoire, who would be glad to give their time in exchange for a certain remuneration. If you would like me to make enquiries for you, it would be the easiest thing in the world.'

She talked rapidly, to cover the other's confusion, but the sound of her voice drew attention upon her, and in a moment the little witch in the chair had whipped round in her seat to stare at her, her painted lips parted in a smile, her dyed curls bobbing round her cheeks.

'You know what it is, my dear, you're too pretty to be a teacher,' she said, wagging a finger and pointing. 'You ought to find a husband. Plenty of young men about, if you know how to look for 'em. Ellen shall bring you home one day, and when you're tired of looking at pictures and playing the harp you shall have a little chat with me. I know all about husbands – I was married at seventeen – and I can tell you what they do and how they do it. . . . No use asking madame here; she wouldn't tell you. Would you, madame?'

She giggled like a schoolgirl, pointing an accusing finger at the Directrice.

The situation had become intolerable. Miss Clarke rose to her feet and spoke sharply to her mother. 'We have taken up too much of madame's time,' she said, 'and doubtless Mademoiselle Busson has a class to attend. I am afraid we must tear ourselves away. . . . Shall I come next Tuesday, then? *C'est entendu, mademoiselle*. It will be a great pleasure for me to enjoy the company of someone of culture like yourself.'

For the first time the daughter unbent, and spoke with feeling. A message flickered in her dark eyes, a signal that said,

'I am lonely. I want you for my friend. I believe we shall understand one another.' And then she bowed her head and passed from the room, the mother tapping after her on her high pointed heels, her cape slipping from her shoulders, the hairless dog peering from beneath her arm. 'Ellen always takes me away just as I begin to amuse myself,' she complained. 'Such a good girl, but – *entre nous* – no sense of humour. You ought to meet my son, mamzelle. He's a lovely fellow, a subaltern in the Army, y'know. The women adore him. . . . No time now for his old mother!'

She winked again, and then, putting up her hand, she whispered in the English teacher's ear, 'Don't stay a governess too long; bad for the complexion. My advice is, take a lover. Nothing like it to put the roses in your cheeks.' She went out rocking with laughter, enveloped in a cloud of scent, the little dog spitting in sympathy and pecking at her ear.

And so started the friendship between Ellen Jocelyn Clarke and Louise Busson du Maurier – who had seen each other as children, though neither of them knew it – a friendship that was to endure the difficulties of near relationship and other strange vicissitudes of fortune, a bond that was strengthened by a certain resemblance between them, both born, as they had been, at the close of the eighteenth century and therefore not belonging to it at all, both imbued with that sense of self-righteousness and propriety that was the inevitable reaction of the new century. A rather pathetic snobbism was ingrained in them as well. Ellen believed herself to have the blood of kings and held her head the higher for it – blind to her slum origin – and Louise spun tales of an old château at Chenu in Sarthe, which she had never seen but took for granted, and clung to the aristocratic memories of her poor dead father, who, for all his Royalist sympathies, had died a schoolmaster at Tours.

Their blue blood was a myth, and perhaps in the secret places of their souls they knew it and suffered accordingly, thus bringing a little grain of bitterness into the conversation from time to time; and it was all very unnecessary, could they but have realised that it was simple honest bourgeois blood that made the best stock in the long run, giving to its descendants a capacity for work and achievement and straight thinking, whereas the other turned to water and produced the idler, the shirker, the weaver of sterile dreams.

Eugénie St Just became a little jealous of the new friend who took up so much of dear Mademoiselle Busson's time, but, possessing a sweet nature, she soon consoled herself with the thought that, after all, Miss Clarke was not a pupil, she was quite old, and that of all the young girls in the *pension*, Eugénie herself was the most preferred.

The only cloud on Louise's horizon was, as usual, her brother Louis-Mathurin, who had abandoned his singing career as suddenly as he had started it, and could now think of nothing but science and making a journey to the stars.

When Louise went home on Sunday to the stuffy little apartment in the rue de la Lune, she found her mother in tears, Adelaide and Guillaume staring open-mouthed, and Louis-Mathurin striding up and down the room blaspheming the saints.

'They were all epileptics, every one of them,' he was shouting. 'I tell you I have made a special study of epilepsy, and the evidence is conclusive. Staring eyes – foaming at the mouth – insensibility to pain – muddled speech – immobility during several hours – each and all of them symptoms of epilepsy. Good evening, Louise. Behold the prodigal returned. Opera has lost the greatest singer of the age. I shall sing no more. I'm going to study science.'

He stood in the middle of the room waving his arms, his mad blue eyes staring down to hers, his chestnut curls springing from his high forehead.

Louise kissed him gently, and held his hand in hers. 'I am glad you have come to your senses about the stage,' she said, 'but what nonsense are you talking now? Come, Louis, be reasonable and calm. You are frightening mother, and the others look as though they had seen a ghost.'

'Nonsense? Who dares to say I talk nonsense?' he exclaimed, flinging her from him. 'There is only one truth in this accursed world in which we have the misfortune to live, and that truth is to be found in science. Your God does not exist; your religion is a mockery. Do you know that when you fold your hands and say your prayers to heaven you are saying them to a billion billion suns all whirling in space, part of an unlimited universe, and that this world was once a ball of sun also, and will either return to fire and burn itself out or slowly freeze and become a dead world, like the moon?'

'Ridiculous and wicked,' said Louise firmly. 'God would never allow such a thing to happen.'

'But, my poor little sister, I have already told you that there never has been, and never will be, a deity. God is an invention of mankind, a sop to the emotions. We are so lacking in courage that we must create a figurehead, a—'

'Enough, Louis,' broke in his mother. 'You shall not utter another word of blasphemy in this room. You were born and bred a Catholic, like your brothers and sisters; if you choose to deny your faith, it is a matter for your own conscience; we do not wish to hear you. While you hold such beliefs, it is better that you stay away from the house altogether.'

Louis-Mathurin ran his fingers through his hair and groaned. 'Misunderstood,' he muttered. 'No sympathy, no enlightenment. Thrown out of my own home and cast upon the streets. It is a fine example of Christianity when a mother will not give a crust of bread to the son she bore. Never mind; I have my pride, I have my unconquerable determination to succeed. One day my fame will be on the lips of the world; the professors of science will call me Master. Already I have in mind the plans of an apparatus that will carry men to the moon. . . . Louise, you are the only one of my family who has ever shown a grain of understanding. Are you going to throw me away too?'

He looked like a great overgrown schoolboy as he pleaded before her, with his long legs and curly hair, a tear cunningly squeezed into his pale-blue eye.

Louise's mouth twitched as she looked at him, and she remembered the hundred scrapes from which she had rescued him as a child – the absurd adventures, the vague wanderings, striking off on his own as he had always done, dilatory, absent-minded, the bad boy of the family. . . . She took his arm and led him out to the passage above the stairs. 'You know you can always come to me,' she said, 'but not storming like this, Louis, not raving of atheism and the devil. Mother has suffered so much in life, and she is getting old. Try and remember that. And it hurts me, who love you and love God, to see you lose yourself so utterly.'

He was not listening to her, though; she could see his vague blue eyes look through her and beyond her, caught in some fancy of his own, and, tightening her grip upon his hands, she prayed for him silently, swept suddenly with a strange confidence that he was a genius, a great personality, and that one day his name would be on the lips of the world, as he had said.

He would make some great discovery, perhaps, to benefit mankind, and when she was old she would walk in the Jardins du Roi and see his statue.

'O Seigneur,' she whispered, 'let Louis-Mathurin become a leader among men and follow Thy will, thinking only of the noble things of life.'

It seemed to her that there was a light on his face that had not been there before, and a new purpose. She saw by his eyes that he was far away, somewhere where she could never hope to follow. She was only a woman, a humble school-teacher, and he was a genius. Suddenly he turned to her, sighing deeply, and, smiling his wistful, trusting smile, he kissed her hand.

44

'Louise,' he began, 'such a little thing – I hate to worry you – I'm in debt again – nothing at all, a matter of fifty francs or so – a mere flea-bite – but if you could let me have the money to-night, now, before I go . . .'

5

When little Eugénie St Just became betrothed to the Duc de Palmella, there was tremendous excitement at the *pension*. She had met him at Lisbon during the summer, and they had fallen in love at first sight. So handsome, so full of promise, and with such a name in diplomatic circles; it was really a wonderful match, for, though she came of a very old French family, she was by no means an heiress, and now she was to marry one of the richest men in Portugal. Louise was almost as delighted as her pupil. That she should have fallen into such good hands (the Palmellas were strict Catholics and extremely cultured: not at all like the Portuguese Jews one saw sometimes in the poorer districts of Paris) was in a way a tribute to her own foresight, for it was she who had persuaded Eugénie that a visit to Portugal would broaden her mind, and that she should take advantage of her cousin's invitation.

It was arranged that the marriage would take place in January, and dearest Mademoiselle Busson, declared Eugénie, would be the most honoured guest at the wedding. 'Whenever you become tired of Paris,' she told her, 'you are to come and stay with us in Lisbon. There will be a room prepared for you always. Sometimes I wonder how I shall exist without your company, and I dare say when my husband is too busy to talk to me I shall sigh for the rue Neuve St Etienne and our conversations together.'

'You will forget all about me in Portugal,' smiled Louise. 'You will be a grand duchess, with hundreds of servants waiting on you, and balls and entertainments every night. You won't have time to think about your old teacher.'

'I will, I will,' protested Eugénie. 'How could you think me so ungrateful, after all that you have done for me? Miss Clarke, be a witness to my words. I vow here, and now, that I – Eugénie de Palmella, as I shall be – will cherish the friendship of Louise Busson du Maurier until I die.'

Ellen Clarke looked up from the pages of music she was sorting.

'All the vows in the world won't bind a friendship,' she said. 'I've seen too many go astray. When you've travelled as far as I have, Eugénie, and seen as much flattery and insincerity, you will know better than to make a vow about anything.'

Eugénie was silent. Miss Clarke was such a cynic. She continually damped enthusiasm. She looked at you with her dark eyes so suspiciously, always on the defensive, as though she expected some unkindness and wished to be prepared for it by striking the first blow. Her very features were aggressive – the prominent nose, the sharp jutting chin – and she seemed to take a delight in saying hard things. 'I suppose you think me foolish to fall in love?' said the girl. 'You will tell me it does not last, and that my husband will tire of me?'

Ellen Clarke shrugged her round shoulders and laughed – the laugh marred by a little inexplicable note of harshness.

'I consider you very wise to make provision for the future,' she said. 'It is not everyone that has the chance of meeting Portuguese noblemen.'

Her words cast a shadow on the glamour, as though the love-match were some sordid bargain, a formal agreement between two interested parties, and poor Eugénie twisted her little hands in distress, looking to her dear Mademoiselle Busson to sweep away the clouds.

'Affection between a husband and wife, when it is fortified by religious understanding, can be a very beautiful thing,' said Louise solemnly. 'I can think of no greater happiness than to attend Mass with a chosen beloved. All earthly joys pale beside united prayer.'

Eugénie nodded in sympathy, consoled immediately, but Ellen Clarke, patting her lank ringlets before the mirror, hesitated a moment before replying.

'It is all very well for you,' she said at last. 'I was never brought up to pray. I am too old now to acquire the habit.'

'No one can ever be too old for prayer,' said Louise gently.

Ellen shrugged her shoulders again. 'You don't understand,' she said. 'Why should you? Faith in an Almighty came naturally to you. You sucked it in with your first milk, in the cradle. I breathed rather different germs; a little malice, a little flattery, a little deception – those were the qualities that came to me. No one ever told me about God. The word was used as an oath before me and that was all. The only religion I have ever learnt was to take care of myself.'

Louise and Eugénie glanced at one another and away again. This was very shocking. It was also very sad. There seemed a gulf between them and Ellen Clarke.

'You must be exceedingly lonely,' said Eugénie timidly.

'Lonely? Why should I be lonely? I have my books and my harp. I would rather be alone than in the company of most people that I've met.'

She began packing her music calmly into her case. Louise grieved for her friend. How terrible, how painful it must be to possess such a cold, hard attitude to life! What an empty future Ellen laid in store for herself! Louise decided that she would burn a candle for her in the Église St Étienne when she went to Benediction. She would burn another candle for Louis-Mathurin. She would pray that both their hearts would be softened and they would learn to love God. She would also burn a candle of thankfulness to St Anthony of Padua for having found a husband for Eugénie. One of the tall, expensive candles, that lasted a day and a night, because, after all, he was the Duc de Palmella. . . .

The intervening months passed rapidly, and it seemed only a few months before little Eugénie was leaning on the arm of her husband, while the bells of Notre-Dame clanged solemnly in the cold January air.

It was a magnificent ceremony; half the nobility of Paris appeared to be there – ambassadors, diplomats, the *entourage* of the Portuguese Embassy, even a sprinkling from the Court itself. And Louise, as Eugénie had promised, was the favoured guest, standing by the side of the bride while high officials and soldiers in uniform, and counts and countesses, bowed and curtsied before her.

How enchanted they professed themselves to make her acquaintance – Mademoiselle Louise Busson du Maurier, the great friend of the Duchesse de Palmella – and how many of them present would have raised their eyebrows in surprise, had they realised that she was a teacher of English in a small *pension*.

It was a wonderful experience, and Louise, who despised the things of the world, could not help blushing a little with pleasure when she heard a voice behind her say, 'I must positively have an introduction to the Duchess's friend. She is much the handsomest woman present.' The voice was a pleasant one, and, turning a little self-consciously, she saw a tall, fair young man gazing down at her with frank admiration in his eyes.

'I am going to take the liberty of presenting myself to you,' he said. 'Palmella told me I might do so. My name is Godfrey Wallace, and I'm one of the secretaries at the Legation. I'm told you speak perfect English.'

'I was born in London, and spent the first fifteen years of my life there,' replied Louise, smiling. 'I should be foolish if I could not make myself understood in your language after that.'

'Ah, but I'm a Scot, Mademoiselle Busson, and we speak purer English in Ayr than they ever do in cockney London. I congratulate you on your accent, which is without fault. You may have heard of my father, Sir Thomas Wallace? He lived in London until quite recently.'

'But I have not returned to London since I was fifteen, Mr

Wallace, and that was many years ago – more than I care to remember.'

'Nonsense. You are trying to make me believe you are more than three-and-twenty, which I deny. I am told that your father, alas, is no longer with you, mademoiselle, but that he possessed property in Sarthe. Is your mother in residence at the château at the moment?'

Louise felt a little bewildered. The handsome stranger obviously was not aware of her position. He was so agreeable, so very distinguished in appearance, it seemed really a pity to enlighten him, unnecessary almost. . . .

'No, we . . . we are in Paris for the winter,' she stammered. 'That is, my mother has a minute *appartement* in the rue de la Lune – you would not know; close to the Jardins du Roi.'

'And how does life *en ville* agree with your health, mademoiselle? You look remarkably well; but, then, doubtless you always do! I suppose you will shortly take a visit to Portugal to see the Duchess in her new home? What it is to be a young lady of leisure! We poor secretaries to the Legation are kept hard at work.' He chatted away to her in the most amusing fashion, paying all sorts of delightful compliments, and really there was never a moment when she could explain that he was suffering under a misapprehension regarding her; that she was not quite the lady of society he supposed her to be.

He expressed his desire to wait upon her mother, and she was able to tell him, quite truthfully too, that Madame Busson would not find it quite convenient at the moment; she was preparing for a visit to Hamburg to stay with her second son, Jacques, in business there; and this immediately led to a discussion upon her brothers – Robert in London, Guillaume presently to repair to Hamburg also – and he felicitated her upon the family enterprise, declaring that he took an intense interest in science and positively must make the acquaintance of Louis-Mathurin.

'Should it not be too much trouble, perhaps your brother

would call upon me at my hotel one evening?' he suggested. 'I dine at five o'clock, and I should be extremely happy to see him, if it would be convenient to him.'

Louise promised to give him the message when she should next see him.

'If you have any friends in England, let me be the bearer of your letters,' he went on. 'It is superlatively easy for me to forward them. Our bag for England is made up every Friday.'

Louise excused herself; he was really too kind, she said.

The afternoon passed all too swiftly, and it seemed to Louise that they had scarcely begun to talk before farewells were being said, the guests were departing, and little Eugénie de Palmella was waving from the carriage, her tall husband by her side, and she was blowing kisses to her friend for the last time.

'How touching!' exclaimed the charming Mr Wallace. 'Time flies, but love and sincerity always remain. Sincere affection deeply rooted no time can erase. I intend, Miss Busson, to take such a sentiment for my motto. Do you approve?'

How could she do otherwise? thought Louise; he seemed to comprehend so perfectly her distress at parting from Eugénie. She dabbed at her eyes with her handkerchief.

'I find I have so much to say in your society,' he murmured to her, as he took his leave, 'that I look forward to our better acquaintance. Have I your permission to write to you?'

Louise found herself blushing like a young girl as she bowed her head.

'It is really very ridiculous,' she told herself; 'he must surely be aware that I am older than he'; and she was put in such a little flutter at the whole business of her meeting with him, and the conversation they had had, that sleep was almost impossible that night, and she was obliged to rise at three in the morning and make herself a cordial.

Three days later she received a letter, penned in a bold, flourishing hand, and she opened it with a slight trembling, her heart beating faster than usual.

'*My dear Miss Busson,*' it ran, '*I have addressed my letter to your mamma's home according to my promise, but on making enquiry I find there is more than one rue de la Lune, and it occurs to me that you may not receive my letter. Were you half aware, dear Miss Busson, how anxious I am to hear from you, or rather to see you, you would not, I am sure, deprive me another moment of that pleasure. My whole and only thoughts are centred upon my new friend. How much I could say that I cannot express with my pen! Pray write me on receipt of this and endeavour to relieve an anxious mind by saying when I may expect to meet you. If I have your permission I will call and see your brother if he cannot call upon me. I shall then at least have the pleasure of conversing of Miss Busson and of becoming acquainted with one so nearly related to her. I must own that I am truly sorry your mother will not be in Paris, as her absence seems to bar the pleasure I shall have in meeting you. But why not, dear Miss Busson, permit me to accompany your brother one day to see you? There surely could not be any impropriety in that? If the weather is fine we could take a walk in the Jardins du Roi; it would be something new to me, as I was never there but once. But I will not urge anything that would not meet with the approbation of my friend. Pray write soon and let me know your wishes in the matter. Accept my sincere wishes for your future health and happiness, dear Miss Busson, and allow me to subscribe myself most sincerely and truly yours,*

'GODFREY WALLACE.

'*Hôtel de Paris.*
    '*Boulevard de la Madeleine.*'

Louise read the letter some five or six times, and with heightened colour she folded it at last and put it inside her bodice. In the bustle of her mother's departure for Hamburg she had no time to answer it, but, as soon as she had gone, Louise hastened round to the Clarkes' apartment in Auteuil to take counsel of Ellen.

She found her friend, as usual, seated in the front *salon* beside her harp, her shoulders more rounded than ever as she crouched over her instrument, and, young woman as she was, there was something almost witch-like in her appearance, with her long nose and pointed chin, her dank locks falling beside her sallow face like an elfin thing. She was a wizard with her hands, though, and as Louise came into the room she paused an instant to listen, pained, as she always was, by the weird beauty of the notes as they fell upon the air. The magic Ellen must have in her fingers, she thought, and how strange it was that by twanging at those strings she could release such a flood of melody and lose herself in sound. Her personality softened with her playing and, as Ellen looked up and saw Louise, a warm expression came into her uncommunicative brown eyes, the narrow lips parted in a smile, and she was no longer a dark witch brewing spells in the flickering firelight, but a young woman who would be handsome if she only smiled more often, who would be graceful if she only straightened her back, and who, in spite of pretended cynicism, held out her two hands to her friend and welcomed her with an affectionate kiss.

'Mother is asleep,' she said, glancing at the couch before the fire; 'we can talk quietly here without disturbing her. She always sleeps after her glass of porter, and when I have played to her for five minutes or so. She can still talk of nothing but the wedding. Now that we see so few people, and seldom entertain, anything in the nature of a function excites her so.'

Louise squeezed her friend's hand in sympathy. She had a vivid memory of Madame Clarke at the reception in the rue St Honoré, more preposterously dressed than ever in very bright green satin, surrounded by a crowd of old gallants – an ex-ambassador, a general in the French Army, and a white-haired monocled marquis who leant upon a stick. Their loud laughter had drawn the attention of the other guests upon them, and the old marquis had suddenly become aware of it and grown rather red in the face, in consequence, while Madame Clarke,

53

oblivious to the sensation she was causing, continued in piercing tones, and with an atrocious accent, to recount what she insisted on calling '*une petite histoire, mon cher marquis, d'une première nuit de noce.*'

It was all very embarrassing, and everyone looked most distressed.

'I want to talk to you about the wedding, Ellen,' began Louise with a pretty hesitation, and she stumbled somewhat diffidently into an account of her meeting with Godfrey Wallace, gathering courage as she continued, and finally producing his letter with a little air of confusion.

'You see,' she said, 'he appears to wish to see me again, and, really, I hardly know how to refuse him, he expresses himself in such language, I . . .'

'Do you know anything of his circumstances?' interrupted Ellen. 'After all, that is the thing that matters most. A secretary at the Legation cannot have more than three or four hundred a year at the most.'

'I hardly see how we can make enquiries without a great deal of embarrassment,' said Louise.

'It is essential that you should know if you wish to continue the acquaintance,' Ellen said. 'Of course, he may have a private income. You said his father was Sir Thomas Wallace from Ayrshire. Depend upon it, they have property there. How do you consider the prospect of living in Scotland?'

'But, my dear Ellen, such an idea does not enter my head! I have only met this Mr Wallace once.'

'His letter is couched in strong terms, then, after one encounter, Louise. One wedding always leads to another, so they say, and you were introduced at the Palmella reception. If he is a personal friend of the Duke's – and you seem to think he is – that would be a guarantee in itself. However, I would tread warily if I were you. The mere fact of being a baronet's son does not necessarily mean he has money.'

'I hardly care about his circumstances, I must confess. I am no fortune-hunter, as you know, my dear Ellen. My position is such that I cannot hope for much out of life. His manner was pleasing, and very respectful. I do not mind admitting to you that I should like to see him again.'

'Then no doubt you will contrive it. For my part, I would go carefully; but, then, I am reserved by nature and suspicious of everyone as a matter of principle. Had I my way, every man would present his dossier upon introduction: "My birth is such, my prospects are so-and-so, and you may cultivate me if you wish." In that way people of breeding like ourselves, Louise, would not have upstarts forced on our acquaintance, and be obliged to suffer common thrusters in our society.'

'Alas, if it were possible. . . . But we are living in an age of ill breeding, Ellen. My mother talks of France as it was before the Revolution, and compares it with the present régime. Everything so vulgar now, so very different from when she was young. The trouble is that there *is* no society nowadays. Titled people to-day received their title under the Empire, and before that they were shopkeepers. What can you expect after that but bad manners and vulgarity?'

'It was certainly a pleasure to see someone like the Duke of Palmella,' said Ellen. 'I suppose his family goes back hundreds of years in Portugal. *Ça se voit.* He showed up amongst the petty noblemen at the wedding. As you were saying, there is no aristocracy in France at all.'

'I think perhaps that is why I was so enchanted with Mr Wallace. There is an indefinable "something" about Scotsmen, I always consider. Such a background behind them, so much history, so – well – so very romantic. The pipes and the kilt. We heard them once in London. I have never forgotten the incident. Since then I have had a fever for Scotland. What a pity, Ellen, that the Stuarts no longer sit on the English throne. There is so much grossness about your present royal family.'

'I was not aware of it,' said Ellen coldly.

'But surely – one has heard such tales – so much drunkenness and debauchery amongst those dreadful brothers; and their morals – quite unspeakable.'

'People of high position are for ever a prey to gossip, Louise. Personally, I know of nothing derogatory to the House of Brunswick.'

Louise glanced up in surprise. Her friend was sitting very straight in her chair, her mouth pursed, her chin in the air. She seemed offended. Louise regretted her words. How strange English people were! Ellen had taken her little criticism of the royal family as a personal insult.

'Of course,' she said tactfully, 'the position of King must be an appalling one. Such a responsibility; so difficult not to lose one's head.'

'So Louis the Sixteenth seems to have found,' said a sleepy voice from the couch, 'and he lost his in a basket, which is more than the rest of 'em do.'

The two friends started in surprise, and Ellen rose to her feet at once. 'Mother, I thought you were asleep,' she exclaimed. 'How long have you been awake?' A satin coverlet was kicked in the air, and a small foot waved a welcome to Louise. 'How d'y do, my dear? Always glad to see you. You're looking very pretty. What's all this about liking kilts and Scotsmen? I know a funny story about a kilt, but I daren't tell it in front of Ellen. I think a thistle came into it somewhere. . . . Use your own imagination. Tell Gustav to bring the lamps, Ellen. I want to get up.'

'You have not rested long enough,' said her daughter.

'Rest fiddlesticks! I'm tired of being on my back. Sit me up and arrange my cushions. That's better. Now I can see you both. What a solemn-looking pair you are! Might have been quoting Scripture from your expressions, instead of discussing a young man and his kilt. I quite agree with you. They're vastly becoming. Can't think why they don't all wear 'em. Save *us* a lot of trouble.'

She shook with laughter, and her little dog, disturbed from

her slumbers, stood up on her spindle legs and yapped. 'Be quiet, Lulu, or I won't give you a lollipop. There's a precious duck. Bark for Boney, then. Good dog. She still barks for Boney, with the poor fellow in his tomb all these years. . . . Tell me about your young man, Louise. I'm in quite a flutter.'

Ellen's eyes flashed a message to her friend. 'Keep a guard on your tongue,' they seemed to say; 'she will never leave you in peace.'

Louise smiled brightly at Madame Clarke. The terrible old lady must be humoured.

'We were chatting of the Palmella wedding,' she said. 'Ellen agrees with me that society has altered for the worse. I remarked upon the pleasing manners of a Mr Godfrey Wallace who was introduced to me. So refreshing to meet someone of breeding.'

'Very refreshing if he wore a kilt, I should say! Did he complain of the draught in Notre-Dame?'

'Mother, you are deliberately misunderstanding Louise,' said Ellen, with impatience. 'There was no question of Mr Wallace wearing a kilt. He is a secretary at the Legation, and is a son of a baronet, it appears – Sir Thomas Wallace, who has an estate in Ayr.'

'Very much in the air, if I know anything of Scotsmen,' clipped Madame Clarke. 'Probably consists of a cow-house and a quarry. Impecunious race, the Scots. Don't have anything to do with him. Who was his father, d'you say?'

'Sir Thomas Wallace, now resident in London.'

'Never heard of him. Can make enquiries, if you like. My lawyer, Fladgate, would find out for me. I still have my spies in London, you know. Nothing much escapes me.'

'Thank you, madam, but it's really of no consequence. I shall probably never meet Mr Wallace again.'

'Pity to lose a beau if he amuses you. I remember in Gloucester Place, when the house was full of officers from morning to night, none with a penny to bless 'emselves with, and how we used to laugh and jest and dress up in each other's clothes! My brother, Captain Thompson, was a gay spark. I shall never forget when he and two of his friends in the regiment put on my petticoats and bonnets and walked in Vauxhall, and I got myself in his uniform and ogled 'em! No one discovered the impersonation. We nearly died of laughing. Imagine George doing such a thing, Ellen! He would rather kill himself.'

'I should hope so, too.'

'Oh! Fie! You and George are both too mealy-mouthed. Do you good to forget yourselves. Don't listen to her, Louise. You enjoy yourself with your Scotsman if you want to, but keep a tight hand on his purse. When it's empty, let him go. No use playing a drowned fish.'

She talked in riddles, thought Louise. What an impossible woman! Poor Ellen!

'Mr Wallace is not likely to need his purse,' she said. 'If we meet, it will be in the Jardins du Roi for a little stroll one Sunday.'

'What d'you want to go there for? Much too exposed. All shrubs and no trees. Go to Versailles. Quite a forest at Versailles.'

'My dear mother, how could Ellen possibly undertake a journey to Versailles in the company of a strange man? The Jardins du Roi is a few minutes only from her apartment in the rue de la Lune.'

'Yes, I see. Very opportune. House only round the corner. Feel a little faint. Must lie down. Young Scotsman offers assistance. Apartment empty. Servant out. A convenient couch. And the rest to nature. . . . Damme, Louise, what a shocking girl you are!'

Madame Clarke chuckled, pointing an accusing finger at her daughter's friend. Louise felt that it was time to go. Ellen wore the usual air of disapproval habitual to her when her mother was present, a flush on her high cheek-bones, her lips pursed. Louise felt for her deeply. She got up from her chair, making some excuse about the lateness of the hour, but she knew that

Ellen was not deceived. Too many acquaintances had departed early from the house because of Mrs Clarke. As she went from the room, Louise was aware of a giggle from the depths of the couch, and a voice that murmured some monstrosity regarding a kilt and a cactus. She returned home with her mind made up, and that evening penned a letter to Mr Godfrey Wallace at the Hôtel de Paris.

Three days later, on a Sunday afternoon, when Louise was preparing to spend her weekly holiday from the *pension* in a quiet reading of the *Life of St Francis*, while her younger sister Adelaide occupied herself in plain sewing, the door flew open and Louis-Mathurin walked in unannounced, followed almost immediately by the secretary to the Legation. The two women uttered little cries of confusion, while their brother – evidently in tremendous spirits – took stock of the situation, holding up his hand for silence.

'I present you both my new friend Godfrey Wallace,' he declaimed. 'From henceforth we are to share board and lodging. We only met last night, but already we have sworn eternal friendship. Wallace believes with me that there is no truth except in the goddess of science. We discussed the stars until four in the morning. Wallace, my friend, sit down. My mother's apartment is poor but honourable. *Bon gentilhomme n'a jamais honte de la misère.*'

Louise could see that he was in his most theatrical mood; his hand was on his heart, his head was thrown back, and he would need no encouragement to burst into song. His absurdities put them all at their ease, and in a moment Wallace was at her side, a world of admiration in his eyes, his hands fingering the book she had laid aside. 'How I honour the saints!' he began at once. 'Had I but the courage, I would endeavour to emulate St Francis, but, alas! the flesh is weak. I called upon your brother as you desired me, and I must felicitate you on the relationship. So delightful a humour, so happy a temperament! And your sister here, such a modest appearance. It is really quite charming to meet with a family who are so lacking in false pride that when they visit Paris they live like the little Parisians – *comme les bourgeois*, as you term it! I dare swear that the contrast to the Château Maurier amuses you vastly.'

Louise smiled uncertainly, her mind in a ferment. Was it possible that he had spent several hours in company with Louis and still had not grasped their true position? 'I fear you attach a certain grandeur to us that does not exist,' she said nervously. 'We are very humble people really.'

He shook his head playfully. 'And your friend the Duchess de Palmella, is she humble, too?' he said. 'No, Mademoiselle Busson, you are one of those sweet persons who like to put humble secretaries like myself entirely at their ease. Your manner would be the same were I a duke. Your brother tells me he owes any good quality he possesses to you. What a nature!'

Louise blushed and laughed. It was really impossible to persuade Mr Wallace. The little party decided to take a turn in the Jardins du Roi, and the four of them set forth, Louise and Wallace a trifle behind the others, for Louis–Mathurin took immense strides which his sister Adelaide was still young enough to admire and wish to emulate.

Wallace offered his arm to Louise, and she took it with a little thrill of excitement, realising that she had never taken any arm but her brother's before. The sensation was really very pleasant, very agreeable.

'Your family must have suffered appallingly under the Terror,' began Mr Wallace in sympathetic tones. 'Your brother was telling me how your father and mother were obliged to fly for their lives to England, and that you were all born there – in exile, as it were. How I feel for you!'

'Yes, I suppose it was hard for my parents,' said Louise, 'but for ourselves I cannot complain. England seemed to be our home. I and my brothers and sister were very happy there. We knew nothing else.'

'Your brother tells me that on your return to France his late

Majesty Louis the Eighteenth made a grant to you all as a mark of his esteem?'

'Why, yes, a certain trifle, of no great consequence.'

'Perhaps not to you, Miss Busson, but to anyone else it would no doubt appear magnificent. To a poor Scot like myself, for instance!'

'I really cannot say. I do not know how you are circumstanced.'

'How I wish you could see my home in the Highlands. The wild scenery would appeal to a sensitive imagination such as yours.'

'Does Sir Thomas vary his time between Scotland and London?'

'Well, no, hardly. . . . That is to say, his health is far from good. The air of Scotland is a trifle damp. He – ah – he is more generally in Town, I believe.'

'You have seen him lately?'

'Why, no, alas! Here I am, chained to my office stool. We are not all free agents like yourself, dear Miss Busson.'

'I am as tied as yourself,' said Louise, determined to brave it at last. 'Did not Louis explain to you that I give English lessons at a *pension*?'

'Yes, he did indeed. What a delightful eccentricity! I was highly amused. He gave me to understand that you could not bear the life of a young lady of leisure. How I wish I were your pupil! I would be very dutiful, I promise you.'

Louise sighed. It was impossible to discourage him. She had always heard that obstinacy was a national characteristic of the Scots.

She could not but feel, however, that Louis-Mathurin, like herself, had glossed over their true position, and that, having once started the little deception, it was going to be exceedingly difficult to unravel the knot.

Godfrey Wallace was not indifferent to her – so much was obvious, even to the passers-by. He stayed close to her like a shadow; his eyes were never off her face, and he sighed from time to time as though oppressed.

He called her 'Dear friend', and 'Dear companion', which flustered her not a little, and he kept expressing his desire to see her often – two or three times a week, if she would permit it. It was flattering, certainly, but somewhat troubling; it looked almost as though he had certain intentions regarding her, and really she had never had the opportunity to consider marriage before.

When, after supper, he finally took his leave, with several protestations and insistences that she should write, her head was in such a whirl from excitement that she felt almost ill. Even Louis-Mathurin, generally in the clouds and oblivious to all but his own concerns, remarked upon her high colour.

'I am rather distressed,' she admitted to him in confidence, 'that Mr Wallace is under a misapprehension regarding us. What have you given him to understand?'

Louis-Mathurin yawned – a signal that he was not entirely at his ease.

'Why accuse me?' he said. 'I have not said anything. I happened to mention that my family had always been staunch Legitimists, and that we possessed a château in Sarthe, and one or two things like that. It is true that the château no longer exists, and I was going to tell him, but he started on some other subject and I forgot all about it. He seems a good fellow, and he knows people of influence. I thought perhaps he could get me one or two introductions. . . . I am working very hard on an invention, as you know, and he declared himself interested. I thought there was no harm in encouraging his interest. Why, Louise, do you turn up your nose at him?'

'On the contrary, I like him. I like him very much. I am only afraid that he will be disappointed in us.'

'My beloved sister, when my invention is perfected we need none of us worry again. We will all be famous. And you shall be the first to accompany me in my rocket to the moon.' He pulled her on to his knee and kissed her, laughing at her trou-

62

bled face, and then he rose from his chair and stretched himself, throwing back his curly head, flinging his long arms in the air, and he began to sing from the pure joy of living, from being young, and impecunious, and gay; the deep notes soaring from him effortless and free, mounting higher and higher until they softened in a whisper, immeasurably sweet, wringing his sister's heart with pain for no reason. Then he waved his hand to her, and, clapping a hat on to his chestnut curls, he strode from the room, forgetting her at once, forgetting his little debts, and his lies, and his God-given gift of beauty, thinking only of the fiery worlds in space and the mad stars.

The following Sunday, Godfrey Wallace called again, and he had scarcely entered the room before he flung himself down on his knees before Louise and demanded her hand in marriage. Scarcely knowing what she was doing, she stammered an acceptance, and in a moment he had swept upon her, straining her to his heart and covering her with kisses, murmuring that she had made him the happiest man on earth, and henceforth his life was in her hands.

He insisted that their marriage must take place at once, immediately. It would be torture for him to wait. But here she was firm. They must bide their time, she said, until her mother gave her consent and returned from Hamburg. The weeks that followed were like a strange delirium. It was impossible for Louise to believe that she, past thirty now, who had never had a proposal in her life, was adored and worshipped by a handsome young man several years her junior, and that she would shortly be a bride like Eugénie de Palmella.

In a fever she wrote to her eldest brother in London, to her mother in Hamburg, to Eugénie in Lisbon; in a dream she prepared her trousseau.

Still no question of money passed between her and her future husband, and she pushed the dark shadow away from her. It could wait until her mother returned.

Once she had tried to broach the subject; she had said something about her little dowry, the annuity to her family from the late King, as being all she possessed in the world to bring to him, and he had smiled, and put his hand over her mouth, saying, 'Surely you do not think I expect more?' and this had relieved her: he must, after all, understand something of her circumstances.

She was, in fact, so bewildered and fascinated by this future husband of hers that even the thought of being married in the Reformed Church was no torment to her conscience. Ellen Clarke did not know what to make of her friend. She was certain that *she* would never be infatuated to such an extent. It was so unreasonable, almost undignified. She was afraid that poor Louise would be sadly disillusioned after several weeks of marriage. Men were all alike in these matters. She had digested enough of her mother's conversation to know that. This Mr Godfrey Wallace seemed presentable enough – well mannered, too – but not at all what *she* would look for in a husband. He was just a little too effusive, and to her, at any rate, his gallantry did not ring quite sincere.

Not that she would tell Louise for the world. Louise was blind to counsel. Her Godfrey had no fault at all. Her Godfrey was perfect in every way. It would be interesting to see if she said the same in a year's time.

As for Mrs Clarke, she was enchanted. 'Such an appearance!' she said. 'Those green eyes, so intriguing! He reminds me exceedingly of Folkestone. You wouldn't remember him, Ellen. But, I declare, the same way of raising his eyebrows and smiling from the corner of his mouth. Tell Louise she must not let him out of her sight until the ring is on her finger. I know these green-eyed men. They are slippery fellows, and love to elude a bargain. I suppose she will have a settlement. What does he propose to do for her?'

'I gather from Louise that there has been no particular arrangement.'

'No arrangement? But she must be mad!' Mrs Clarke looked

aghast. 'You don't mean to tell me that Louise has tumbled into this without seeing to her interests? Without a settlement she will not have a hold on him at all. I have never heard of such a thing in my life!'

'I consider her rather foolish,' Ellen agreed, 'but the fact of the matter is that Louise is in such a state of excitement over the whole affair that she will listen to no one except her wonderful Mr Wallace.'

'A few weeks of married life will soon cure her of that,' said her mother. 'Nothing like it for clearing the system. As good as a purge. Do you good yourself, Ellen. Why don't you find a young man to love you?'

'I am perfectly content, thank you.'

'You are too sober, you and George. I wager he leads the life of a monk in India, bless him.' She kissed her hand to her son's miniature and smiled affectionately, and then fell to pampering her dog, forgetting him at once.

Two days before Madame Busson was due to return, a letter came from her at Hamburg to say that Jacques had taken the small-pox, and that she could not possibly leave him until he was perfectly well again. There was also the fear that Guillaume, who had just arrived there, might contract it also.

Louise was at once for postponing her marriage, but Wallace would not hear of it, becoming pale and nervous at the very suggestion, declaring that the suspense had already been more than he could bear, and that if he had to wait another week for his angelic Louise he would not answer for his reason. Swayed and flattered by this excess of adoration, the bride consented to his wishes, and on the fourteenth of April, eighteen hundred and thirty, the marriage was solemnised at the Église Suisse.

The register ran as follows:

'*Lundi, quatorze avril, mil huit cent trente.*
'GODFREY WALLACE, *secrétaire, né à Craigie, comté d' Ayr en Écosse, fils majeur de Sir Thomas Wallace, baronet, et de Rosina*

Raisne, son épouse; et LOUISE BUSSON DU MAURIER, *née à*
Londres, fille majeure du feu Robert Busson du Maurier et de
Marie-Françoise Bruère, son épouse; ont reçu la bénédiction
nuptiale par le ministère de Jean Monod, ministre du St.
Évangile, et l'un des pasteurs de l'église reformée consistoriale
du départment de la Seine séante à Paris, soussignée.
'(*Signé*) J. MONOD, *Pr.*'

Louise made her responses in a dream. Was it really true, she
wondered? Could it be possible that she was Madame Wallace?
She felt the ring on her finger – how bright and new it looked
– and she gazed up at her tall husband, whose manner, now
that the ceremony had actually taken place, had lost all its agitation and was collected and calm.

'The dear fellow believed he was not sure of me,' Louise
told herself, and, catching sight of her face in the mirror, she
could not help noticing how well she looked, her golden hair
arranged in loose curls, the white veil thrown back. Rather like
a nun, taking her final vows; and she wondered how she would
feel if, instead of becoming the bride of Godfrey Wallace, she
had indeed been wedded to Holy Church.

The reception, partly because of Madame Busson's absence,
and partly at Louise's own request, was a small one; not even
Mrs Clarke had the time or opportunity to be offensive, and
as soon as the health of the bride and bridegroom had been
drunk, Mr and Mrs Godfrey Wallace left for the Hôtel de Paris
in the Madeleine, which was to be their temporary home.

The happy pair dined alone at five o'clock, and during the
meal Louise noticed that her husband's nervousness had
returned. He ate sparingly, and now and again he glanced over
his shoulder as though he expected to be interrupted.

'Are you ill, my love?' questioned his bride, and at once he
reassured her, pleading a slight headache, the excitement of the
day.

The meal over, they went upstairs, and Louise, who was

herself naturally a little upset at the prospect of conjugal life, made play of unpacking her clothes and arranging them in the wardrobe, more to give herself countenance than anything else; while her husband paced up and down the room deep in thought, his hands clasped behind his back.

Finally he came over to her, and, taking her hands in his, began to speak in tones of great confusion.

'My beloved wife,' he stammered, 'I hardly know how to express myself. . . . I am all agitation. What you will think of me I dare not say. The fact is this. I – I am momentarily embarrassed for money. An unlucky speculation . . . one thing and another . . . my life at the Legation . . . in short . . . well, you understand that I am entirely without the means of supporting you. At this moment, I have less than a hundred francs.'

Louise stared at him without comprehension. Did he mean he was unable to pay for their lodging here at the hotel, for their very food?

'I don't quite understand,' she said. 'Do you mean you have not sufficient for our board here? Will they not trust us until you obtain the money?'

He blushed and smiled, more embarrassed than ever. 'Ah, but there lies the difficulty. How can I obtain it? My intense love for you, dearest Louise, has forced me to play this little deception. My fear was so great that I should lose you, and if you knew the truth you would cast me from you. My dearest angel – better to confess here and now – I am a penniless wretch. My father disinherited me five or six years ago. I have not a sou in the world. I must throw myself upon your charity.'

Louise looked up at him in great distress.

'But, Godfrey, how can I help you? My poor little annuity will never keep us both.'

'Oh, but you are such a capable little manager, you will do wonders. My tastes are not expensive. We will live very well. It is only that I am such a brute to depend on you. I daresay that when your château is fully restored your brother will make

67

some provision for us – he would give me a place as supervisor in the factory. In the meanwhile, your allowance from the State . . .'

His wife turned very pale. She sat down on a chair and began clasping and unclasping her hands.

'I am afraid there has been a terrible mistake,' she said. 'There is no question of the château being restored. It passed to other hands when we returned to France. I do not even know where it is. My father was unable to claim it; everything was unsettled. He died in proverty at Tours. My mother had a little income from her people in Brittany, and we have been living on that. I endeavoured to help by becoming English teacher at the *pension*.'

Wallace had turned as pale as his wife. He stared at her in horror. 'But your annuity,' he said, 'your annuity from Louis the Eighteenth?'

'I tried to tell you,' she cried in agony; 'it was a form of courtesy, nothing more. Two hundred francs a year.'

'Two hundred francs a year?' he thundered.

She nodded, terrified at the expression on his face. 'But I understood from everyone you were an heiress!' he screamed. 'Mademoiselle Busson du Maurier, with estates in Sarthe, a personal allowance from the late King. I assumed as much from your brother. He never denied it. And your friendship with the Duchesse de Palmella, how do you explain that?'

'She was my pupil at the *pension* – I taught her English – she became fond of me.'

He rocked on his feet as though she had struck him in the face.

'Oh, my God, my God!' he said. He began to sob like a little child. He sat down on the bed, his face in his hands, swaying to and fro.

She sat beside him without a word, swallowing now and again from fright, her hands, very damp and tense, folded in her lap.

Presently he got up and went out of the room. She thought perhaps he had gone for a glass of water, and she waited, expecting him to return at any minute.

He did not come back. She heard the chimes of midnight, and one, and two, and three; and still she sat there, stiffly, like a poker, her hands folded, her face towards the door.

She tried to make a picture of him in her mind and it would not come. Already his features were indefinite, his colouring blurred. The only face that came to her unbidden was her brother's, Louis-Mathurin; it kept laughing up at her out of the darkness, inconsequent and careless, with his tight chestnut curls, his impudent blue eyes.

6

For three days Louise remained secretly at the hotel, saying nothing to her family or her friends, pretending hopelessly to herself that Godfrey Wallace would return to her. On the fourth day the manager of the hotel became suspicious – he had never known a bride spend the first days of a honeymoon alone – and he demanded payment for his room. His manner, that had been obsequious before, changed abruptly, and he was now insinuating, a bully, bluntly telling Louise that she had been deserted, and that it was the fate of all women who married husbands younger than themselves. Louise, near to breaking-point, summoned her courage and began to pack the clothes she had unfolded so happily four nights ago. She would not remain to be insulted, and the stinging words of the manager found a place in her heart and rooted there. She could not but wonder how much of truth there was in his suggestion. The whole tragedy had come about through her own sinful pride. She had led Godfrey to believe she had money and possessions, and he, penniless himself, had seized his opportunity and won her to him by words of flattery that she should never have permitted.

He had never loved her. So much was plain. He imagined her rich and desired her money. Had he but a grain of affection for her he would never have left her on the first night of their marriage. She could forgive his lies and his deception, she could forgive the expression on his face when he learnt that she was as poor as he; but this last insult – no, that she could never forgive. A bride deserted on her wedding-night! She could never hold up her head again. How the girls at the *pension* would stare, how the Directrice would sneer. And Mrs Clarke – Louise could hear the broad, lascivious laugh, the coarse jest; she could see the wagging finger, the shake of the head, and she could picture the pity in Ellen's eyes coupled with a pursing of the lips and 'I told you so.' The shame of it! The agony and the bitterness, remaining to the day she died!

As she prepared to leave the hotel, the manager presented her with a six-page document as a bill – arrears of rent owed to him, he insisted, by Mr Wallace; and Louise, rather than argue with him, delved into her little savings and settled the sum. Then she took a *fiacre* and drove out to a convent at Versailles where she had friends amongst the nuns, and where she had often gone to retreat.

They received her amongst them, asking no questions, and there she nursed her wounded, bitter heart, praying for counsel, begging for courage to face the world again. She wrote to her family and to Ellen, explaining briefly what had happened, and desiring them to do nothing in the matter – neither to communicate with her nor to seek her out until she felt strong enough to have word with them. As to her husband, they were not to pursue him. If he loved her he would come back to her. If he did not love her, then she had no wish to see him again.

Her letters were a thunderbolt to the family.

Madame Busson, in Hamburg, ran distracted amongst her German friends, declaring that her daughter had been outraged and betrayed, and was only pacified when a note of explanation came from Adelaide saying that Louise had at least been married, and bore a ring on her finger in proof; the register had been examined, and the pastor questioned, and, even if her husband was a scoundrel and a rogue, she was Madame Wallace, of blameless reputation.

Robert, in London, put forth enquiries respecting the Wallace family, and found Sir Thomas to be an impoverished old gentleman of no standing in Scotland, who had seen nothing of his son for years. Louis-Mathurin, who was in great distress and blamed himself for having encouraged the secretary in the beginning, rushed out to Versailles, and with tears in his eyes begged his sister for an interview. It was permitted. She came into the little waiting-room very pale and dignified, but as soon as she saw him the composure of the last weeks deserted her and she burst into tears.

'The scoundrel, the villain, I'll see that justice is done!' swore her brother, shaking clenched fists and breathing fire, part of his anger due to the realisation that he had been as big a fool as his sister, and that his wonderful invention still lacked a patent, and himself the support of influential friends.

In spite of Louise's wishes and her repeated injunction that she did not wish her husband to be hunted down and traced, matters moved swiftly. It was soon discovered that Godfrey Wallace was wanted for swindle and theft; that he had forged papers at the Legation; and was, in short, a rogue.

Even his pretended intimacy with the Duke of Palmella was false; the Duke wrote from Portugal denying all knowledge of the fellow beyond having met him once in a café. He had gained admittance to his wedding by an air of assurance and a bribe to the servant at the door.

'I told you green eyes were never to be trusted,' said Mrs Clarke to Ellen. 'If Louise had listened to me, she'd have tied him down to a settlement and now she would have had the laugh of him. But to get herself married without any surety, and then not a penny from it, not even a wedding night – well, I had a good many strange experiences when I was young, but, damme, I never had that!'

'I distrusted him from the first,' said Ellen; 'he had a sly way of looking under his lashes that I always found most disagree-able, and he used to caress his whiskers with his long fingers – quite horrible to my mind.'

'Horrible my foot!' said her mother. 'The man may have been a rogue, but I wager he knew what to do with his hands. More than Louise did, I dare swear. He was the double of

Folkestone, I shall always insist. These green-eyed men have scurrilous characters, but such amusing habits.'

She sighed in retrospect, her mouth full of lollipops, and then, demanding loudly paper and pen, she set herself to write to her lawyer, Fladgate, enquiring in language strong and to the point why her dividend from the Duke of York was so monstrously overdue.

Meanwhile poor Louise languished in the convent, spending most of her time on her knees before her crucifix, and finally, on the eighth of July, a letter was brought to her bare little room by a meek, round-eyed nun.

The letter was penned in the bold, flourishing hand she knew so well. The postmark was Calais. Louise waited a moment; her emotion was almost too strong to bear. Then she took courage and broke the seal.

This is what she read:

'*Ah, Louise, your most wretched Husband has at last met with his merits. I have arrived at Calais and at the instigation of your brother Louis have been arrested and thrown in Prison for no less a crime than that of* SWINDLING *and having abandoned my* WIFE. *Whatever my errors have been my conscience is clear as to that. I can call my God to witness that I am innocent of having abandoned my wife. My separation from you was momentary to avoid the disgrace of having made away with another person's money at a wretched Gambling Table. The hopes of gaining money to clear off debts I had already contracted was alone what induced me to the rash act. If your Heart is not entirely shut to the voice of Pity, for God's sake write to me, and endeavour to obtain the influence to release me from this base Cell. I will meet with patience the just reward of the Law and shall only live for her by whom I was once loved, and whose picture is for ever engraved in my heart. One word to the Duke of Palmella might effectuate my pardon, my dearest Louise, and I will endeavour to atone to you for my Base crime. Oh, pardon*

or at least pity your once beloved Husband. Write and tell him
that you are not so miserable as he is; then he will meet either
death or any other Punishment the Law may award.

'*I cannot write any more, but let me once more entreat a*
single line from you.

'*I am, unalterably yours,*

'*Your Husband*

'GODFREY WALLACE.'

'He loves me still,' was her first thought; 'he has remained true
to me in spite of everything. I have only to send the money and
we will be together again. My married life will no longer be an
empty lie.' In a fever of excitement she dressed herself in her
outdoor clothes for the first time in many weeks, and set out
for Paris. When she reached the apartment in the rue de la Lune
she found her mother just returned from Hamburg, preparing
to visit her at Versailles. Yes, it was all true. Godfrey Wallace had
been found. A letter from Louis-Mathurin had come that
morning. He was in Calais, and the wretch in prison at his instigation. 'But he must be released at once,' cried Louise. 'I cannot
bear that he should suffer the indignity of a cell. There is no
time for a letter to reach Portugal now, though I know Eugénie
would help me. Somehow we must obtain the money and send
it immediately. My husband has acted rashly, even wickedly, I
admit, but he loves me still and lives only to be united.'

Once more she was deaf to reason. The solid wisdom of her
Breton mother fell on closed ears; she could not or would not
listen. 'He has failed you once and he will fail you again,' warned
Madame Busson. 'What you do now is the act of a madwoman.
He will never return to you.'

'He must! He shall!' stormed Louise, her usually gentle
expression tormented with repressed anger and longing. 'His
letter is a proof of his affection. As soon as he is liberated he
will come to me.' She ran round and round her little circle of
friends like a blind mole, begging five francs from one, five

from another – securing eighty from Mrs Clarke, who in a sudden fit of generosity gave her a ruby ring to sell, declaring she could not resist a woman so pathetically and violently in love as Louise, even if she were the biggest fool in France.

The money was collected and dispatched. A line of protest came from Louis-Mathurin. Another letter from Louise threatening she would come to Calais herself if her husband was not liberated immediately. Then silence. Everyone waited for the reply. Louise, with her eyes on the door of her mother's apartment, sat from morning till night expecting the door to open and her wretched and adored husband to stumble to her arms.

On the twenty-second of July, Adelaide, who had been watching from the window for the *facteur*, rushed downstairs to the concierge and came up again with a letter bearing the Calais postmark. Louise snatched it from her, tore the seal, and read it aloud.

> '*My ever-lovely Louise, I am at the moment about to embark for England. I have, this morning, the 19th, been liberated at your instigation and with the money you sent, and at three I leave this accursed land of France for ever. Rest assured that I will soon relieve you from your anxiety. I soon expect the pleasure of embracing the only object of my heart, and you will soon receive money sufficient to defray all expenses. Your ever-loving Husband has nothing in view but the Happiness of his Dearest Louise. Ah, conceive what I have suffered on your account; words cannot express my feelings. Endeavour to pardon your unfortunate Husband. I will write on my arrival in London, and will soon procure means to embrace the only object of my heart.*
> '*Ever your sincere lover and husband,*
> '*G. WALLACE.*'

The little group listened in silence, and when Louise had finished she read it over again to herself. Then she raised her eyes and looked at her mother.

75

'You see,' she said slowly, 'he thinks only of my happiness. In two or three weeks he will send for me to join him in England.'

Her mother did not answer. Adelaide got up from her chair and went quietly from the room. Louise went on sitting with the letter in her lap.

She knew now that she would never see Godfrey Wallace again.

It was provident that Eugénie de Palmella should write at this moment from Lisbon, saying she was expecting a child in October, and she could not possibly face the ordeal unless her dearest Louise was by her side. Madame Wallace decided to leave France at once for Portugal. Once away from Paris and all that reminded her of her miserable husband, she could pick up the threads of her old life, giving to Eugénie and to Eugénie's children that store of affection that filled her heart. She could do more good, so she argued, by serving others than by shutting herself up in a convent, which had been her original intention. 'But for Fate intervening,' she wrote to her friend, the Duchess, announcing her arrival, 'I might now be in the same happy state as yourself, and we could have looked forward to motherhood together. Now this can never be, and I am a widow in all but name. Therefore, dear Eugénie, I take this opportunity to dedicate myself to you and your family, and you may make what use of me you like. I will be nurse, companion, governess, should you so desire it, and in watching those expressions of conjugal bliss between you and your husband I will find myself recompensed in some measure for what I have lost.' So poor deserted Louise set forth for Portugal, the romance of her life ended, and the momentary lustre gone from her for ever. She was thirty-five, and she looked older. There were threads of white now in her soft gold hair, and lines of disappointment circled her mouth. Louis-Mathurin, only a few years her junior, looked a boy beside her. She kissed him with great tenderness when she said good-bye; he was like a child to her still, and the fact that he had been instrumental in the furthering of her unfortunate marriage was a link between them rather than a barrier. 'Remember, I expect to hear great things of you,' she said. 'Eugénie and I will read of your invention when it is perfected, and everyone in Lisbon will envy me for possessing a famous brother.'

'We shall be making journeys to the planets in ten years' time,' he told her eagerly. 'You can leave Lisbon in the early morning and arrive at the moon to drink your tea. I only need a few months and my invention will change the face of the world. Life will become so much fuller, so infinitely more worth while; the universe itself will be open to us. Only a few months more, Louise.'

'You must not tire yourself by working too hard, dear.'

'Tire? I never tire. My energy is boundless. I drink of the elixir of life itself. At this moment I am as one of the gods.'

She smiled at his absurd enthusiasm, and then, as she embraced him for the last time, he whispered his final message in her ear.

'It might not be entirely inopportune,' he said, 'if you should mention to your friend the Duke that your brother is on the track of a great invention, and that he is only prevented from giving his invention to the world by a regrettable lack of money. . . . Should the Duke show interest, he might even . . . well, you understand, Louise . . . just a hint . . . just a casual word dropped at the right moment.'

His sister looked grave at once. 'I do not want Eugénie to feel her friendship is only of value because of her husband's position,' she said; 'I love her for herself alone, not for her wealth nor her title.'

'Of course, of course,' he assented rapidly; 'nothing would be further from my intentions than that you should trade upon her affection in any way. No, no, indeed. I am far too proud to accept favours from anybody. A Busson would never beg.

Bon sang ne sait mentir, as I always say. No; *it is* only a little hard that the loan of a few francs stands between me and fortune. A handful of coins from the pocket of a nobleman who would not even notice their absence may mean all the difference between fame and starvation. The world and future generations will be deprived of the greatest invention of the day because of a tiny scruple. It does not matter. Better perhaps that the world should retrogress rather than advance. . . . What do I care?'

'Hush, Louis. Don't speak so wildly. I did not mean to hurt your feelings. And if I can interest the Duke in your schemes, I will, I promise you. There, let that content you.' He was all smiles at once, his blue eyes impudent as a child's, and she carried away with her to Portugal this last vision of him as he waved farewell; his tall, slim figure, all arms and legs, his snub nose, and his chestnut curls blowing in the summer wind.

Meanwhile, in her apartment at Auteuil, Mrs Clarke had been in correspondence with her lawyer, Fladgate, as to the possibility of laying hands upon Mr Godfrey Wallace. She was pleased to think she had a certain amount of influence still in London, and she had only to set her spies, as she termed them, to work and they would soon be hot-foot upon his trail.

Meddling in other people's affairs had always been her greatest pleasure, as her former career proved, and, now that she had retired from that profession to which she had given the best years of her life, advancing age and declining beauty having necessitated her withdrawal from business, she took an intense delight in probing into the little misfortunes of her few remaining friends, with a word of advice here and a suggestion there, thrusting her tip-tilted, inquisitive nose into many matters that concerned her not at all. Beyond betraying certain confidences, destroying faith between friends, and breaking one or two marriages, she did very little harm in a general way. Her quick wits and sharp tongue were always at the disposal of those who did not need them, and so her life, in retirement, was not really as empty as might be supposed.

The sad story of Louise Busson and her scapegrace husband, who had been so remiss as to desert his wife on the night of her wedding, was a situation after Mrs Clarke's heart. It was so full of possibilities. While she commiserated over the poor bride with her daughter, shaking her head wisely and declaring what she would have done in her place, she would change her manner when gentlemen were present, and the story became, on those few nights when she entertained the riff-raff of the decayed *noblesse*, the *pièce de résistance* of the evening. Old marquises and white-haired counts, who had not sniggered so heartily since Marie-Antoinette was lampooned in the passages at Versailles, staggered home to bed with the tears running down their cheeks.

'*Mais elle est épatante, cette Madame Clarke!*' they gasped, their hands to their sides, fancying themselves once more as young blades tripping through the obscenity of the eighteenth century; while Mary Anne, her raddled face heavily painted and her lashes darkened, shook in silent mirth at the memory of her successful evening, and how old du Croissant had spilt his wine down his shirt-front and Le Remilly had hiccuped his soup over the napery.

Such a good thing Ellen had been at the other end of the table, and had neither observed their manners nor heard the story. Poor Louise, it was really a monstrous shame, but the incident of the wedding night did so lend itself to exploitation, sighed Mary Anne, wiping the tears of laughter from her smudged lashes, and she and Ellen would be asked to dine with the Marquis on the strength of it. So few amusing people nowadays. Such a dearth of wit. Everyone so prim and proper and middle-class. Bourgeois, they called it here. She thought of the old parties in Park Lane and Gloucester Place, and the broken glass strewn on the floor, and the split wine, and how no one had ever been in a condition to walk to his carriage, but must

79

always send for his servant to carry him. Oh, Lord! for the guttering candles, and the rich meats swimming in sauce, and the red wine, and the strong perfumes, and the handsome young officers, with their oaths and their hot hands, making improper proposals in the dark corner of the drawing-room. . . . Here she was, an old lady over fifty, with rheumatism in the left leg and wind under the heart, and she had experienced quite a flutter when du Croissant had dropped his handkerchief under the table and in fumbling for it had touched her ankle swinging beneath her petticoat.

Poor Louise, she little knew the merriment she had caused; and Mrs Clarke sat herself down in a pang of remorse and badgered the unfortunate Mr Fladgate to continue his search for Louise's husband.

The mission was partly successful. Word came that Wallace had been heard of in Chatham, as having enlisted in the service of the East India Company, but in what particular position it could not be discovered.

Fladgate was then instructed to proceed to Chatham, to the offices of the company, and make enquiries as to the delinquent; but whether he omitted to do so immediately is not certain; at any rate, by the time he did arrive in Chatham, Wallace had disappeared. A vessel had left Gravesend for India at the end of the month, and he was believed to have been on board.

To pursue the adventurer to the East was more than Mrs Clarke could accomplish, and, though she did write to her son George, whose regiment was stationed in India, desiring him to keep his eyes open for a green-eyed young man with side-whiskers, she had no further hope of success.

Louise, stitching baby clothes in Portugal and making the inevitable comparison between herself and Eugénie, bore the news with composure. Godfrey at least was alive, and in good health, as far as was known. If he wished to hide his shame in the jungles of India, she had no power to stop him. All she could do was to pray to Almighty God that he should be shown the error of his ways and would repent before he fell to utter damnation.

She wrote to her brother, begging him to call on Mrs Clarke and thank her for the trouble she had taken, bearing also messages to Ellen. And Louis-Mathurin set forth one September afternoon, rather bored by his mission, knowing very little of the Clarkes beyond what he had heard from his sister, and having a vague memory of a painted old lady, preposterously over-dressed, at the unfortunate wedding. He had no recollection whatsoever of the daughter.

Arrived at his destination, he was informed by the concierge in his *loge* that Madame Clarke lived in the apartment on the second floor.

He proceeded up the narrow flight of stairs, his thoughts a hundred miles away, and as he climbed he was aware of music somewhere, borne down to him from the landing above. The sound was muffled, almost insensible, like dream music heard by a sleeper before waking. He paused to listen, and there it came, clearer now, from behind the door on the second landing, the soft rippling notes of a harp, sweet and unexpected on this stale September day. Someone was playing Schubert's Serenade. Strange choice for a harpist, thought Louis-Mathurin, and he waited, smiling, to see how the unknown player would manage the little echoing accompaniment that follows the melody. Half consciously he began to hum under his breath, turning the handle of the door as he did so, and, when the door opened to his touch, he walked straight into the apartment without thinking, never pausing for a servant to introduce him, his whole self lost in the plaintive beauty of the Serenade, his favourite song, which had come to him thus unbidden. That his visit was unexpected, and his hostess a stranger, mattered not at all to Louis-Mathurin, who had only to hear Schubert to be possessed. Like a sleepwalker he passed into the *salon*, tracing the harp to its source, and Ellen, brooding beside her instrument, looked up suddenly and saw him advancing towards her like an apparition, a tall, scraggy figure with vague blue eyes and scarlet curls, singing the Serenade as she had never heard it sung before. Her magic fingers faltered, were idle a moment, as the thought flashed through her mind that the servant must have lost his reason to admit a visitor without permission, but her hesitation was unnoticed by the stranger; he was entrapped now in the flow of his own song, and the ceasing of her music would not release him.

She fell in with his mood then, a passionate victim to his voice, and, forgetting those formalities and conventions usually dear to her stern temperament, she took up the thread of her song once more, compelled to follow him who had followed her before. The harmony was perfect; neither destroyed the other; and the two dissolved into one another without knowing, obeying some blind instinct of which they had no waking knowledge, making their little talents an unconscious gift to God. It was as though they were momentarily suspended in time, with no past and no future, and the necessity of daily toil, of food, of plodding the hours, was something with which they no longer had concern. The petty meanness of their natures fell from them, and his lies and his poses and his dishonesty were taken from him with her narrowness, her intolerance, and her pride. They were stripped of their poor sins, and were now no more than naked children with a love of beauty.

Then the song finished. The last ripple of the harp vanished to nothingness. His whispered breath sank away, and died, and, though the magic was no more and they were only a man and a woman smiling a little foolishly at one another, something of themselves had made union in the invisible and would continue into eternity.

'You are Ellen Clarke,' he said. 'Louise never told me you were a musician. How many hours I have wasted, when I might have known!'

'I saw you at the wedding,' she said, 'but you looked different then, almost another person. I had no wish to talk to you.'

'I am glad we've found each other like this,' he said. 'Music has spared us the absurd formality of introduction. Had I come into this room behind a servant I would have bowed to you, and handed you my sister's letter, and we would have chatted inanities for five minutes, and then I would have bowed again, and you given me your hand, and we would never have seen one another again.'

'And because it hasn't happened in that way, what shall we do?' she said.

'Why, we shall discuss life, and death, and how unhappy we are, and why we do not believe in God, and how Euclid was the greatest man that ever lived; and, when we are tired of that, you shall sit beside your harp again and I will sing for you.'

'I remember now, Louise has often told me about you. You are a scientist, which she does not quite approve, and you are an atheist, which frightens her.'

'Louise should have been a nun. She does not exist in the world at all. She has never heard of Galileo, of Bruno, of Copernicus; she prays to the saints (who, by the way, were epileptics, all of them), and confesses her poor little imaginary sins to a fat priest who does not listen, and, if he does, he has no business to.'

'Were you not brought up as a Catholic?'

'Of course I was, that's why I'm an atheist. I read a book about the Inquisition when I was ten, and saw a picture of the Massacre of St. Bartholomew when I was twelve, and I've hated Catholicism ever since. Catholics have persecuted thinkers and philosophers since the beginning. If I had my way, I would hang every priest from the nearest tree.'

'I'm inclined to agree with you. But, then, I've never had any religion at all.'

'We shall agree famously, then. We are both free-thinkers and we both adore music. There is no better base for companionship. What do you know of science?'

'Very little. I desire to know more. History has always been my favourite subject, and I've read more books than I can count.'

'We will read together; or, rather, I will read and you will listen. I am glad you are different from the usual type of young woman, who simpers behind a fan and demands pretty compliments.'

'I have never expected or received a compliment in my life.'

'Why should you? You are not beautiful. There, you see, I pay you your first compliment by telling you the truth! No, you are not beautiful, but you have very striking features. You have a Roman face. You should be on a coin.'

'A pair of nut-crackers, my brother used to say.'

'No, that is harsh. A true brotherly remark. You have very expressive eyes. How old are you, I wonder?'

'Two years younger than Louise.'

'Then you are the same age as myself. We become more and more alike. And you spent your childhood in England, as I did, and you grew up in France, even as myself. We may even have travelled here on the same boat!'

'It is quite likely. We left England in the March of 1810.'

'So did we! But this is amazing. Why has Louise never told me all this?'

'We have never discussed it.'

'And you have known her how long? Two years, is it? And I have known you ten minutes, and already understand you better. I shall visit you often. Do you mind? Now that Louise has gone to Portugal there is no one willing to listen to me when I talk about myself. I feel stifled in the rue de la Lune. My mother does not understand me, and Adelaide is too young. I have a feeling you will listen.'

'Yes, and talk too! I have held my tongue for thirty years and have grown rather tired of silence. My mother is a rattle, and two talkers in a family do not always make for peace.'

'So you sit with your embroidery while she converses?'

'On the contrary, I play the harp and do not listen. Beyond playing, I have no talent with my hands. I hardly know how to sew!'

'Better and better. I detest domesticated women. That is why I have never married. *Soupe à la bonne femme* and babies' flannels and discussions about small-pox in the neighbourhood – it would not do for me at all!'

'Nor I either, I cannot bear small-talk. That's why I am such a failure in society. Let me but argue, or criticise a book, or damn a politician, and I will continue until two or three in the morning. But my mother will have none of it. She must be amused.'

'I believe you are a very dutiful daughter. . . . But wait, I am forgetting my mission. Here is a letter from Louise, addressed to Mrs Clarke. Will you open it?'

'No. She dearly loves a letter. She has so few these days.'

'You are unselfish as well as dutiful. Louise bade me give you many messages, and I have forgotten them all. Perhaps I will remember them in the night and then I will come out to you to-morrow before I forget them again. God save my soul! Is this your mother?'

He stared incredulously at the open door, through which a strange vision in white had made its appearance. Mrs Clarke, her hair newly curled and dyed, and arranged in the latest fashion on the top of her head, advanced to meet him, dressed as though for a Court presentation in a satin gown whose designer had intended it to be worn by a child of seventeen.

Her arms and shoulders, carefully whitened to alabaster, were well preserved, but all the powder in the world could not conceal the lines in her throat and the wrinkles on her hands, which were like little monkey's paws.

'I know who you are,' she said roguishly, shaking her head at him. 'You are Louise's brother. The family likeness is ridiculous. But where have you been hiding yourself all this time? Why have we never seen you before?'

85

Louis-Mathurin bowed politely. 'Madame, the loss is entirely mine. When my sister mentioned her friends the Clarkes, she omitted to tell me that Miss Ellen possessed a sister. You are she, I presume?'

'Oh, fiddlesticks! None of your nonsense, Mr Busson. I was a married woman and a mother before you drew your first breath. You are quizzing me, I know.'

'Madame, I would not dare to do so for the world.'

'Oh, so you pretend. I know your sex too well. Lived with 'em and foxed 'em since I was seventeen. How do you like my gown?'

'I have not noticed it. The wearer holds my attention.'

'Damme, what a liar you are! I saw your face when I entered the room. I know I'm an old woman, but I can't help it. So few pleasures left, and, dear Lord! how I adore a new gown. Ellen here doesn't give a fig for such things. What have you both been talking about?'

'Madame, we discovered we are affinities. Born in the same year, with the same tastes, there is scarce a subject upon which we don't agree.'

'Don't tell me Ellen has found a twin! I won't countenance it for a moment. Sir, do you think I'd make the same mistake twice?'

'Surely Miss Clarke was not a mistake?'

'I rather fancy she was, Mr Busson. It's so long ago I really can't remember. No doubt I was as absent-minded then as I am now. I never did pay much attention to little details. . . . Poor Ellen, what a disgraceful mother you have! She's such a good daughter, too, Mr Busson, I wouldn't part with her for the world. Only for a rich husband with several thousands a year.'

'Perhaps Miss Clarke has something to say in the matter?'

'Miss Clarke would much rather not be discussed at all,' said Ellen firmly.

The laughter was general, and the little group moved into the inner *salon*.

'Here's my Lulu, my precious Lulu,' exclaimed Mrs Clarke, reaching for her obnoxious toy dog, who immediately set up her ridiculous yapping at the sight of a stranger. 'Is she not the sweetest thing you ever saw? Kiss the gentleman, then, Lulu. Brave man, you stand it well! Her breath is unbearable; her darling teeth are bad. Ellen, order tea. Poor Mr Busson is exhausted.'

She sat down on the couch, patting a place beside her for Louis-Mathurin, who realised with a shrug of his shoulder that escape was impossible.

'So nice to have a presentable young man in the house,' sighed Mrs Clarke. 'We have all the riff-raff here, I'm afraid. Not very amusing for Ellen. And the old men don't take to her. She's not sweet and pretty enough, and she can't flirt. Neither of my children flirt, Mr Busson. They leave all the work to their poor mother.'

'But in very capable hands, madame.'

'Oh, fie, you dog! I suppose you think I'm going to flirt with you. If I were twenty years younger I would, and I wager you'd have liked it. You chestnut-headed men are always warm-blooded.'

'My blood runs like ice in my veins, Mrs Clarke.'

'Pooh! I don't believe it. If it does, it has no business to. Can't think what is the matter with you young people. My sweet George won't look at a woman, so he tells me. There's his portrait. Is he not the handsomest thing you ever saw?'

'He certainly appears to wear his uniform to advantage, madame.'

'Uniform, fiddlesticks! My George would be lovely without it. You should see a man stripped before you judge his full beauty.'

'You are a connoisseur, Mrs Clarke?'

'I was, my dear boy, I was. Don't tell Ellen. She's so easily shocked. When you've entertained half the English Army in your house, you can't but know something about 'em dressed and undressed!'

'You must have been a great help to the Service, madame?'

'Help be damned, Mr Busson! The service relied on me entirely. Not an ensign, twenty-five years ago, but got his commission through me. Were he presentable he got something else in the bargain. The dear fellows. Always very grateful for the least little thing. I tell you, sir, in those days there was scarce a man in the Army I didn't know something about, from the Duke of York down to the drummer-boy.'

'Indeed, madame! How very commendable! I had always heard that the Battle of Waterloo was won on the playing-fields of Eton College. Is it possible that there has been some error, and it was really won on the person of Mrs Clarke?'

The old lady shook with laughter, poking her companion in the ribs.

'Oh, delightful! Exquisite! Why did I never think of that myself? I tell you what, Mr Busson, you've got a very pretty wit. They'd love you in Town. You can sing like an angel, too. I heard you just now. You ought to train for opera.'

'I intended to. Family obstacles, madame, prejudice, one thing and another.'

'Nonsense! With your appearance you'd have made a fortune. I was on the stage once; I know all about it. I tell you I've heard all the best singers in Town and on the Continent, and I've never heard such a fine natural voice as yours.'

'You do me honour.'

'I speak the truth. What is your profession, then?'

'I dabble in science, madame. I invent machines. One day my name will be on every person's lips as a great creator.'

'How very amusing! What do you invent?'

'At the moment I'm engaged upon a miraculous machine that will carry us all to the moon.'

'But, my dear man, does anyone want to go to the moon? I'm sure I have no desire to fly through the air. What would we do when we got there?'

'That, madame, I confess, has not occurred to me. No doubt

we will explore the territory; come upon strange beasts, strange men even. . . .'

'Strange men, my foot! If they were made any different they certainly would not amuse *me*. I shouldn't know what to do with 'em.'

'Ah, Mrs Clarke, but what fun it would be finding out!'

'Do you think so? I fear I'm too old. Couldn't begin all over again at my age! Hush! Here's Ellen with the tea. We must behave ourselves. She's such a prude. Ellen, my love, I've taken a great liking to this young man. He's quite a wit. Much more amusing than his sister. Poor Louise, we are all very fond of her, Mr Busson, but she has never made me laugh.'

'She takes life too seriously, madame. She has always done so. And now, since that unfortunate marriage, I wonder whether she will ever smile again.'

'What a dreadful affair! Quite shocking. I was grieved beyond measure. Such a nice-looking young man, too. You were all deceived in him. And then to desert her in that manner, on her wedding-night. I suppose no one will ever know the truth of that little episode.'

'I think it kinder not to enquire, madame.'

'Oh, very true and proper. Much kinder. Still, one cannot help wondering. Your poor, dear sister, so inexperienced . . . if she had only . . . however, she would never have taken advice from me.'

'What would you have suggested, madame?'

'I'll tell you another time. When Ellen isn't here. Now, you tell me what *you* would do if your wife ran away on your wedding-night.'

'Sleep alone, I presume, madame.'

'Oh, fie . . . and you an inventor! Ellen, I am sure you are going to forget Lulu's tea. Three lumps of sugar, and let it cool first.'

'Lulu has had her tea, mamma.'

'Then give her another saucer. . . . Well, Mr Busson, what were we talking about?'

'Philosophy, madame.'

'Were we? I thought it was something much more amusing. I am such a scatter-brain. Nothing stays in my mind an instant. Pray continue.'

Louis-Mathurin smiled at Ellen over his cup and saucer, and she nodded imperceptibly. He began to recite some of the sayings of Marcus Aurelius, and, while Mrs Clarke stared at him vacantly and fell to yawning and caressing her dog, her daughter sat with her chin in her hands, her solemn eyes dark and broody. 'She's like a witch,' thought Louis-Mathurin, 'a young, sombre witch, brewing spells in the half-light. When she was a child she must have had an elfin face, with that pointed chin. I wonder what she is thinking about.'

He continued talking while Ellen listened, and Mrs Clarke became more *distraite*, picking her teeth with a brooch.

'Dear Lord,' she said at last, 'this is very slow. Mr Busson, why don't you sing to us?'

'If your daughter will accompany me on her harp.'

'Ellen, sit down to your harp for mercy's sake. If I must go to sleep, I would rather do it to music than to philosophy.'

And so they played and sang together again, happy and at peace with one another's company, Louis-Mathurin with his head thrown back and his hands clasped behind him, Ellen crouching round-shouldered beside her instrument, her eyes upon his face. Sweet German melodies, and country songs from Provence, and English ballads he had heard as a child – all these Ellen knew as well; and, while they lost themselves in music, Mrs Clarke rested on her couch, swinging her foot in time, and watching the shadows creep into the room, her mind misty with old days and older songs, of light and laughter, of carriage wheels rattling in the Mall, of those autumn evenings five-and-twenty years ago when the Duke of York came riding to Park Lane.

Louis-Mathurin became a frequent visitor to the Clarkes' apartment in Auteuil. Now that Louise was in Portugal the rue de la Lune had nothing to offer; his mother frankly disapproved of him, and was already making plans to return to Hamburg to her elder son, Jacques. Adelaide had gone as companion to friends of the family at Tours.

Robert, in London, had become too Anglicised altogether, and Louis-Mathurin had no intention of following his example and wearing a tall hat in the City, and sitting at a desk from nine till six. Louis lived, so he liked to think, on a different plane from the rest of his family, and because he was vague and temperamental, and a bit of a genius, why, then, he must have sympathetic friends around him who would understand his moods, and listen intelligently to his schemes for inventions, and not look solemn and religious when, like all clever and artistic people, he got into debt now and again.

Mrs Clarke frankly adored him, and declared she would give him her last sou if he asked for it. Luckily for the somewhat precarious state of her finances, he did not, but from the extravagant way she talked she might have had millions in the bank, and a thousand important persons in England waiting for her word of command. Whether this was really so he could never discover, but at least it was of interest to know that she received an annuity from some royal personage in London, according to her mysterious hints and whispers, and that at her death this annuity would come to Ellen.

Fortune, as always, was a fickle jade, and science a hard mistress. It was extraordinary how slow the world was to recognise the value of the inventions that Louis-Mathurin put before it. He would meet men of reputed influence in Paris who seemed to be all agog at his schemes, when he explained them over a liqueur in a café, but when it came to looking at papers over an office table their enthusiasm waned almost immediately, and they would fall back upon the most absurd excuses – the times were bad for launching new enterprises, the risk was too great, nobody had enough money. They were all as slow as sheep and terrified of a gamble. Good God! thought

Louis-Mathurin, if I had half the money some of these fellows have, I'd be ashamed to let it lie idle in the bank as they do. If I did not want to spend it I'd give it away. But to hoard gold when it might be put to helping unfortunate inventors like himself, it was a lasting shame to the country!

He bewailed his ill luck to the Clarkes, and stormed up and down the room raving at the humdrum men of business who knew nothing of acids, and hydrocarbons, and nitrates – without which they couldn't exist – and thought only of lining their fat bellies with *bœuf à la mode*: while he, Louis-Mathurin, starved in a garret with one guttering candle, working like a fiend until the dawn on an invention that would change the face of the world.

And he looked so romantic and picturesque, with his fiery curls in disarray and his long arms flying out in all directions, and his pale-blue eyes glaring at both of them, that the Clarkes were quite thrilled and disturbed, wondering if he would break anything or tear the curtains or throw the china out of the window. 'Something must be done. I will write to Fladgate,' declared Mrs Clarke, as though her unfortunate lawyer was a fairy who produced golden eggs out of a basket; and, anyway, she thought, it was time the royal family were jogged into discomfort by the reminder of her existence; her dividend had been lower the last time and no excuse given. 'Fladgate will have a word with one or two influential friends in Town,' she said significantly. 'It is monstrous that your inventions are ignored in France. I wager you will have a very different reception in England. You leave it to me.' And she set to and wrote a stinging letter to the wretched lawyer, saying that her interests were not being watched; she suspected that someone was selling out her stock and deliberately withholding her dividend, and if the matter was not attended to immediately she would publish something exceedingly derogatory to the reputation of a Certain Person, which she was sure was the very last thing anybody desired in England at the present time. 'I wish to offer my protection to a brilliant young French inventor,' she added, 'and this I cannot do unless I delve into a little capital. You might remind Lord Folkestone that it is a long time since he was kind enough to give me his news, and you may hint that I have in my possession an extremely indiscreet letter of his which I very much doubt whether his wife would care to see.' She worked herself up into a fine indignation over the whole affair, signing her name with a flourish – 'Mary Anne Clarke' – in her hard, pointed handwriting; and, looking over her shoulder, she saw that Louis-Mathurin had ceased raving, and was poring over pages of music with Ellen, their heads very close together. 'I wonder if she has fallen in love at last,' was her thought. 'He is certainly charming, and sings exquisitely, but, dear Lord! no money at all until he succeeds in his inventions. Still, she is over thirty, and no looks worth speaking of, and hardly likely to marry anyone important. I could allow her something, I suppose. . . . I should be very lonely, unless George came back from India.'

'Let us try "Der Nussbaum",' said Ellen. 'The piano accompaniment is very lovely, but I dare say I could transpose it to the harp. And you can cover my mistakes so well by singing a little louder. It is meant to be a gay, rippling song, but you have such a quality of sadness in your voice that we shall probably both end by weeping!'

Her brown locks fell gracefully for once on to her shoulders, framing her pointed face, and she was flushed with pleasure and excitement.

'She is almost handsome to-day,' thought Louis-Mathurin. 'That light dress becomes her; she should never wear drab colours. And she has a positive talent for knowing the songs I like best. Perhaps she is only round-shouldered from crouching so much over her harp. I like being with her. She has a quick brain, and can be witty when she chooses. I wonder how much truth there is in this story of the annuity. . . .'

He smiled at her, taking the song from her hands, and he

began to sing the ballad of 'Der Nussbaum' in his own inimitable way − very softly at first, like a whisper, bringing to the
simple, unpretentious song about a nut-tree an almost unbearable note of pathos that at once brought a lump to Ellen's
throat and a little lost feeling of depression for no reason.

'Why must he sing like that?' she wondered. 'I can see by
his eyes he is not unhappy; he smiled at me just now. It is
unconscious in him, this quality of sadness; it is a funny thread
in him he knows nothing about. . . . How I hope his inventions are successful. When he is angry he is like a disappointed
child. He ought to have someone to look after him. . . .'

And so they drifted, hardly aware of it, into a sort of depend-
ency upon one another, an attachment that was like a necessity. He came nearly every day to the apartment, and they talked
together, or played and sang, and, because of this mutual love
of music, a sentiment grew between them that became stronger
every day. They thought alike on many subjects, and when they
disagreed they would have an argument upon it, the discussion
acting like a stimulant to their brains, both enjoying the battle
without loss of temper.

Ellen suddenly discovered how lonely she had been before he
had become her companion, and how wasted those hours had
been when she had sat alone with her harp, or brooding over
her books. And then, no man had shown an interest in her before,
or desired to talk to her. They came to the house to be amused
by her mother; the plain daughter did not entertain them.

Louis-Mathurin brought an element of gaiety into her life
that had not been there before. His spirits were infectious, and
she, who until now had rather despised laughter as being shallow
and insincere, wondered why she smiled so often, and hummed
light-heartedly. She was even merry, as a child is merry, and
merriness was a thing she had never experienced. He made
ridiculous love to her mother, who declared herself fifteen years
younger in consequence, and even forgot to pet the offensive
Lulu when he was present, and while autumn drew to winter

and the evenings were dark, and the shutters bolted early, the three of them would gather in the *salon*, talking or making music, when Mrs Clarke watched them from the couch before the fire, winking, her tongue in her cheek.

No word was spoken, and yet they were aware instinctively that this intimacy must lead them somewhere; it could not always continue thus. George was coming home in the spring, and wrote to his mother suggesting she should join him in England for a time – he might be stationed there indefinitely – and Ellen did not seem to care for the thought of leaving France, so that really if there was any suggestion of marriage it might work in rather well.

Mrs Clarke would make Ellen an allowance, or some arrangement could be come to with Fladgate about the income, and, what with the inventions and one thing and another, no doubt they would manage somehow.

'You know, when I die, the money goes to Ellen,' she told Louis one day, and he had not said much; he looked rather vague, as though money was something he never touched; but a week or so later Ellen came into the room very flushed and excited and said that Louis-Mathurin had proposed.

Mrs Clarke burst into tears at once, highly emotional, and, when Louis followed Ellen into the room in tremendous spirits, rather like a swimmer who has taken the plunge at last and has emerged well satisfied with his performance, she fell on his neck and called him her 'son', her 'dear handsome fellow', and said that he had made her the happiest woman in France.

'We must all live together,' she declared (at which Ellen and Louis-Mathurin looked a little perturbed), 'and my beautiful George will join us, and perhaps he will marry too, and I shall have lots and lots of grandchildren, and you will all amuse me from morning till night.'

A hundred plans were discussed as to the future, but it was decided that nothing should be definitely decided until George returned.

'He has such a head on him,' said his mother: 'he will solve all our difficulties.' And Louis-Mathurin kissed her on both cheeks and told her she was a marvel, thinking rather dubiously that a subaltern's pay did not come to much, and if George Clarke was as stupid as he looked in his portrait he was not likely to come forth with any brilliant suggestion.

George arrived in England with his regiment, and crossed to France at the first opportunity. He proved to be a fine-looking, presentable fellow, extremely slick and well groomed, with excellent manners and a pleasant disposition, a trifle pompous at times, but never enough to be objectionable, and Louis-Mathurin took a liking to him at once. It was arranged that the marriage would take place in Paris as soon as possible, and that Louis and Ellen would continue to live there for the present. George would return to England, taking his mother with him, which was a much better plan than the idea of all living together, which would have been very trying for a newly married couple.

George expected that his regiment would be stationed for at least four or five years at home, and during that time he could perfectly well act as companion to his mother, and, as one or two years might be spent at Dover, it would be easy enough to cross to France to see Ellen.

Mrs Clarke seemed well satisfied with the arrangement, as the thought of living with her handsome son and keeping open house for his military friends sounded extremely amusing; it would be almost like old times having scarlet coats about the place again; and she would give little dinners, and entertain, and probe a curious finger into all their love affairs, and give advice, and really it would be very delightful; she would hardly miss Ellen at all.

As for Ellen, over thirty years was a long time to spend as her mother's shadow, and she could not help longing for personal freedom.

She would exchange her mother for a husband, it was true,

but Louis-Mathurin could never be as exacting as Mrs Clarke had been; he read, he had many interests — his science and his music; he was not of a nature to be bored.

Ellen looked back over the years she had spent at her mother's side since she had grown up — their travels on the Continent, and her mother's endless search for amusement; how she could never be left alone; how she must always be entertained, must always find someone or something to gossip about; and how they used to wander from town to town in Italy and France, never settling for long at a time, a restless, nomad existence for no particular reason except that her mother must not be bored. Paris had seemed to content her; the riff-raff of the town, as she termed her small circle of friends, served as a distraction, and Ellen had been able to go to the museums, and study pictures, and practise her music. But lately she had yawned more often, and tapped a restless foot, and Ellen, who knew the symptoms, had guessed she would be on the move again.

Louis-Mathurin had been a temporary amusement, but, once the wedding was over and there was no more excitement, Mrs Clarke would need a change.

She was all over George, of course, whom she hadn't seen for five years, and the novelty of being with him would keep her happy for a year or so. After that, well — they would have to see.

As for Louis-Mathurin's family, they appeared resigned to receive another heretic in their midst. Louise had paved the way with the unfortunate Godfrey Wallace, and it was only hoped that this new marriage would not turn out the same.

Ellen Clarke seemed a quiet, respectable, well-educated young woman, even if her mother was not all to be desired. However, one could not be particular these days, sighed Madame Busson; everything had changed so appallingly for the worse during the present century; people were so mixed, and the dukes of to-day were the butchers' sons of yesterday; it was all very different from when she had been a girl. True, her head was safe on her shoulders now, when it had not been then, but she had to scrape and save every sou. It was very trying.

Louise wrote from Lisbon saying that her prayers had been answered, and her two dearest friends in the world – Ellen and her brother – were to be joined by God's holy love at last. It had long been the secret wish of her heart, she said, and their happiness was also hers. She prayed for them both continually. She had even arranged for a special Mass to be sung in their name. Candles burned night and day for them in the cathedral. Little Eugénie, safely delivered of one child and already expecting another, joined in the prayer that they would be blessed likewise. In fact, the happy pair were overwhelmed with good wishes for the future; it was almost embarrassing.

They were married at the British Embassy a year almost to the day after Louise's wretched wedding in the Swiss Reformed Church, and left immediately afterwards for a honeymoon in Brittany. Mrs Clarke departed for England, on the arm of the attentive George, much to the concern of the harassed lawyer, Fladgate, who dreaded her reappearance after all these years.

'*Ellen and I ramble on the rocks, and listen to the sad waves, and feel the wind in our faces,*' wrote Louis-Mathurin to his sister in Portugal, '*and sometimes we read Chateaubriand aloud to one another, and sometimes I sing, and she nods her head in approval. But, whatever we do, we are supremely content in each other's company, and look forward to the future without fear.*

'*All that I ever said against marriage I now realise to be unutterably foolish and untrue. My one regret in life is that you have not been so fortunate as myself. Please remember me to the Duke and Duchess, and bear in mind that your brother is still a poor inventor without influence. . . .*'

'We must always remember, my love,' said Louis to his wife, 'that if our relations are forced on us we can at least choose our friends. The Palmellas would do anything for Louise, and Louise would do anything for me. You see the link between us? In a world as uncertain as the present it is a mistake to lay all our eggs in one basket. I am an incurable optimist, and if I fail in one thing I shall succeed in another. Let us drink to fame and fortune, and last, but not least, to ourselves!'

He smiled at her across the table, very handsome and debonair in his new blue double-breasted coat with the velvet collar, his side-whiskers carefully trained to his cheekbones, his tight chestnut hair framing his forehead; and Ellen, her sharp features softened already, and the perpetual little frown smoothed from her brow, smiled back at him, raising her glass in her hand, drinking to that problematical future which had perhaps – who knows? – been mapped out for them long before their birth, and which all their hopes and fears and expectations might never alter now.

Part Three

In the middle of March, 1834, Louise Busson received two
letters from Paris. One was in her brother's handwriting,
and this she put aside for the moment; the other had been
forwarded to her from her mother's old apartment in the rue
de la Lune, and bore a foreign postmark. She scanned it more
closely, turning it over in her hand, and then, with a sudden
sense of foreboding, she perceived that the stamp was an Indian
one. The writing was unknown to her, but she knew that this
was news of Godfrey at last.

Louise was alone in her room. Eugénie had driven out somewhere with her children, and the Duke was away from home.
Whatever news the letter contained, she would have to bear it
alone. She hesitated a moment, glancing at the statuette of the
Blessed Virgin on her prie-dieu, and murmuring a prayer; then
she broke the seal and opened the letter. If Godfrey was
returning to her, and this letter announced his arrival, he would
find her prepared.

The letter was brief, and the signature that of a stranger.

*'Madam, – I have to perform the unpleasant duty of informing
you that Mr Godfrey Wallace died at this place in September
last. It was his last request that I should inform you of it. Some
obstacles arose, together with a want of opportunity, which
prevented me from carrying out until now this afflicting duty.*

'I am, madam, your most obedient servant,

'H. ELGAN,

'Clerk, East India Company,

'Bombay.'

That was all. No word of explanation. No mention of the illness. Not even a short account of how he had lived in India, of his business, of how he had earned his bread. Simply that he had died there. Nothing more than that. Whether he had suffered much, endured great hardships, repented of his former sins and come finally to God, she would never know. All that remained now for her to do was to have Masses said for his soul, and pray that they would meet in Purgatory. She would wear widow's weeds, of course, until the end of her days. She began to cry softly to herself, thinking of the terrible finality of his death. There had always been the hope, somewhere in the depths of her heart, that he would come back to her – changed, no doubt, altered perhaps sadly for the worse, a drunkard even, or an incurable invalid, but at any rate he would have been her husband and they could have made a life together.

She had pictured herself in an attitude of mercy, bending over his recumbent form, soothing his poor brow. He would have been entirely dependent on her. Now she had not even the consolation of his grave to visit; the weekly pilgrimage was denied her. The only crumb of comfort lay in the stranger's words. 'It was his last request that I should inform you of it.' So he had not forgotten her. He had clung to her at the end. She wondered what she had been doing at the actual moment of his death. Last September. The date not given. There had been a fête in Lisbon on the fifteenth, and a great procession through the streets, the carriages decorated. Banners had waved and the people had thrown flowers. She had followed the procession in a carriage, too, in company with a Portuguese gentleman – quite respectable, of course – but how heartless and terrible if it had happened on the day that Godfrey had died. She could not bear to think of it. Mechanically she took up her other letter and opened it, her brother's familiar handwriting awaking no chord of response in her heart. Her thoughts were all for her poor dead husband.

  '. . . *And so we intend to name him George, after Ellen's brother,*

Louis, after myself, and Palmella, as a mark of respect towards your amiable friend and protector.' What in heaven's name was this, then? She hastily re-read the opening phrases of her brother's letter. *'You will rejoice to hear, dearest Louise, that Ellen gave birth to a son yesterday, the sixth of March. She stood the ordeal well, and the child is strong and beautiful. I have already dedicated him to science. May he live up to our expectations. Ellen's mother crossed over from England to be with her for the event, and is full of her first grandchild, whom she declares to be the image of myself. We have all three been discussing his future, and realise the importance of a string of initials before his name. . . .'*

Dear Ellen, and Louis-Mathurin; how pleased she was that their union had been blessed with a child, and how selfish of her to be so wrapped up in her own sorrow that she had read the letter without understanding the content.

George Louis Palmella Busson du Maurier – how noble it sounded! The child would at least have a good start in life, with such remarkable names. The Duke would be gratified, no doubt, at the mark of attention paid to his family. He took such a kindly interest in all that concerned the Busson relatives. Louise wiped away the tears that she had shed for her husband, and, lighting the candles on her prie-dieu, she knelt down to offer a prayer for her young nephew.

Meanwhile the infant himself lay asleep in his cradle, blissfully unaware of the excitement he had caused, still wrapped, for all he knew, in that lovely pre-natal darkness to which every man, in his lonelier moments, wishes to return. The Bussons had an apartment on the first floor at No. 80 in the Champs Elysées, quite close to Mrs Clarke's former lodging, and with Ellen's allowance from her mother and Louis-Mathurin's occasional contributions they managed to live, if not lavishly, at least in reasonable comfort.

Ellen was a good manager, and careful. The latter was extremely necessary, as only a few months of marriage proved to her that Louis-Mathurin had no more idea of saving than a child in arms. It was as though the money sense, given in full to some and only in moderation to others, was in him entirely lacking.

He would set forth in the morning from the apartment 'to work', as he termed it, in his laboratory, very sunny-natured and happy, singing at the top of his voice, and with fifty francs or so in his pocket. When he returned to his luncheon at noon he would still be in the same excellent spirits, but the fifty francs would be gone. 'Give me some of the housekeeping money, my love,' he would say to Ellen, with an affectionate kiss. 'I will return it to you directly I can get my loan back from Dupont, but he is such a forgetful fellow.'

'You should not lend money to your friends,' Ellen would complain. 'It is a very bad principle.'

'I know, dear heart, but I never can refuse a loan. I am too good-natured; I cannot hurt a fellow's feelings. Besides, when my invention is accepted, we need never worry about lending money again. The whole world can live on us.'

'I don't know that I want to share my home with all the world,' Ellen would say.

'The trouble is,' her husband would sigh, 'that I was born to have possessions. Had the Revolution never shaken France, and had my father been rewarded properly for his loyalty, we would be living in our château now, with acres of land belonging to us, and as many servants to wait upon us as you wished. You would do nothing all day but play the harp. Heigho! How pleasant it would be. The peasants would bob to us as we passed in our coach, and I would fling them gold. Charlotte, are you not sorry that I am not a great landlord?'

He would lean back in his chair and address the one servant who waited at table now. She would giggle, and hang her head. 'Oh, monsieur . . .' she would simper, fumbling with her apron. 'I should make you housekeeper, Charlotte,' Louis would declare magnificently, 'and you would have the right to behead the

106

inferior servants if they displeased you.' Louis-Mathurin would spear his meat as a hunter spears his game, and the little maid would giggle again. Louis-Mathurin adored an audience. Ellen would frown and look displeased. She did not approve of chatting to servants. It did not pay to be familiar. One always regretted it in the long run.

'How does your business go?' she would say to Louis, to change the subject.

'It does not go at all,' he would answer cheerfully; 'but, then, I am used to that. It would astonish me if it were otherwise. However, in a month or so I hope to tell a very different story. I met a man this morning – in fact, we had a little refreshment in a café – and it appears that he has an uncle who has a very influential friend who would be just the person to show a practical interest in my invention. I am meeting this man again to-morrow, and we shall discuss the project further.'

'You spend so much of your morning in these cafés,' Ellen would say, 'that it is small wonder you never do any business.'

'Ah, but that is just where you are mistaken,' he would assure her. 'More business is done in a café than ever is done in an office. Everyone knows that. In fact, I am so well pleased with my morning's work that I propose to take a holiday this afternoon. Let us drive out to St Cloud.'

'But, Louis-Mathurin, the expense – the hiring of the carriage?'

'Pooh! my love, who cares for such things? A Busson is above such wretched considerations as money. Old père Jean at the corner will take us, and I will pay him at the end of the week.'

And she would shake her head at him for his extravagance, forgiving him in her heart because he smiled so sweetly at her, conducting her to the *fiacre* later as though she were a queen and the *fiacre* a golden coach. But, all the same, she could not but worry privately at his total want of responsibility, his childish casting aside till tomorrow of the cares of to-day.

When her son was born, she hoped that the status of fatherhood would steady him, make him think more seriously of the urgent necessity of earning money; but, though Louis-Mathurin appeared delighted with his son, fondled him, kissed him, and even sang him to sleep occasionally, he did not mend his casual, impecunious ways. Ellen would not admit to herself that she was disappointed in him. She was too proud and too reserved. But the lurking regret was hidden in her all the same, and suffered for its repression. He was like the grasshopper in La Fontaine's fable, who sang and amused himself all the summer, and made no provision for the winter. Yet no one would have been more hurt and astonished than Louis had she attacked him for his ways. He believed he worked very hard as he played with his strange-smelling chemicals in his funny little laboratory. She had gone with him sometimes, and watched him, observed his air of concentration, his pale-blue eyes fixed in utter contentment on his bottles and his instruments, humming a song under his breath; and to her there was something pathetic and childlike in the intensity of his interest. It hurt her; she had to turn away her head.

'If only he would earn settled money in some steady profession,' she thought, 'and could keep this chemistry as a hobby'; and she began to plan for the child she was expecting, determined that she would find in her son – for of course it would be a boy – all that she lacked in her husband.

She had the tiger quality from the first – the fierce affection of a mother who has suffered a certain disappointment as a wife, mingled with the rather primitive selfish pride of any female who gives birth.

Ellen was not a young girl when she married, and she was over thirty-six when her son was born, therefore the event seemed to her of even greater importance than it would had she been in her first youth, with child-bearing comparatively easy. She had never expected to marry, never believed she would become a mother, and the very act of producing a child appeared to her stupendous, a tribute to her own powers, and a really brilliant piece of work.

108

The boy was beautiful, too. No round shoulders here, no nut-cracker features, but the snub nose and the crop of curls she would like to have possessed herself. There had never been such a child, of course. He was not only ten degrees hand somer than other babies – she felt quite sorry for Madame Painé's baby next door, such a plain, pasty-faced little thing, quite bald too – but he was much more advanced. He cut his teeth earlier; he sat up straighter; he smiled sooner, though the doctor declared this to be wind – very unfeeling of him, thought Ellen, as if she could not recognise her own child's smile when she saw it. She was determined to lavish upon him all the affection and interest that her own mother had never lavished upon her. She would not spoil him – she would be far too careful for that – but she would see that he had every quality necessary for his future happiness.

She, as a child, had been left to the care of servants; she had been obliged to bring herself up. Not so her son. Already she began to think out his education, what books he would read, what languages he would study, so that at an early age he might be a paragon of culture and learning and courtesy, a brilliant example of what a mother could do for the child she had borne.

The baby appeared to possess his father's sunny temperament, which was perhaps as well, as a sulky disposition would be difficult to work upon, but she could only trust that he had not also inherited his father's weaker qualities – his lack of money-sense, for instance, and his carelessness, and his habit of getting into debt. It sounded all very well in theory to be impracticable and a dreamer, but it did not make for success in the world, as far as Ellen could see. It would be as well if the boy had some of her own determination.

Meanwhile her mother, who had returned to England, kept writing to her suggesting that she and Louis should pay her a visit, bringing the baby with them, and why not have the christening ceremony over there, for as George Clarke was to be a godfather nothing could be more suitable? The Bussons played with the idea for a year, and finally, in the April of 1835, when the child was thirteen months old, they crossed to England and stayed at Rotherfield, in Sussex, where Mrs Clarke had taken a house, and there George Louis Palmella was given his string of Christian names and made a child of God into the bargain. His Uncle George had just been promoted, and everyone agreed that Captain Clarke sounded very well, though his mother declared that in her day, when she had influence, he would have been a colonel long ago. He was due for foreign service again before long, and the problem of 'what is to become of mother?' would arise once more, to be anxiously discussed between the brother and sister.

'Why not live over here with her?' urged the soldier. 'The country air would be extremely beneficial to the child, and you would have an English nurse. I may as well tell you that I haven't much desire to see my nephew grow into a Frenchman.'

'How can we live in England when Louis-Mathurin has his work in Paris?' said Ellen impatiently.

'But, my dear sister, I have no wish to hurt your feelings, and I have the utmost regard for Louis – only, what exactly is his work?'

'He has his laboratory,' replied the sister, a little put out by the direct question; 'he has made several contributions to science – and – and he was working on a new invention just before we came here.'

'That rocket-to-the-moon idea?' persisted Captain Clarke. 'I have not heard him mention that very lately.'

'I believe he has been obliged to give that up for the time,' said Ellen shortly. 'There was some technical difficulty . . . and of course our problem is always the same: no capital, no backing behind any enterprise.'

'Do you find you manage comfortably on the allowance mother makes you?' he asked her.

Ellen flushed, and avoided the direct question in his eyes. 'Sometimes it is a little difficult,' she said. 'Louis is a child in many ways; he does not seem to understand the value of money.'

'I thought he understood it very well,' said her brother drily. 'Since you have been here he has borrowed twenty pounds off me.'

The moment he uttered his words he regretted them. He saw that the shock was severe to Ellen, but because of her loyalty to her husband she would not betray it. Only her mouth tightened and her eyes looked darker than usual.

'I am sorry for that,' she said quietly. 'You shall have the money at the end of the month, when my allowance is due.'

'Nonsense,' he said uncomfortably. 'I don't want it returned. I can well spare it. I don't wish to hurt your feelings, or say a word against Louis. But, after all, mother makes the allowance to you, and it is not inconsiderable, and even a fool can see that you don't spend the money on yourself. . . .'

'The child makes a difference, of course,' said Ellen, her back to the wall. 'His clothes, and his food, all his little necessities. You as a bachelor can have no idea of the expense of a child.'

'I am sorry, Ellen; but I have always been plain-spoken, as you know. Living quietly as you do, you should manage very well on your allowance. But when it comes to supporting your husband as well, that is another matter. However, do not let us talk of it again. It is embarrassing to both of us. If you are ever in want, my dear, write privately to me.'

Ellen said nothing. Her heart was too full. She turned with relief to the child, who came into the room at this moment, swaying unsteadily on his little feet in a first attempt at a walk. He blundered along without seeing her, looking very vague and exactly like his father. When she swooped upon him and covered him with kisses, he said, 'Papa, Papa,' and looked over her shoulder, which hurt her unreasonably. Louis-Mathurin came bursting into the room, waving a letter in his hand, in a tremendous state of excitement. 'Palmella has been made

111

Portuguese Ambassador in Brussels,' he shouted. 'He and the whole family are leaving Lisbon in June, when he goes to take up his appointment. What a splendid thing for him, and how delighted he must be. Here is a letter from Louise, full of their plans.' He looked as happy as a schoolboy as he crossed the room to his wife. She forced a smile, thinking of that twenty pounds he had borrowed from George; but her discomfort was lost on him; he sat down by her side and began reading the letter aloud.

'Brussels, Brussels, who's talking about Brussels?' said Mrs Clarke, wandering in from the garden, swinging an absurd *chapeau de paysan* on a velvet ribbon.

Since she had lived in Sussex she had become passionately rustic, and went about dressed like a Watteau shepherdess, much to the confusion of her family. 'I dote on Brussels,' she declared, forcing a sticky sweetmeat into her grandson's mouth when his mother was not looking. 'You remember we went there in 1818, Ellen; you passed your twenty-first birthday there, I do believe. Such charming people. Most hospitable. Always giving parties. I can't think why we ever left. I rather think I lost money at a gambling-table and had nothing left to pay our lodging bill, and that brute Fladgate would not send my dividend in advance. . . . An absurd fellow called François de Burgh followed me everywhere.'

'I don't recollect the people,' said Ellen. 'I spent most of my time in the galleries, looking at the pictures. Nobody ever followed me.'

'I am pleased to hear it, my love,' said her husband.

'I suppose I am unfortunate,' sighed Mrs Clarke, 'but the men have always pursued me, since I was ten or twelve. Why, only yesterday, in the village here, I wandered out to take the air, dressed quite simply, as you see me, and I had half a dozen great fellows round me in no time. I was quite alarmed. Anyone would think I was poor little Lulu.'

'Oh, come, mother, what a comparison!' frowned her son.

112

'I wish you would be more careful what you say. For the Lord's sake don't talk like that in front of Colonel Greville. I should have to send in my papers.'

'My darling boy, what have I said now?' asked his mother, all innocence. 'You and Ellen are so hard on me. Louis, I appeal to you.'

'Madame,' he bowed, 'I will defend you to the last. If I might suggest, however, that your phraseology is apt, sometimes, to be a little unhappy . . .?'

'You are all so prim,' she protested, 'it will soon be impossible for me to open my mouth. It's a vast pity you did not hear the conversation in the old days. I can remember in Tavistock Place once, I said to Sir Charles Milner — he owned a large racing stud at the time — "Charles," I said . . .'

'That will do, mother. Let Louis read his letter,' said her son firmly. 'You can tell me what you said to Sir Charles Milner another time.'

Close companionship with his mother had taught him that her reminiscences were inevitably of an undesirable nature, and he grew hot under his collar at the memory of one or two of her stories, declaimed in piercing tones at a dinner-party given by his commanding officer.

'This appointment of Palmella's to Brussels,' whispered Louis to Ellen, 'has come at a most opportune time. We must profit by the occasion.'

'You mean we shall be in close touch again with Louise?' said his wife.

'Why — yes, partly that,' he said. 'The fact is, dear heart, business in Paris has not been very successful of late. I have several bad debts, through no fault of my own. It has occurred to me that perhaps Palmella would see his way to helping us over a difficult time.'

Ellen was silent. She knew now what she had suspected, but never admitted, before. Her husband had no moral sense where money was concerned. He would borrow from her, from her

113

brother, from the Duke – from anyone, in fact – without the smallest compunction, and without the least hope that the money would ever be returned.

'I should not care to make Louise uncomfortable in any way,' said Ellen. 'After all, the Palmellas are her friends, not ours. I hope you will not do anything that is likely to prejudice her with them.'

He smiled vaguely; he did not appear to hear her. He began singing softly to his little boy, rocking him up and down on his knee.

The Bussons returned to France at the end of May, and Louis-Mathurin at once wrote to his sister proposing a visit to Brussels. Ellen was firm, however; she had no wish to set off on another journey; it would unsettle the boy, and she herself had been suffering from headaches lately. If Louis cared to go he must go by himself. Louise appeared delighted at the prospect of seeing her brother again, and said that her dear friends would be only too pleased to offer him their hospitality. So Louis-Mathurin departed for Brussels in excellent spirits, his brain bursting with propositions to put before the Portuguese Ambassador, while Ellen remained behind, rather more sallow than usual from an attack of jaundice, and her temper a little shorter in consequence. She was determined to save money while he was away, and really it was a wonder how far she was able to stretch her allowance when he was not there to borrow from her, and she did not stint herself in the least: she had all she wanted, and the boy too. 'When he returns I will be firmer,' she said to herself. 'I will tell him that we cannot continue as we have done'; and she wondered what he was doing in Brussels, missing him considerably in spite of herself, missing his singing, his laughter, and his infectious spirits.

June was very warm in Paris, and Ellen felt far from well. She supposed that this was the result of jaundice, but when she consulted a doctor at last he told her she ought to know better;

the symptoms were unmistakable, and she was going to have another child. Ellen was furious. Nothing could be further from her intention. She was not young, and she had no wish to go through the process again. Nor could she afford it. Her whole interest was centred in her one boy, and he satisfied her maternal instinct to its capacity. Now the precious child would be unable to have her undivided attention; he must share her with another. She almost hated the unfortunate unborn rival. She would never love it as well, that was quite certain. She wrote off at once to Louis telling him the news, the letter a stream of reproaches, as though her poor husband had committed a felony, saying that she was nearly dead with worry over the affair and how they were possibly to afford this new expense she did not and could not see. To her surprise and indignation, Louis wrote back with perfect composure. It would be excellent for the boy to have a companion, he said; he was inclined to be spoilt as it was. Another child would do him a world of good. There was not the slightest need to worry. He had explained their circumstances to Palmella, who, with his wife, had shown the utmost consideration. Their suggestion was that the apartment in the Champs Elysées should be relinquished for the time being, and that the Bussons should come to Brussels. Palmella would give Louis a position in his suite, and they would live in complete comfort. The child would be born in Belgium, and the services of a Flemish nurse could be obtained to look after both children. Louise would love her companionship. Nothing, in fact, was wanting. The future was rosy for them all.

At first Ellen was inclined to protest. She disliked plans being made behind her back. Louis had no business to take a decision without first considering her. She had half a mind to write back at once and say she would not hear of the idea. And yet – how pleasant to see dear Louise again, and live in the company of really well-bred people like the Palmellas, and not worry about money, and have a nurse for the boy. Perhaps, after all,

115

the plan was a good one. Brussels was a delightful city. They would meet interesting men and women. So it was decided upon. Louis-Mathurin returned to pack up his family, and the Bussons moved to Belgium towards the end of the summer.

Exactly what services Louis-Mathurin rendered to the Duke of Palmella during the three years they spent in Brussels it would be difficult to say. In the *entourage* of every ambassador there are one or two persons, possibly more, who pocket a handsome salary for doing absolutely nothing. They write a few letters, pay a certain number of official visits, are to be observed hurrying down corridors with important-looking documents under the left arm, a frown of concentration on the forehead; they are greatly to the fore at State functions, where they manage to obtain front seats for their family, they wear ribbons on their lapels at levées and balls to distinguish them-selves from the common herd, and they are always among the first to nod mysteriously and whisper behind the hand if there is any question of a national or Court intrigue. To-day these fortunate gentlemen are somewhat impolitely referred to as 'hangers-on'. In the year 1836, at the Court of His Majesty King Leopold of Belgium, it is rather doubtful if the word existed. At any rate, Louis-Mathurin Busson du Maurier fulfilled the part to the best of his abilities. His patron, the Portuguese Ambassador, if not of vital importance to the future of inter-national politics, was at least a cultured and charming gentleman. His wife, who had been Eugénie St Just, was equally sweet and gracious. The Palmellas were, in fact, so generous that Louis-Mathurin was able to live for many months without borrowing money from his wife.

It was a pleasant change for Ellen. They had a comfortable apartment in one of the suburbs of the town, and two servants, besides a Flemish nurse. The nurse immediately won the approval of Ellen by developing a violent affection for the dear boy. She called him 'mannikin'; which he, struggling with his first words, at once translated into 'Kicky'; and so, ironically enough, if the trouble that was taken over naming him be remembered, George Louis Palmella Busson du Maurier became Kicky, and remained Kicky to the end of his days.

His brother, Alexandre Eugène, who was born on the ninth of February, was equally unfortunate. He was immediately dubbed 'Gyggy' by the first-born, who, far from being jealous of the new baby, was perfectly enchanted by his appearance.

Ellen, when she actually held the infant in her arms for the first time, was a little resigned to his existence, but really he was nothing like the child Kicky had been, and had her own prominent nose into the bargain. She rather resented the fuss that was made over him. The Duke and Duchess of Palmella were his godparents, and Louise also, the condition being that Alexandre Eugène should be baptised and brought up in the Catholic Faith.

Ellen did not approve of this at all. She could not understand Louis agreeing to the arrangement, with his atheistic views. It would make it so difficult, too, when the boys were older, going off to different churches.

'What does it matter?' said her husband carelessly. 'When they are grown up they will believe exactly what they like. It would be absurd to throw away the advantage of having Palmella as Eugène's godfather. Should anything happen to me, his future will be assured.'

'And what about poor Kicky then?' said his mother indignantly.

'Your brother George is his godfather. Don't tell me that he can't afford to keep an eye on him. Our sons need have no fear, Ellen; they will do very well.'

'I don't approve of Roman Catholics,' said Ellen stubbornly.

'I don't approve of any religion at all,' said Louis-Mathurin. 'It doesn't matter whether Eugène says his prayers to a pillar of salt as long as he has good manners, and is kind to animals, and considers other people besides himself.' And he went off to Brussels, humming a song under his breath, his mind full of

117

a new invention he wished to show the Duke, and which had been refused already by every scientist in Belgium.

So little Gyggy was baptised in a flood of holy water and in strings of Latin, and had candles burning for him night and day, thanks to his devoted Aunt Louise, who prayed for him unceasingly, and to show his gratitude, and in revenge perhaps for the names with which he had been saddled, he proved himself as possessing, even in the cradle, a character of complete and utter frivolity.

Kicky had drunk his milk without a murmur; Gyggy spat it back in his mother's face. Kicky had done his little business where he was told; Gyggy did it on the drawing-room floor. Kicky piped an eye when he was scolded; Gyggy chuckled loudly and blew bubbles. Kicky was a silent child, sitting for hours with his face in his hands, listening to music, his small person throbbing in sympathy to the strains of his mother's harp; Gyggy, with a smut on his nose and a torn pinafore, cut the strings with a pair of scissors. Ellen could hardly be blamed if the elder were her favourite, seeing that the younger was nothing but a nuisance from morning till night; but had she known anything of psychology she would have blamed herself.

The two brothers were devoted: that, at least, was a blessing. And the gentleness of the one balanced the boisterousness of the other.

Ellen was a little vexed when the younger outstripped the elder in size and strength. At two, Gyggy was as tall as Kicky at four. He threw a ball straight: he ran faster; he climbed a tree like a monkey while Kicky was dreaming in the lower branches. He was a comic from his first moments. He had only to pull a face and the servants were in fits of laughter. His elder brother would try to copy him, and the result was tragic. Kicky only succeeded in looking pathetic. There was something touching about his face, about his whole personality, that was impossible to explain. People longed to protect him for no reason. They felt, 'This child must not be hurt; it would be unbearable if he suffered in any way,' whereas they knew that Gyggy would not care; he would whistle and run away.

Kicky was pathetic in the same way that his father was pathetic when he sang; they had that same irrational quality of tragedy.

It was as though, locked in both of them, something was imprisoned that yearned to escape. When Louis-Mathurin sang, it was like an angel weeping, an angel exiled from paradise who wanted to return. Life was a burden that must be cast aside. 'I am alone,' he cried, 'unbearably alone. I am lost, I am cast down, there is no virtue in me.' Just a song, perhaps, thrown carelessly to his friends after dinner – the 'Nussbaum', or his favourite Serenade – and at once – he had only to lift his voice above a whisper – that strange and touching quality was there, the prayer of a man who had never prayed, the lament of a soul that had no God. He would stand with his hands behind his back, his handsome head thrown back, well satisfied with his performance, thinking nothing of the gift that came so naturally to him; and his very unconsciousness was his tragedy. Upstairs in his cot, Kicky would listen, his hands clasped round his knees, the tears running down his cheeks – and if his mother had gone to him then, and kissed him, and questioned him, he could not have answered: he only knew that in the depths of his little being he and his father were one; they suffered and endured; they were blind people struggling in the dark.

Pain and beauty were allied; there was no dividing-line between them; and this intensity of beauty, this concentrated glory that was his father's voice, made it the harder to bear. Gyggy, flushed and asleep beside him, his thumb in his mouth, smiled in his dreams at the memory of stolen plums, but the music did not come to him. So Mary Anne had smiled, perhaps, when she read her first letter from the Duke of York.

How many minute, invisible, intangible threads go to the making of a single human being, and what a strange jumble of hereditary impulses must have been this young Kicky and young

119

Gyggy. Was Gyggy a charming waster all his life because his grandmother had been a wanton? Was he a rebel because his mother had not wished him born? Was Kicky a meticulous draughtsman in maturity because of Louis-Mathurin's scientific exactitude, and because Ellen had talent in her fingers? Did that longing to escape from his surroundings, that almost unbearable nostalgia for the past, exist in him because his father's father, Robert Mathurin Busson, had been denied his country and had lived in exile for over twenty years? What sort of legacy could this Robert Mathurin hand down to his children, all born to him in an alien land when he was over fifty, but a sense of yearning and frustration, a desire to return, an ache for things known and experienced in the subconscious mind and in the blood? On the borders of Brittany and Anjou, whence their seed had sprung, the inhabitants are dreamers, mystics, superstitious with their inheritance of old legends; and the air is soft there with a quiet melancholy, and rain falls often, and there is a mist upon the land. An exile from this country, torn roughly from the soil, and transplanted into the busy streets of London city, would be bruised and shaken. He would not recover, and the roots that sprang from him would grow awry.

Some would have agony of spirit, and some a wild, unreasoning gaiety, and all would have that restless yearning for the past, a blind searching for security, even as lonely children long unconsciously for that blessed peace which is pre-natal darkness.

Kicky was the son of his father and his father's father. He was an artist and a dreamer, even as they had been, but he typified the men and women of his day sharply, satirically, to a fine exactitude, with the same precision that his father showed when analysing his mixtures in the test-tube.

And his powers of concentration, his determination to succeed, his fight against poverty and blindness, his indomitable will?

Louis-Mathurin had none of these qualities, nor had his

father before him. The pleasant, sweet-natured, melancholy Bussons of Sarthe had not such fortitude. These fighting qualities were bequeathed to him by a woman, a woman without morals, without honour, without virtue, a woman who had known exactly what she wanted at fifteen years of age, and, gutter-born and gutter-bred, treading on sensibility and courtesy with her exquisite feet, had achieved it laughing – her thumb to her nose.

8

L ife might have continued indefinitely in the same easy manner for the Bussons were it not for the fact that the Portuguese Ambassador was recalled to Lisbon in the autumn of the year 1838. It seemed that his presence was required with greater urgency in his own country than it was in Belgium. Whether this was really the case, or merely some manœuvre in diplomacy, cannot be discovered; at any rate, the result upon the fortunes of the Busson family was the same. Their presence in the ambassadorial suite would no longer be required. Nor was it suggested by either the Duke or the Duchess that the Bussons should return with them to Portugal.

Louise, of course, in her position as governess to the little Palmellas, went to Lisbon with the family. It is possible that Louis-Mathurin had played his part as inventor to the Ambassador, or whatever his official position was supposed to be, with too great a zeal. There comes a time in the life of every patron when his patronage becomes a burden to him rather than a pleasure. At first it may be rather amusing to consider flying to the moon, or turning sand into gold, or making diamonds out of broken bottles, especially when the process to be employed is described vividly and convincingly by a blue-eyed charmer with flaming curls, who sings delightfully after dinner to one's guests, but when the charmer continues to pocket loans indefinitely without any sign of the rocket being produced, or the bags of sand becoming anything but sand, or the broken bottles bearing the slightest resemblance to a diamond, there is nothing amusing about it any longer.

Mademoiselle Busson had such high integrity of character that it would be out of the question to hurt her feelings, but surely, if her brother were really the genius she made him out to be, he would have achieved some particle of success by this time. Artistic temperament has been made too often the excuse for inefficiency. The poet who waits for inspiration will never put pen to paper. The artist who blames the atmosphere for his blank canvas had better grow potatoes: they would prove more profitable.

The Duke of Palmella had become a little weary of Louis-Mathurin and his moods. He expected inventors to be like conjurers, and wave a magic wand. If Monsieur Busson had no magic wand, he had no business to call himself an inventor, and he must take his bags of sand elsewhere. There was no laboratory for him in Portugal. Farewells were courteous: there was no hint of ill feeling on either side. The little godson was embraced by the Duchess and bidden to be good; messages of goodwill and good faith were exchanged; sister and sister-in-law embraced with tears, and the Palmellas and the Bussons went their separate ways.

There was no longer any advantage in remaining in Belgium, and so it occurred to Louis-Mathurin that one of the few persons he had never bothered with his existence was his elder brother Robert, who was the only member of his family who had remained in London and made his home there. He had a business in the City, was unmarried, and would no doubt be delighted to see him, his wife, and his two boys. The Bussons went to London.

Whether Robert was delighted to see them or not has never been ascertained; he was a strange, melancholy fellow, with black moods – the Busson heritage – and was, in fact, destined to end his days in a madhouse; however, his spirits must have been on the upward grade when his brother called upon him, for he made him an allowance – nothing tremendous, of course, for he was not a rich man, but enough to enable Louis-Mathurin to spend a year in London enjoying the first instalment. The Bussons took a house in Marylebone – 1 Devonshire Terrace – and here their youngest child was born – a daughter, Isabella – in 1839.

Strangely enough, Ellen did not resent the arrival of a third baby. Both she and Louis were delighted to have a girl. She would be the companion when the boys went out into the world. She was a pretty baby, too, with golden curls – very much like Louise had been as a child, according to Louis – and Ellen looked forward to dressing her well, and having her admired.

The unfortunate Gyggy was the only one of her children to whom she felt an antagonism, and the boy played up to it unconsciously, striking the note of disobedience whenever possible, jarring her with his noise when she was tired, committing all the minor sins of childhood so infuriating to a parent whose temper, even at the best of times, is easily irritated.

Ellen was now forty-two, and bringing a third child into the world at that age, especially in those early Victorian days, was hardly a pastime. That she survived, and was apparently little worse for the ordeal, showed remarkable strength and endurance. There was a certain toughness somewhere in the Clarke strain, and Ellen possessed it in full measure. That lean jaw of hers and the Roman nose were not altogether a misfortune.

If motherhood did not wear down her constitution, however, it had a certain effect upon her nerves. Her temper, never her sweetest quality, became shorter than before. She was 'touchy', or, as they said in those days, easily 'put out'. Little things fretted her from day to day – tiny domestic details, housekeeping, the health of the children, Louis-Mathurin's incurable optimism in the blank face of poverty; and it became more obvious now from month to month that he would never succeed as an inventor, that their fortunes would remain in the air, where they had always been.

Robert Busson had done what he could for them, had acted generously enough, and he was not likely to do more. Ellen disliked London, she had lived too long in France to appreciate anything but French ways; besides, the living was very much dearer in England; it stretched her slender income to its widest capacity. Her brother George was due for India again, and Mrs Clarke kept writing from Dover, where the regiment was stationed, and suggesting that her daughter, and Louis, and the children should make their home with her, for a while at any rate, during George's absence. She had been over to Boulogne once or twice from Dover, and was full of its praises; so cheap, she said, so picturesque, so very amusing. And really she felt like Ellen; she was getting weary of England: the eternal fogs, and the rain, and the people all so formal and dull, everything so altered since she was young. It made her sad, too, to open her morning paper and find all her contemporaries dead or dying; soon nobody of the old days would be left at all. She had quite a mind to settle down in Boulogne when George went back to India, take a comfortable apartment in the best quarter, and the Busson family could come and stay with her until Louis-Mathurin's ship came home, which it surely would one day; she was always writing letters to people about him and his inventions, but people were bad-mannered and careless these days, they did not reply: anyone would think she had no influence at all. Ellen was not at all sure she wished to share an apartment with her mother, but as the weeks went by it looked as though they would have no alternative. Louis-Mathurin ruined his chances by having some disagreement with his brother. Robert was already becoming strange in his behaviour, and his attacks of black depression, when he never spoke a word, increased rapidly. He had already made one attempt at suicide, known only to his brother, and perhaps because of this knowledge he nursed a strange mad grudge against Louis, turning against him suddenly for no given reason, and Louis, lacking tact, lost his temper and told Robert he was going off his head.

The man to whom insanity is a dread approaching menace has little humour where his reason is concerned. Robert never forgave Louis-Mathurin, and the allowance was stopped as suddenly as it was begun. Poor Robert, the first tangible result of the Terror upon the Busson family, conceived, as he had been, in the flight to England nearly fifty years before, was left alone to face the horrors of his darkness. Louis-Mathurin, with a shrug of his shoulder and a happy air of irresponsibility almost equally insane, went off to Boulogne to live on his mother-in-law, complete with wife and children, his ideas for inventions still buzzing to no purpose at the back of his mind and not a penny in his pocket because of them. It was really very lucky for Kicky and Gyggy and little Isabella, and all the future gener- ations; that their kind grandmamma had succeeded so well in her profession that she was able to live in honourable retire- ment and keep them all clothed and fed. But for her generosity, and the allowance she paid her daughter, the Busson du Mauriers would have fared very ill indeed. It is even doubtful whether they would have survived at all.

Of course, it is not every woman who rises to such heights in her career, and can boast of an annuity from the Duke of York.

As a matter of fact, Mary Anne Clarke was incorrigible. She was never quite certain whether she could not have done better for herself and her children if she had refused the annuity and relied upon blackmail instead.

There was something rather too solid and dull and secure about an annuity; and in blackmail there is that delirious element of uncertainty that gives such a zest to life; there is all the fun of reading over the old indiscreet letters and imagining the scarlet face of the recipient when he reads his copy. Besides which, the resulting 'hush-money' is often of far greater value than the sober annuity, with its maddening little dividend every quarter.

Now that the Duke of York had gone to his fathers, where

it is to be hoped letters of no kind are sent or delivered, it occurred to Mary Anne that she might do business with his brother, the Duke of Cambridge.

Not in the old way, of course. She was over sixty and she had retired. There was no question of that. But, after all, she had one or two ancient letters from his late lamented brother that made very amusing reading, and if she cared to publish her memoirs she would include them in it, naturally; and a certain publisher up a back street in London had offered her vast sums for the sole right to print and publish the work in England. She had had secret dealings with him just before she had left for Boulogne. All behind George's back, needless to say. The dear boy would be furious if he knew. It seemed such a waste, though, all that material in the back of her mind going to nothing because of a silly scrap of paper signed over thirty years before. Now that the Duke of York was dead it was an ideal opportunity to break her contract. The book would have a tremendous sale in London, the publisher had intimated; everyone would talk about it, and her portrait would be published in the papers, and all the old notoriety, which, truth to tell, she had missed sadly during the years of retirement, would be hers again. She would give such presents to the family, too; a piano to Ellen, and a fitted-up laboratory for Louis, and ponies for the darling boys, Kicky and that scamp Gyggy, and wax dolls for Baby Isabella; and for herself – why, some new dresses, perhaps, and a carriage and groom. But really the pleasure to herself would be sitting in a comfortable chair with her mouth full of lollipops, reading the scandalised reviews in the English papers, and imagining the high colour and staccato fury of those persons whose sensibilities had been offended by her too excellent memory.

So Mary Anne sat herself down in her airy, comfortable apartment in the Grande Rue, Boulogne, chuckling to herself now and again as the flow of rhetoric tripped off her pen on to the paper. She wrote with extreme facility, and at the other

127

end of the room Louis-Mathurin paced up and down, singing softly to himself, while Ellen stitched laboriously at blouses for the children.

'Wooden fingers,' mocked her mother, looking over her shoulder. 'You play the harp like an angel and you can't make anything but blouses for your boys. When I think of the embroidered dresses you and George wore in Tavistock Place, and there you sit, like a seamstress, stitch, stitch, taking a week upon one sleeve!'

'I protest,' said Louis-Mathurin, pausing in his stride. 'Ellen does very well indeed. My children are by far the best turned-out of any I have seen in Boulogne. Simplicity is the keynote of good breeding. *Bon sang ne sait mentir*'; and he bowed to his wife in extreme courtesy, his hand on his heart, a sure sign that he was without money again, and would come to her later in the day with his innocent blue eyes and a request for a small sum to tide over the next few days.

No doubt but she wore embroidered dresses when she was young, thought Ellen with some bitterness; and much happiness they brought to her too. Poor, lonely child that she had been, left with servants at the top of the house while her mother entertained below. At any rate, her children should not make the same complaint when they were older; their education and health were not neglected, even if they were only dressed in plain blouses. She called sharply to Gyggy, who was banging a drum with a stick, and bade him quit his noise and find his brother, because it was time for his spelling-lesson and he must have longer at it to-day, having missed ten minutes yesterday by going to the port with papa to watch the boats come in.

'Can I not go with papa again?' pleaded Kicky, his brown head appearing behind a couch. 'I like the boats better than my lessons.'

But his mother shook her head firmly, and, putting aside the little white blouses, she reached for the spelling-book – how well he knew the dull brown cover and the black lettering; no pictures at all – and, drawing the boy to her, she began to spell the words to him gently, watching his eyes.

He repeated the words after her wistfully, his hands on her knee, but he was too well brought up to wriggle and cry when his papa, still humming light-heartedly, strolled from the room to fetch his hat, *en route* for the harbour, the fish smells, and the clattering cobblestones.

'You would not like to grow up ignorant, like the little boys who run barefoot,' said Ellen. 'They wear ragged clothes, and go hungry, and sleep in the gutter at night. Their mammas do not teach them to read.'

Kicky said nothing. He thought he would very much like to be a little harbour boy. But he was far too kind-hearted to say so.

> '*Maître Corbeau, sur un arbre perché,*
> *Tenait en son bec un fromage,*'

recited his mother, and the boy solemnly intoned after her, the words coming parrot-like from his mouth, the satire hopelessly wasted; while Gyggy, securely hidden by his grandmother's petticoats, pulled all the buttons off his blouse, heedless of the spanking that would come to him, delighting only in the fact that it was such a pleasure to feel naughty.

No doubt his grandmother would have agreed with him; she was feeling rather naughty herself. She knew perfectly well that the publication of her memoirs would be strictly against the letter of her contract, but the Duke was dead, and what did it matter? Besides, she wished to justify herself in the eyes of the world. She had been treated abominably in 1810. She had not forgotten the lampoons, and the mud flung at her carriage, even if everybody else had done so. It was superlatively easy to nurse the grievance over thirty years, and she would return the mud now in full measure.

Unfortunately – or perhaps fortunately for the Busson family, at any rate, who depended on the secure annuity for their future bread – a stinging reply from the lawyer, Fladgate, put the whole matter on an entirely different basis.

Here is his letter, written from his office in Craven Street, in March 1841:

'*Dear Madam, – The Duke of Cambridge's solicitor has called upon Messrs Cox & Co with reference to the deed of trust under which your annuity is paid, in consequence of a letter addressed by you to His Royal Highness, and Messrs Cox & Co have referred the gentleman to us.*

'*It appears that you contemplate the publication of some work in which you consider the Royal Family has an interest, and which you propose the Duke should in fact purchase in lieu of allowing its publication.*

'*The object of the application made to us was to ascertain whether or not the proposed publication would be a forfeiture of the annuity – which it most unquestionably and clearly would be.*

'*Now under the circumstances I cannot let matters come to such a crisis without begging you to pause before you throw away the income in question or forfeit the advantages secured to your daughter.*

'*I am, in fact, doubtful at this moment whether in strictness the annuity is not gone, from the facts stated in your letters, but I do not think there would be any wish on the part of those interested to press unduly hardly upon you, and am of the opinion that at the present moment there is nothing to apprehend. A performance, however, of the threat of publication would at once put an end to payment, which would most unquestionably never be resumed.*

'*From the Duke and his advisers I am confident you will obtain no answer at all to your letters, and any further application will only lead to a discussion of the point whether any further payment whatever should be made.*

'*I need hardly remind you that the condition for the grant of the annuity was the fact that all papers connected with the business in question were actually destroyed. It appears from your letters that this is not the case.*

'*Begging you for the sake only of yourself and daughter (for no other persons really feel very great anxiety on the subject) to pause before you act,*

'*I remain, dear Madam,*

'*Your very old servant,*

'*W. M. FLADGATE.*'

Short of ignoring her claim altogether, there was little more the lawyer could do to damp her enthusiasm. The irony of his letter was not lost upon her, and the tail sentence, 'for no other persons really feel very great anxiety on the subject,' was like the flick of the lash to Mary Anne, who liked to imagine the whole of London Society in an uproar.

Had Fladgate the impertinence to insinuate that she was not, and never had been, of the slightest importance? Damn the annuity! The memoirs would be published when and how she liked. It was impossible to keep the secret to herself now. She was far too angry to hold her tongue. Mary Anne in a temper was the same Mary Anne, even if she was sixty-three. The whole household was in an uproar. Plates were smashed, cushions were torn, the servants were cursed and dismissed in one breath, and the flow of language that poured from the painted lips would have done credit to the most hardened fish-porter in Billingsgate, where, in all probability, she had learnt it in the first place. The children were sent to play in the bedrooms while their grandmother threw the china about in the *salon* – a pity they were not permitted to join in the fun – and Ellen, very tight-lipped and shocked, demanded to know what it was all about. The idea that her mother contemplated publishing her memoirs was appalling enough – all that old disgusting scandal raked up again to make publicity for them; it was quite dreadful; and George would have to send in his papers; but to consider for a moment forfeiting the annuity, which was to come to Ellen after her mother died – that was not only appalling, it was wicked, treacherous, and quite unforgivable. She went white to the lips at the bare prospect. How were they to live, she questioned her mother, how were the children to be clothed and fed? How dared she call the income 'her money' when legally it was held in trust for Ellen and the children? Did she realise that by forfeiting the annuity they would none of them be able to exist at all?

It was such a surprise to Mary Anne to see her daughter lose her temper that it acted as an antidote to her own, and she found herself screaming out to the servant, whom she had dismissed ten minutes before, to bring brandy at once; Madame Busson was not very well.

Ellen looked very ill indeed; her naturally sallow complexion had turned almost green. 'God knows,' she was thinking, 'I do not need the money for myself. I have never spent a penny of my allowance on anything but necessities. If Louis made but the slightest effort to find some settled position I would not be obliged to humble myself as I am doing now. But to see the annuity, the only hope that stands between us and complete and utter poverty, thrown away through a spate of ill humour and pride . . .' No, it was too much; it was too unkind. She thought of Kicky, and baby Isabella, and Gyggy too – all of whom depended on her care and prudence for their existence – their small, trustful faces, and oh, especially that look of blind confidence in Kicky's eyes. She felt like an animal guarding her young, her claws sharpened, her teeth bared.

Her mother was considerably impressed. She was almost alarmed. She made all sorts of promises to pacify her daughter, and, although it was bitter cold weather, the middle of a particularly unpleasant March, she opened all the windows in the apartment and stood fanning herself in the draught, she felt so hot and breathless. The storm blew over. The memoirs were laid aside – for the time. The atmosphere in Boulogne was never quite the same again, however. There was something uncomfortable about it, something false. Ellen always had the impression that her mother was signing papers behind her back, coming to some black agreement with a publisher, and one day she would find herself without a penny to her name. She spoilt the children, too. They were getting out of hand. Even Kicky copied his brother nowadays, and was often noisy and rough. All sorts of undesirable people came to the apartment – her mother had a peculiar knack of picking up acquaintances and making bosom friends of them for a month or so, tiring of them rapidly – and that atmosphere of shallow insincerity Ellen had always detested, and associated with her mother's manner of entertaining, pervaded the place continually. She could not bear the children to grow up in it. She began to hate Boulogne, and long for a home of her own, however, small, however modest.

And then Louis-Mathurin came back from a visit to Paris full of plans and projects for a new portable lamp he was in the process of inventing, and which was definitely going to make their fortunes at last.

A group of men were interested, a company had been formed, and the patent taken out. Louis-Mathurin had fitted up a bedroom and a laboratory in the Faubourg Poissonnière, where he could work undisturbed; but now that his prospects looked so much brighter in every way he desired to have his wife and family with him, and he had, in fact, already seen about taking an apartment in Passy.

Ellen was so overjoyed at leaving Boulogne she would almost have consented to living in the Morgue. Luckily for them all, the Busson fortunes were not yet reduced as low as that, and one June morning the children piled themselves inside the stage coach with all the family boxes and packages beside them, and, waving their small hands gaily to grandmamma at the window, set off for Paris.

133

It was a very pleasant apartment that Louis-Mathurin had taken in the rue de Passy – on the first floor, *au-dessus de l'entresol* – and all the windows except the drawing-room, which had a stone balcony looking down upon the rue de Passy, faced in the opposite direction, on to the rue de la Pompe, for the house was a corner one. This particular apartment was called '*Le Cabinet de Physique*,' because Louis Seize was said to have used it as a blacksmith's laboratory – making locks and keys was his hobby, it seems; anyway, the name decided Louis-Mathurin to take up the lease, and he refused to consider any of the other apartments in the house.

There was a garden at the back, a delight to the children, and a green gate in the wall that led to a private avenue, all tangled undergrowth and mystery. And away behind this was the Bois itself, the enchanted forest, stretching surely to eternity, thought the children; a paradise with no beginning and no end.

It was these years in Passy, between 1842 and 1847, that Kicky was to describe nearly fifty years later in *Peter Ibbetson*. The story is fictitious, of course; there was no pale little Mimsey Seraskier in reality, who played with Peter by the Mare d'Auteuil, no big dog Médor who padded beside them over the fallen chestnuts; but the old yellow house is there, with the gallery, and the green shutters; and Louis-Mathurin sings through those first pages as the beau Pasquier, and Ellen plays her harp as Madame, though Kicky had disguised her, with the gentle hand of a dutiful son, as a beautiful young woman with golden ringlets. All the familiar sounds and scents of Louis-Philippe's Paris, his pleasant bourgeois Paris, that filled Kicky's small ears and nostrils in those early years were to be stored up and remembered with a strange yearning, an almost unbearable sense of nostalgia, half a century later.

The *maison de santé* is there; and the proprietress, Madame Pané, though Kicky called her Pelé in *Peter Ibbetson*; and the Major Duquesne (with an 'ois' on the end of his real name),

and the Capitaine Alladenise, and the Colonel Voisin, the Doctor
Lombard — the Napoleonic heroes, they were called; and
Madame Liard, the grocer's wife at the corner of the rue de
la Pompe, just opposite the rue de la Tour — though her moustache was an invention, and Kicky wondered, fifty years later,
whether she was still alive and would consider it a libel: for
she was a very handsome woman in 1842. They were all friends
to Kicky, and Gyggy, and the baby Isabella — the fruiterer
Guénier, and the butcher Bouchez, both in the rue de Passy,
and old Doctor Larchez, who lived to a great age.

Kicky painted no portrait of his comic prodigal brother, and
grandmamma Clarke in Boulogne was left severely alone, as
was his Aunt Louise and the Palmellas — a strange omission,
when they were all so intimately concerned with the family.
The villain of his book — the wicked Uncle Ibbetson — cannot
by any manner of means be turned into Kicky's real Uncle
George, nor can the polite and rather frigid Duke de Palmella
be transplanted from Lisbon and made scapegoat for the part.
Disappointing to say, Uncle Ibbetson was an invention of Kicky's
brain, and Ellen Clarke would have been exceedingly shocked
had she lived to know of his creation.

When Kicky wrote *Peter Ibbetson*, fifty years later, he shut
his eyes and dreamt true, very much as Peter did in the book.
He saw the past through the eyes of his own boyhood. He ate
soupe aux choux and *vinaigrette de bœuf bouilli* and drank claret
at one franc a bottle; he fished for tadpoles in the Mare
d'Auteuil; he pushed his little wheelbarrow through the garden
gate to the mysterious tangled avenue; he was a child again,
with a child's lovely inconsequence, pottering happily from day
to day. Everything was joyous and *couleur de rose*, as he said to
himself. But he did not see, because he had not seen as a child,
that this sunny, blessed existence was precarious, toppling, and
insecure, even as his own first childish steps. He did not see
the anxious care with which his mother saved the poor threads
of her income so that Kicky and Gyggy and Isabella should

eat their *soupe à la bonne femme* and dig their patch of garden *sans souci*. He never knew of the debts, the harshly worded letters from creditors, that awaited his father, 'le beau Pasquier,' when he climbed the stairs to wish his son good night, singing softly, as though the house of Busson had no care. He remembered his mother's smile as she sat beside her harp; the puckered frown he never saw. He heard all the melodies of those days, the singing and the playing, but the strained silences, the anxious letters that Ellen penned to Louise in Portugal, and the little sums sent to her in return, while Louis-Mathurin visited reluctant firms with his portable lamp and obtained an order here and there by luck – these he did not hear, these he did not see.

Kicky and Gyggy chased butterflies in the golden Bois, and flung themselves breathless beneath the trees, watching the sunlight play at patterns with the leaves; and at night Ellen faced her husband across the round table in the *salle à manger*, her shoulders drooping, a little querulous note in her voice.

'I am tired to death with washing and scrubbing them,' she was saying. 'The first money that either you or I get, the boys shall be put to school. I will willingly stay a few months at some inn, with baby, without a maid, a few miles out of Paris. It would cost but a trifle for one person and child. The boys should be placed at a proper English school. We must find some way of arranging it.'

He consoled her, of course; there was no need for such economy. The portable lamp would bring them all the money necessary. Yes, he would guarantee a school for the boys. Next year perhaps. That would be soon enough. They were forward and intelligent boys, both of them, thanks to her handling; they could both read and write; they had an appreciation for beauty – Kicky at any rate.

'There must be some way of arranging with your mother to have the money in advance,' he suggested. 'The money is due to you at her death. Have you written to her?'

'I tried to discuss it before we left Boulogne,' said Ellen wearily. 'She calls the income "her money", as though she can do what she pleases with it. I don't see that there is any redress unless we go to law. You know, she talked to me as if I knew nothing of her affairs, and that agreement she signed in 1809. Sometimes I think she is senile, or else she takes me for a perfect idiot. If only George were at home . . .'

'Louise wrote me from Portugal this morning,' said Louis. 'Palmella is coming to Paris; he has not been well. I must endeavour to meet him somehow, and show him my invention. What a pity that it is not Eugène's birthday!'

'A birthday present would not solve our difficulties,' sighed his wife.

'*Bon gentilhomme n'a jamais honte de la misère*,' said Louis cheerfully. But he had said it too often to sound convincing, and Ellen could only smile a little wanly, and shake her head. A certain number of people were buying the portable lamp, but so far the world in general appeared unmoved by its creation. She could only hope that time would show an improvement, and meanwhile the Busson family must live on credit and long promises.

Her sister-in-law, Louise, understood the position better than anyone else, and her letters were a great comfort to Ellen, even if they were rather strongly diluted with religious maxims. She sent them small presents of money now and again, which Ellen was almost ashamed to take, and she made frocks for baby and smocks for the boys. It was very sweet and understanding of her, and so much more useful than if she had continued her original practice of presenting Gyggy with *Lives of the Saints* three or four times a year, which she had done at Boulogne. She ended her letters with: '*Almighty God, however, knows what is best for us, and, humbled by our involuntary abjection, we must find comfort in becoming resignation and hope,*' and other little sayings of the same nature, which Ellen skipped. But in the postscriptum she would add, as though it were of no importance, that she was sending them a hundred francs under separate cover, and that she had taken the opportunity yesterday to speak to a certain Baron d'Alosta, who was to pass through Paris in a week or so, about Louis-Mathurin's invention.

> '*The Baron has paid me an order for one thousand francs,*' wrote Louis to his sister, in great jubilation, after his arrival, '*and to this favour he added that of being extremely civil, and I think him a very nice fellow.*
>
> '*The amiable Duke has also called at my chambers in the Faubourg Poissonnière, but I was unfortunately not present at the time. He left word that he was going back to Portugal the following day, and so I was deprived of the pleasure of seeing him.*'

Perhaps the amiable Duke left his call to the last day of his visit on purpose. He knew his inventor too well.

> '*I was very sorry to miss him,*' continued Louis-Mathurin, in great concern, '*because I intended to talk to him of a doctor whom I know, that has performed some extraordinary cures of epilepsy, which, if I am not mistaken, is the nature of the Duke's complaint. However, this could not be, and so we must say no more about it. I need not tell you how happy I should be, if I could be instrumental towards his cure. He was so kind as to leave a number of books for his godson, who was very much delighted, and very sorry not to see him.*
>
> '*Baby bursting with delight at her chain, and Master Kicky much delighted with his album, and Ellen and I admired your new style of purse, etc., etc.*
>
> '*But I must say another word about the Duke's present — that is, how well it was chosen for a little fellow of Eugène's age — supposing that he were more advanced in his studies. They are interesting for a child, and instructive, full of engravings of which children, and ours in particular, are so fond; and at the*

same time got up in a style to do honour to the library of a little maîtresse.

'*We are all well here, and I can say the same of Jacques's family, whom I heard from a short while since. I am going to give you a little business to attend to immediately on the other sheet, which will give you no other trouble than putting it in proper hands. I am sorry I could not show my invention to the Duke, because he is, I think, capable of understanding the immense difficulties I have overcome and the great importance of the thing from every point of view.*

'*Thine ever affectionately,*

'LOUIS.

'*I am happy to see the Marquis had fine weather over. Best wishes and compliments to all the family.*'

There is nothing more distressing than the little prods and nudges of a poor relation, when you are already poor yourself but, according to them, bathing in the glamour of influential friends. Poor Louise, governess to the Palmella family, must have passed many a sleepless night with Louis-Mathurin's suggestions under her pillow, screwing herself to the objectionable task of presenting them to the Duke and his friends at a suitable time; wearing that rather anxious smile, that over-bright expression that betrays the petitioner whose mission is doubtful of success. She must have wondered sometimes how secure was her own position, with Eugénie a woman of over thirty now, of great dignity, proud to be one of the leading ladies in the land, while she, Louise, grey-haired and approaching fifty, was, after all, only Madame Wallace, her old English teacher. She had always been a little afraid of the Duke, anyway; he was so reserved, so cold. The complete aristocrat in every way. He had never called her anything but madame, and she had been with them now for fifteen years.

She sometimes wondered if the Brussels episode had anything to do with it. Nothing had ever been said, of course. It was just the feeling. But when she mentioned her brother, or any of the family, there was a tiny almost imperceptible pause before he replied, and she would cough nervously, with a little rush of embarrassment. It was really very good of him, then, to leave cards on Louis-Mathurin in the Faubourg Poissonnière, even if he left his call to the final day. And to send books to his godson too. It showed a very proper feeling. The Baron d'Alosta, on the other hand, had not escaped so easily from the family. Louise had a delightful note from him, written in extreme haste, saying that he had had the pleasure of making her brother's acquaintance (parting with one thousand francs into the bargain), and also that of her two little nephews and her charming little niece, who, he declared, was Louise's portrait.

They presented him with a superb bouquet of flowers, it appeared, and desired him to know that whenever he passed through Paris he would find a welcome for him in the rue de Passy. Louise did not doubt it for a moment. She was certain that her brother would give the Baron the warmest welcome possible, and furnish his Portuguese mansion with portable lamps in every room. Her only fear was that the lamps in question might not work.

Poor Louise; she was devoted to Louis-Mathurin, but what a pity it was that he had never been to a school for inventors, and had wasted those years singing at the Conservatoire. Her heart bled for him when his inventions went astray, as they nearly always did. And, really, all this talk about burning hydrocarbons with air did not sound very convincing. How terrible if the lamps blew up and did someone an injury. She was quite uneasy about them.

She was uneasy, too, about the Duchess, who was expecting another child and was in a weak state of health. Eugénie had never been strong, and constant child-bearing had undermined her constitution. The air of Portugal did not agree with her either. It was unhealthy and damp. Louise herself suffered considerably from rheumatism. A boy was born to the Duchess on the thirteenth of March, 1844, and Louise, who kept a diary, wrote an account of the confinement in her thin, pointed handwriting. The child was premature, and two days later Eugénie began to lose strength. Her rapid decline, and her death on the nineteenth of March, the day after Louise's own birthday, were all subscribed minutely in the diary.

'*When I went to see her,*' wrote Louise, on the day she died, '*I found her in the act of begging pardon of all those persons who were near her, and as soon as she saw me she put out her hand, asking forgiveness for any offences she might have given me. Shortly after this she received the last rites of the Church with angelic composure, joining in all the prayers that were said for the occasion, after which she seemed truly happy and resigned to whatever might be God's will. As I went to embrace her I told her I could not help envying her. She knew what I meant, and smiled. We had often spoken together on the subject of a happy death, and of the protection of St. Joseph for that happy moment.*

'*She then begged I would pray very much for her, and write to her godson (one of my nephews) to pray for her, promising to do the same for him when she was in heaven. She told me it would give her much pleasure if I did as much as I could for little Eugène on earth. In a few hours she became delirious, but seemed to know me, and even called me loudly by name, and asked me to render some little service. The priest soon after this told her that he was going to give her the last absolution; she was quite disposed, and, to her best, answered all the prayers for a departing soul. She particularly recommended me frequently to throw holy water over her and on her bed at the last moments, because (she said) "the temptations of the devil are very great, and much to be dreaded at the hour of death." Some time before she died I proposed to rub her arms and legs, hoping it might afford her some ease, as she was in great pain, and much in want of rest. She hesitated, and asked if I did not think it would* be too much indulgence. I said I thought there could be nothing wrong in so doing, as she was sick. She then consented. She said — and this was earlier, after she had made her last confession — "I have no reluctance to die. I hope I shall go to heaven, but I am afraid of remaining long in Purgatory." When asked if she felt quite resigned, "I only wish that God's will may be done," she was frequently heard to say.

'To her husband she said, "Above all things I entreat you never to commit sin."

'She put me in mind of the happy moments we had spent together at the pension and begged me to remember her always. She always had a great devotion to the Blessed Virgin, and she told me she wished to be buried in blue and white, the Holy colours. Towards the end she wandered somewhat in her mind, and I heard her murmur, "A week ago only I was very well, I had my little boy, and was so happy. . . ." After a calm agony of three hours, and as if she had been accustomed to die, she joined her God, in whose presence she had always steadily walked, loving His commandments above all things, and avoiding with scrupulous care the least thing likely to offend Him. As a duty I pray for her, feeling, however, convinced that I do better asking her to pray for me, begging of Almighty God to grant me, through her intercession, those virtues of humility I so much wish to obtain, and which have merited her eternal happiness.'

So little Eugénie, Duchess of Palmella, was laid to rest in the great black mausoleum in Lisbon, surrounded by all the old departed dukes, and forgotten generations of Palmellas, while the cathedral door was draped in sombre purple and the deep bell tolled solemnly, and poor Louise Wallace, weeping bitterly for the friend she would see no more, knew that this phase of her life was over now for ever, and she would not be wanted in Lisbon any more.

The new-born baby did not long survive his mother, and the Duke had other plans for his older children. The services of a governess-companion were not required. When the Duchess's will was read, it was discovered she had left a handsome legacy to her friend, which, on careful investment, would make sufficient income for Louise, and by living inside it suitably and economically she need not work again. It was a great wrench to leave Portugal, when it had been her home for fifteen years, but the children had never been as dear to her as the mother, and with Eugénie gone there would be little reason to remain. The climate had never suited her, and her rheumatism was now a permanent disability. Next year she would be fifty. She had a desire to return to France again, to her brother, and her brother's children, and, though she was far too thoughtful and discreet to make her home with them, or to force her company upon them in any way, she wanted to be close to them, to offer help should it be needed, and to fulfil her promise to her dear Eugénie by supervising the upbringing of her little godson, Gyggy.

She returned to France at the end of the summer, and went at once to the convent at Versailles, where she proposed to make a home for herself among the kind sisters. How good it was to see them again, but above all to see the Busson family, and her brother Louis-Mathurin, who, with all his strange vicissitudes of fortune, his debts, and his inconsequence, was the same snub-nosed fellow she had adored for nearly fifty years.

He was, of course, working on a theory – some mixture of oils that was going to revolutionise industry – which he tried to explain to her at great length; and she nodded and smiled and pretended to listen while he drew impossible diagrams on paper. Dear Louis, he had not changed at all; he was forty-seven, and looked absurdly young. He sang, too, as charmingly as ever, as poignantly, as tragically; she sat in the corner of the room and cried, as she had always done. And Ellen played the harp – good, kind Ellen. She looked a little older, of course; it was only to be expected; and Louise had forgotten that she was so very round-shouldered, and her chin so pointed, but she was such a splendid mother to the children, and had brought them up beautifully; they were really exceptionally gifted and brilliant, especially Kicky.

Such a thoughtful little fellow he was, running to fetch a cloak for fear his aunt should catch cold by remaining too long in the draughty drawing-room; and he had written a pretty poem to his mother, quite charming; she begged for a copy of it. Gyggy, too, was well grown and handsome; just a little noisy, but never mind, it was only high spirits; his handwriting was extremely neat and bold for his age, and the Duke, his god-papa, would be very pleased, she told him. And, of course, there was dear baby Isabella, the pet of the family, with her golden ringlets.

'God bless them all,' said Louise, as she drove back to Versailles after her first visit, shivering in the cold carriage, 'and may Ellen be rewarded for the exemplary care she takes of them. Time will bring all things round, and with it, please God, compensation for protracted annoyance.' Good days no doubt were at hand, and Ellen and Louis had an invaluable consolation in possessing such fine, clever children.

9

In 1847 Kicky and Gyggy were sent to school at the Pension Froussard in the Rond-Point de la Nouvelle Avenue de Saint-Cloud, and the family moved from Passy to a small apartment in the rue du Bac.

The portable lamp had involved Louis-Mathurin in various legal difficulties; he had sold a third of his share in the patent to a man called d'Orgeval, and d'Orgeval died, the share reverting in some peculiar way to Louis-Mathurin again, who immediately sold it to a gentleman called McNeish, who from his name ought to have known better. Then d'Orgeval's brother appeared, and declared the transaction illegal, and altogether Louis-Mathurin was very well relieved when he rid himself of the whole business, lamps and all, though his wife was the poorer by a few thousand francs. It was only what she had expected all along. But this time she was firm. Not another franc would he have for his inventions until the boys were put to a good school, and she interviewed Monsieur Froussard herself and found that his pupils were comfortably boarded and well fed, and the education the best to be had in Paris.

Latin, French, Greek, English, German, besides chemistry, mathematics, and physics – all these subjects were part of the general school curriculum, and Ellen was pleased to hear that there was only one half-holiday a week.

Of course, the boys *could* have been sent to one of the Parisian public schools. And far cheaper it would have been for poor Ellen, with her slender income. But the daughter of Mary Anne Clarke and – according to her firm belief – a Certain Personage, was certainly not going to have her sons brought up with the butcher's boy and the baker's boy. They must be educated at a private school and no other, and also they must work hard as a return to their self-sacrificing parents, and go up for their *bachot* at the Sorbonne in four or five years' time.

Meanwhile, Ellen and baby would live in lodgings, if the small apartment in the rue du Bac proved too expensive, and Louis-Mathurin must picnic in his room in the Faubourg Poissonnière. That he had passed his fiftieth birthday made very little difference to the incurable optimism of her husband. He still believed that his ship would come home, and was for ever meeting people who knew someone who knew somebody else who might be very useful, and there would be curious little gatherings in cafés, and they would come to no particular decision, but part after several hours with firm handshakes, and mysterious nods, and great rustlings of important-looking documents.

Louis-Mathurin plunged his charming, inefficient fingers into so many empty pies that it is almost impossible to keep any track of his movements, but he was constantly away from Paris at this time, going to Toulon, to Dijon, to Brussels again, and frequently backwards and forwards to London.

He had discovered a new method of gaining easy money which Ellen did not know as yet, and which he hid from her with the disarming cunning of a child – that of speculating. It was a wonder he had not tried it before. He began to read the financial news. The figures were a delight to his scientific mind, and one or two little plunges were a great success. It was a great feeling to have a small original sum doubled, or even trebled, without working for it. And all so much easier than asking for a loan, for with borrowed money you were never quite free from the uncomfortable sensation that the lender would like his money returned.

He made many new friends, of course, over this new hobby, and involved himself in all sorts of projects that came to nothing, but he felt extremely knowledgeable and important when he travelled to London to 'watch the market' for one of his cronies, some sharp-eyed fellow, perhaps, who lived by standing tiptoe on the fringe of the Bourse crowd passing on information.

At any rate, the fever kept Louis occupied, and he had no time now to take his sons to the Mare d'Auteuil and fish for tadpoles, or carry little Isabella on his broad shoulders, and hum 'Der Nussbaum' in the drawing-room after dinner. Ellen had Louise for company, and the two visited one another, Ellen taking baby out to the convent at Versailles, where she was much petted and admired, or Louise coming in to Paris and sitting with her sister-in-law in the apartment in the rue du Bac – not nearly as charming as the old yellow house in Passy, but with a lovely view over Issy and Vaugirard.

They talked about Louise's rheumatism, which was not improved, and Louis-Mathurin's digestion, never very good, and Isabella's beauty; and Louise recounted at long length the history of all the Palmella aunts and uncles, and what they said and did in Lisbon, which Ellen found very interesting – after all, the Palmellas had been the first family in Portugal for generations – while she in her turn gave her own firm views on politics, and they both shook their heads over poor Louis-Philippe, who had had to fly for his life when the Republic was again declared. Whatever subject was discussed, they generally returned to the most absorbing one – that of the children.

Ellen spoke for Kicky, and Louise for Gyggy – being his godmother, she felt the responsibility of a parent – and it was a little hard for both of them when their school reports came in, written in Monsieur Froussard's neat, small hand, and the work of both boys was subscribed as '*très inégale.*'

'After all the trouble I have taken with them,' said Ellen, 'to throw away their chances of a good education. It is enough to make one cry. Gyggy I can understand – he has always been impossible – but for Kicky to have "*Médiocre*" for Latin and "*Peu attenif en classe*" for his English lesson, I can't understand it; he was always attentive to me.'

'Perhaps it is the novelty of working with other boys,' suggested Louise the peacemaker. 'It is bound to seem strange to them at first. And I do not consider Eugène impossible at all. His behaviour has been exemplary when he visits the convent at Versailles.'

'Only because you give him a good dinner,' said his mother sharply. 'He knows which side his bread is buttered. Of course he is good with you; you always send him back with a cake or with an apple or some nonsense.'

'His natural disposition is affectionate,' said Louise. 'I sometimes think that you and Louis are unnecessarily severe with Eugène.'

'I suppose you think we should praise him for his report,' replied Ellen. 'Look at this, if you please. Character, "*Très léger*"; conduct, "*Peu regulière, et souvent indocile*"; writing, "*Médiocre*"; Latin, "*Médiocre*"; every subject on the list has either "*Médiocre*" or "*Peu du travail*" by the side of it. The only thing that is "*très bonne*" is his health. Kicky's report, poor as it is, is brilliant in comparison. But let us find the general remarks at the end. Du Maurier Un – du Maurier Un is Kicky of course – "This pupil is inattentive in class, and spoils his natural ability by aping the antics of his younger brother." How can Kicky be so ridiculous! He is wasting all his talent. . . . And, heavens, Louise, what on earth do they mean here about Gyggy? Are they suggesting he is not quite right in the head? Du Maurier Deux. "The parents of this pupil should watch him very carefully. It may be that the child has an inherited tendency to insanity, and such a tragedy should be averted at all costs".'

They stared at one another in horror, Ellen white to the lips.

'Your brother Robert,' she whispered, 'is it possible . . . have you ever heard of it before in your family?'

Louise shook her head. They were both thinking of Louis-Mathurin and his total want of money sense, his complete lack of responsible feeling. Was there not something – hardly insane, of course – but *peculiar* in him, that he had lived his whole life long without these qualities?

'Gyggy has always been different,' said Ellen, in hushed tones. 'Punishment has no effect on him, he does not seem to mind. He lies, too, a thing Kicky has never done.'

'Louis-Mathurin lied terribly as a little child,' whispered his sister, 'and he does sometimes to-day, you know that. You do not mind my saying it?'

Ellen nodded. She knew only too well; she had suffered so often from his fairy-tales, those gay embroidered evasions that he invented, like his portable lamp, for no good rhyme or reason.

'Do you think we should take Eugène to a doctor?' she said gravely.

'Better to put your trust in Almighty God, Ellen,' replied Louise, 'for He alone can cure our mental ills. I will burn a candle for him to-morrow at Mass, and intercede on his behalf to St Anthony, the lover of little children.'

Meanwhile the unselfconscious Gyggy played to his heart's content in the garden of the Pension Froussard, cheeking the Directeur with adorable *sang-froid* and making faces behind his back, to the huge delight of his companions. He was a natural comic, and they loved him for it. His droll foolery was genius to them, even if it did look like insanity to his masters, and whether it was in class or in the playground the pranks of du Maurier Deux were the greatest amusements of the *pension*.

Du Maurier Un was not in such demand. He tried to be funny and only succeeded in being a poor imitation of his brother. The boys would have none of it; they waved him away impatiently. 'No, not du Maurier Un, we want du Maurier Deux,' they would shout, with all the callous indifference of the very young; and Kicky would wander away, delighted that Gyggy was so popular, but distinctly uncomfortable that he himself was such a failure.

He longed to be very tall, and immensely strong, and the

149

handsomest boy in the school, and it was his misfortune that he was slightly smaller than medium height, not particularly muscular, and, now that his fair curls had become brown and straight and his apple cheeks sallow, he was not even very good-looking. He used to brood by himself and imagine he was the leader of brave adventures, the rescuer of fair maidens, the hero of a thousand battles, the one boy in five hundred who would dash into a burning house to save the inhabitants; and he would sit at his desk, his eyes very broody and vague, his mind full of Monte Cristo and the Château d'If, with he himself suddenly transplanted there, a dagger between his teeth. '*Du Maurier Un*,' called Monsieur le Directeur, in a voice of thunder, '*faites attention, pour la troisième fois!*'

He pulled himself together then, with a supreme effort, and tried to concentrate on the Latin grammar that was so dead and dusty by comparison, but the meaningless words tied themselves into knots, and he reached for his stub of pencil and began caricaturing the Directeur on the back page of his *cahier*.

The likeness was surprisingly good; so good, in fact, that Kicky had to black it out as soon as it was finished, in case the Directeur saw it and was offended.

He hated hurting people's feelings. He could not bear the little flush that rose on the cheek-bone, the sudden droop of the mouth, and the almost invisible clouding of the eye. Cruelty in any form was abhorrent to him. The dumb suffering of animals, the more articulate pain of children, the voice of grown-up people raised in anger, even if they were unknown to him and merely passers-by in the street – all these things gave him a feeling of deep sorrow, absurd and unreasoning.

This detestation of cruelty was the second strongest quality in his nature. The first was his love of beauty: beauty of face and of form; the beauty of people. This developed in him with the approach of adolescence. He became increasingly aware of the latent loveliness in every man and woman. A young girl, tapping along the cobbled street in her high pattens, with a shawl about her head – the tall, straight pose of her as she walked – it was breathtaking, incredible. And it was not just because she was young, because she was pretty. He had the same feeling of love, of intense appreciation, when he saw an old man in his blue blouse standing by the quayside, a pipe in his mouth – and the pouched, wrinkled face, the sagging lines, the bulbous nose, were like revelations to him of the beauty that existed everywhere.

A child absorbed in some plaything, the little mouth pursed, the lashes folded upon the rounded cheek – this was something that must not be lost; and he would try to capture it with his pencil on the fly-leaf of his book, but it eluded him. That woman kneeling on the banks of the Seine, wringing her washing in muddy water – the curve of her back was exquisite in some strange, indescribable way, and so were the folds of her stuff dress. There was such grace in her movement. A dark coil of hair kept falling over her shoulder and bothering her. She shook it back impatiently, and then wound it round her head with a quick, deft gesture, stabbing the end with a pin. That was where you were defeated, thought Kicky; you could not draw movement, however much you tried. It was denied all artists for ever. You had to be content with repose. An old lady, asleep in her chair, her hands folded on her lap, and her chin just touching her lace collar – he would try to draw this; but the scrawl on his blotting-paper was very different from the quiet, unconscious patience of the old lady he had seen in reality. He gave up the attempt with a shrug of his shoulder, and in half a dozen strokes he had sketched young Dauveynes with his mouth open, his close-cropped hair that always stood on end like a scrubbing-brush, his round, enquiring eyes. Caricatures were so easy, beauty so elusive.

If Kicky was not amusing in person, at least he was funny on paper. Even his companions, critical schoolboys as they were, admitted as much. He could catch their expressions to the life. The dumpy little mathematical master, the terror of them all,

Kicky had him in a moment; his heavy brow, his thick nose.

'*À moi, à moi,*' they would cry, clamouring round him, each one eager for his own portrait; and Kicky would oblige, pleased at this sudden popularity. It was little wonder that his school reports made poor reading for his mother.

Those were good days, though, at the Pension Froussard, full of mad escapades and light-hearted chatter, and pranks, and squabbles. Kicky wrote about them in detail in *The Martian* many years later, when he was sixty instead of sixteen, with his hero, Barty Josselyn, a glorified edition of himself and Gyggy rolled into one. Happy, irresponsible days; swimming in the Passy bath and round the Ile des Cygnes in the summer, or skating in winter on the lake in the Bois, eating roasted chestnuts afterwards in the dark. Long rambles in Paris itself on half-holidays, along the quays towards Notre-Dame perhaps, where funny old men sat fishing with incredible patience and never caught anything, but did not seem to mind; and browsing over books that had no covers, and sometimes rather strange illustrations (*pas pour la jeune fille*); and so across one of the bridges to catch the omnibus in the rue de Rivoli, and back home for supper in the rue du Bac, before returning to the *pension*.

Soupe à la bonne femme and *fromage de Brie*, and perhaps, if it were the right season, *fraises de Bois*, Kicky's favourite dish (poor Gyggy was not asked for his); and, when they had finished, Louis-Mathurin would break into song and delight them all, even old Charlotte who waited at table, while little Isabella was sent to the piano to perform to her brothers. She really played quite excellently for a child of ten. Sometimes Aunt Louise came over from Versailles, if her rheumatics permitted, and she would get Gyggy in a corner and ask him when he was to make his *première communion*. Surely it was time? Would Monsieur Froussard arrange it, or should she come to see him at the *pension*?

Gyggy would pull the necessary solemn face, and said he hoped it would be soon, and perhaps his dear god-papa would send him a present from Portugal?

Louise thought this not unlikely, but warned her nephew that, if he did, the present would presumably be a book of a religious nature; at which he looked so disappointed that she pressed three francs into his hand when his mother's back was turned. The visits of Louise very often clashed with those of George Clarke, who had returned from India; and, while the boys admired his boots and his curling moustache – for he was still very handsome, although he was well over fifty – Louise found pleasure in his voice and his manners, and most especially in the little air of gallantry with which he addressed her.

He had left the Army, promotion being unlikely, and now talked of settling down, whether in England or France he could not make up his mind. His mother seemed content in Boulogne, and until her death, at any rate, he would make his home with her. Louise felt sorry for him: he seemed lonely, at a loose end, and she thought how terrible it must be for him to be obliged to live with that dreadful Mrs Clarke, whose tongue, by all accounts, was more pungent than ever. She had brought out her memoirs after all, but they had been translated into French and published in Paris, which was the only way she could safeguard the annuity. A most scandalous book. Louise had peeped into it. Ellen had never mentioned it at all. There must have grown a coolness between her and her mother, thought her sister-in-law; and a very good thing too. She did not like to think that the dear children had such tainted blood in them. It was most unpleasant. Captain Clarke was very unlike his mother. So polished and courteous.

He seemed to be paying Louise a considerable amount of attention. He asked her opinion on all sorts of subjects; what she thought of the English countryside and the English people, whether she were fond of children, and (rather tactlessly, but quite unintentionally so) whether she considered the best time for men and women to marry was the early thirties.

Ellen was delighted that her brother had taken such a fancy to Louise. It brought her out of herself, and she was inclined

153

to become too convent-minded at Versailles. To hear her chatting, quite unconcerned, of marriage, and young people, and the affairs of the day, was a welcome change after the rather narrow tittle-tattle of the convent. She was still very charming-looking, after all, even if her pretty fair hair had disappeared in Portugal – something to do with the climate – and she was quite bald under the grey wig; but her gentle expression was unchanged, and so were her mild blue eyes. If little Isabella was as pretty as that when she was past fifty she would do very well.

Now she came to consider it, mused Ellen, stitching laboriously at one of Kicky's shirts, Louise and George were much of an age for one another. George was the elder, perhaps by a year or so. Nothing could be more suitable. They would settle down together exceedingly well. The union would make up to Louise for all she had lost twenty years before. And George had always been the sober, steadying sort, hating nonsense of any kind. There would be nothing romantic in such a marriage, naturally; but, then, one did not expect romance when one was past fifty. One needed companionship, and a comfortable home. It was only superficial people, like their poor silly mother, who needed this constant excitement and amusement until they were over seventy.

Ellen stabbed severely at her shirt; her brows contracted. Even if things were very uncertain here in Paris, she thanked goodness she was no longer in Boulogne. What an influence for the boys and Isabella . . . and that dreadful book!

She glanced up and saw that Kicky was drawing a caricature of his Aunt Louise.

She coughed loudly, and frowned, putting on her 'pained' expression that worked magic with him always, and the boy pushed away his paper at once, flushing scarlet, and reached for his *devoir des vacances*.

'If that is how you employ your time at school, your papa and I might have saved our money,' she said, in a low tone.

Kicky said nothing; he buried his head deeper in his book. How terrible if mamma showed the drawing to Aunt Louise, and she realised how life-like was the curled wig. He had not meant to be unkind. And she would think he was laughing at her, and would return to the convent at Versailles and sit thinking about it in her uncomfortable little room filled with crucifixes, dominated by that distressing oil-painting of Jesus Christ pointing to His bleeding heart.

He passed the remainder of the evening in agony, worrying about the possibility. His mother had forgotten the drawing already, however, and was thinking what a pretty bridesmaid Isabella would make.

She knew her sister-in-law so well by now that it was not the slightest embarrassment to question her on the subject, when George had returned to Boulogne. 'Has it struck you, Louise,' she began, in her blunt, straightforward way, 'that George is paying you a considerable amount of attention?'

Louise coloured ever so slightly, and hesitated before replying.

'He has certainly been very courteous,' she admitted, 'but I put that down to good breeding and good manners. There is something about a man who has been in the Army . . . I remember, one of the Palmella cousins was just the same. His attentions were most marked one summer at Lisbon.'

'Oh, but George has never been one of these deliberate compliment-paying gallants,' said his sister. 'He is much too genuine for that. To tell you the truth, I have scarcely heard him mention a woman's name. No, I thought it a little odd that he questioned you so closely on marriage. Of course, he knows your sad misfortune in the old days; I know he was not trying to draw you on that subject. It looked to me as though he was making some allusion to the future. Did he commit himself in any way?'

'He remarked that it was not until a man reached years of discretion, as he had, that he could know his own mind. He said something about fifty-five being the prime of life.'

'Did he really? I should call that very suggestive.'

'He told me he felt lonely very often, now that he had left the regiment, and he knew so many of his old friends who had married and settled down that sometimes he had a yearning to the same. People of our age, he told me, need sympathy and love, and did I not agree, and was I not lonely at the convent?'

'My dear Louise, that practically amounts to a proposal!'

'Oh, Ellen, do you think so?'

'I consider it significant, at all events.'

'You put me in quite a flutter. Really, I have never considered such a change at my time of life, with my rheumatism, and one thing and another. . . . Why, Ellen, I hardly think I could accept.'

'Nonsense, Louise. It would be just the thing for you. I am not too fond of that convent, I don't mind telling you. And George is so tactful and thoughtful, I am sure he would not presume upon you in any way, just because you were his wife. He would make every allowance for your health and tastes.'

'Oh, as to that, I am sure I am quite as capable of fulfilling the duties of a wife as anybody else. We were all born, you know, when my father was over fifty. Not that I compare myself to him, of course. I am not suggesting that I could have any children. But still . . .'

'No, naturally. I understand perfectly to what you are alluding. I feel certain George would be most considerate in every way. Depend upon it, he has gone back to Boulogne to come to a decision. He is a slow thinker, he always has been – very unlike my poor mother – and it may be some time before he makes up his mind. You must not become impatient.'

'I am hardly likely to do that. After all, I should need no preparation. I'm not like a young girl, who must have a trousseau. All my things are in good order. A night-gown or two, perhaps. However, there is time enough.'

'So you are determined to accept him?'

'Why, Ellen, since you yourself seem so much in favour of

it, I hardly know what argument to bring against it. I have a great regard for your brother, and I believe I could make him happy. I think, even, that it would be selfish of me to refuse him. It would be unnatural on my part.'

'That is what I feel. Well, Louise, no need to tell you how happy it would make all of us. I will say nothing to Louis until George tells him himself.'

The months went by, however, without the gallant Captain coming to his great decision, and it looked as though his thinking-powers worked more slowly than his sister had supposed. Or perhaps he considered that Louise had not given him enough encouragement. At any rate, he came to Paris for the New Year of 1851, and went again without as much as a hint regarding marriage. He was as courteous as ever – in fact, most studiously polite – and told Louise a long story about killing snakes in India which she found very enthralling; but he made no mention of his lonely state in Boulogne. Louise wondered whether he dared not trust himself. These quiet men, who had spent many years in the wilds, sometimes lost their heads when the moment of passion arrived. She was deter-mined to be prepared for any eventuality. After all, she was not ignorant; she had been married before.

The prospect of a change in the near future made her life a little unsettling. She could not give her whole mind to her godson Gyggy, who was about to make his *première communion*. And yet she must not fail him in this most critical moment of his life. It was so difficult for him, poor fellow, being the one Catholic of the family. His father and mother did not take the slightest interest in the affair. Louise shook her head as she thought over his last report from Monsieur Froussard: 'This child is in need of encouragement, and some evidence of affec-tion on the part of his parents. They would then obtain a great influence over him'. It was rather unfortunate that Ellen, and Louis-Mathurin as well, were determined to be hard on the boy, whatever happened.

157

'What nonsense!' his mother had said, when she read the report. 'As if we treated Eugène any differently from the others. Let him show some consideration to us, that is much more to the point.'

Louise thought it best not to argue, and she went off to buy Gyggy his armlet, and his *cierge*, and his white trousers, and the lace for his shirt. If his parents did not see that he was properly dressed for his confirmation, then his godmother must. He showed himself so grateful, too, when he received his things; it was really quite touching.

'*Thank you so very much for the dear little image,*' he wrote from school, '*I shall put it in my prayer book and keep it always, and I hope that after my first communion I can come out to you at Versailles. If you ever go to Lisbon again to visit my god-papa, I wish you would keep a little place for me in the steamboat and take me with you. How jolly it would be. All that is just my fancy, you know, and it will never arrive, but I do fancy it. Pray answer this letter, for it gives me such pleasure to receive letters. Papa is in London, and mamma talks of going too and taking baby with her. I shall miss them exceedingly if they go, but I do not suppose that they will miss me.*

'*Let me come to see you at Versailles very soon.*

'*Your affectionate nephew,*
'E̲U̲G̲È̲N̲E̲.'

And then, in a postscript, in tiny handwriting: '*I have not had any pocket-money for a very long time.*'

Louise swallowed and blew her nose. It was so exactly like his father. . . .

She sent him a waistcoat, and a white cravat, and all his little necessities, putting ten francs in the pocket of the waistcoat, and of course he forgot to write and thank her, which was more like his father than ever.

She thought, perhaps, that being confirmed and making his

first communion would have a sobering effect on his nature – he looked so sweet and solemn, dressed in his muslin blouse and carrying his candle – but at the end of the term, when his report came in again, the statement of the Directeur was worse than ever: 'This pupil merits punishment because of his laziness and his thoughtlessness. After his first communion he should have tried to make up for the past, but he has made no effort at all. He is the bottom of his class.'

Ellen was so angry she could scarcely trust herself to speak to him.

Thank heaven that Kicky, at any rate, would do her credit when he went up for his *bachot* at the Sorbonne, which he was to do in the summer. Monsieur Froussard had great hopes of him. When he had passed, and had taken his degree, he was to study chemistry. He had been dedicated to science since his first birthday, and Louis-Mathurin would hear of no other career for his eldest son. Kicky was seventeen on the sixth of March, and did not look much like a prospective scientist. He was always curling up in corners and reading Alfred de Musset, and Lamartine, and had conceived a tremendous passion for the works of Lord Byron, especially *Don Juan*. He was vague and dreamy and rather sentimental – everything that a successful chemist should not be – and now that his voice had broken he showed promise of becoming almost as good a singer as his father. He adored music, and once – when he had summoned enough courage – he asked his mother whether it would be possible for him to go in for music instead of science. She looked very grave, and said it would break his father's heart. So Kicky sighed, and put the thought away from him. It did not occur to him to tear his hair and rush from the house, as Louis-Mathurin had done at his age. He was too fond of his home, of his family, of all the little familiar things that went to make his daily life. He did not want these things to change. He wished that time could stand still, or even go back – anything rather than go forward. This business of growing-up, and becoming a man, and facing the future – he did not care for it at all.

If only one could stay seventeen for eternity and it could be always summer weather, he thought; and one could run, and swim, and talk into the night with one's friends, and laugh and be sad again, for no known reason. And there would be poetry to read, and music to listen to, every day and every night, and no strife, no cruelty, no poor suffering, wounded things, no tormented hating of one another. He knew he should be studying Horace and Cicero, in preparation for his *bachot*, but instead of this he reached for his pencil and began to draw Isabella's profile as she sat at the piano. . . .

A week before Easter, George Clarke came over from Boulogne, having first written to Ellen to say he had news of great importance.

Ellen smiled to herself, and invited Louise to tea on the Sunday.

So George had come to his decision at last. She would see that he had ample opportunity to declare himself, unless he had already done so by letter, which was probably the case. Louise arrived from Versailles in a new bonnet and rather flustered generally, declaring that she had heard no word from Captain Clarke herself, and was it not a little premature, assuming he would announce his intentions to Ellen before giving a hint of them to the most interested party, who was of course herself?

Nonsense, her sister-in-law replied; George was shy by nature, and he probably wished to consult Ellen first. All Louise had to do was to remain her quiet, charming self. Ellen and George would do the rest. She was glad that Louis-Mathurin was in London again – something to do with his poor brother, who had just died – as tact was not his strongest point, and he might make some unfortunate allusion to Louise's first marriage.

George turned up at six o'clock, rather red in the face and self-conscious, and had scarcely been in the room two minutes before he turned to his sister and asked her permission to make a statement of great importance.

'Why, certainly, George,' she said, beaming upon him, and glancing significantly at Louise, who sat with modest eyes upon the ground.

The gallant Captain coughed and puffed out his chest. 'I – ah – I am going to be married,' he announced, 'and let me tell you here and now I consider myself the luckiest fellow in the world to have won her affection. She's the sweetest, purest thing God ever made, and I'm so happy and delighted and proud that I – that I – well, Ellen, my dear, words fail me.'

'We have been expecting this for some time,' said his sister happily, 'and we know that you have made the best possible choice.'

'Ah, but wait until you see her,' cried George; and he went swiftly to the door and put his head into the passage. 'Georgie, my sweetest heart, come in and be introduced.' His sister stared at him in amazement, and Louise, who had said nothing at first, glanced up like a startled deer.

Before they had time to speak, or even look at one another, George reappeared, smiling and fatuous, holding by the hand a blushing, giggling girl of about nineteen, absurdly over-dressed and exceedingly lovely.

'Let me present to you Miss Georgina Lewis, the future Mrs George Noel Clarke,' declaimed the gallant Captain, and he beamed upon the company with all the delight and self-satisfaction of his fifty-five years.

Ellen made a tremendous effort to control herself, and, composing her horrified features into what she imagined to be a welcoming smile, she advanced towards the happy couple. 'We are all very pleased to make your acquaintance,' she said. 'Kicky, Gyggy, and Isabella, come and say how-do-you-do to your new aunt.' The boys, open-mouthed, shook hands with the beautiful vision who looked exactly the same age as themselves, and Kicky, at any rate, blushed furiously when she kissed him. Ellen did not dare glance at Louise as she too came forward with a little breathless message of congratulation, but plunged at once into an offer of tea – a fresh pot was just appearing, and would not Miss Lewis like to take off her bonnet and make herself comfortable.

Miss Lewis gave a small cry of affectation – 'Oh, dearest Mrs du Maurier, call me Georgie, *please*' – of which request the impudent Eugène took immediate advantage, and, handing her the remaining piece of bread-and-butter, murmured, 'Have a handsome husband, Aunt Georgie.'

His nonsense broke the ice, and in a moment they were all seated at the table, talking excitedly, even Ellen forgetting her shock to question her brother on the whys and wherefores of this sudden betrothal. Only Louise sat silent, plucking a crumb of bread, her poor mouth twisted in a smile that nearly cracked her face, and a high, unnatural spot of colour on either cheek-bone.

'We met a year ago in India,' George was saying. 'She came out to be with her brother in the regiment, and we gave her a dance for her eighteenth birthday. Of course, I did not have a look-in. The young fellows swarmed around you like bees round a honey-pot, didn't they, Georgie?'

Georgie pouted and shrugged her shoulders.

'Anyway, she didn't think much of me then. I was an old fogey. I did not count at all. And then my haughty young lady must go riding, and her horse must run away with her, and I don't blame him – do you, Kicky, my boy? Anyway, the old fogey brought her back, and after that she did not think he was quite so ancient!'

He leant back, his thumbs in his waistcoat, his eyes devouring her.

Georgie kissed the tips of her fingers to him across the table.

'Well, to cut a long story short, we became good friends,' continued the soldier, 'and there was something of an under-standing between us when we left India. I spoke, and her brother spoke for me, but Miss Georgie did not know her own mind, and why should she, bless her, when she had barely reached nineteen? She came home to England, and I went to Boulogne. We corresponded. I took mamma into my confidence, and mamma asked her to stay. She has been staying with us now for a fortnight. And the day before yesterday she made me the happiest man on earth.' Tears of joy came into the Captain's eyes at the recollection, and he flourished a handkerchief and blew his nose.

'Of course, your *angelic* mamma has been our good angel,' gushed the adorable Georgie. 'She is just the sweetest person in the world. I positively *dote* on her. She has *loaded* me with presents, and given me frocks, and taken me everywhere in Boulogne. We have had the *greatest* fun. We love all the same sort of things, and are the *best* possible companions. We laugh and talk together, and make a joke of everything. George gets quite jealous, don't you, my love?'

George shook his head at her, his eyes swimming, his mouth a little open.

'And when do you propose to get married?' asked Ellen.

'Just as soon as this precious girl can arrange her trousseau,' said George tenderly, 'and you know what you women are. Must have all your little fal-lals. It doesn't do for a mere man to probe into such things. But mamma is seeing to it all. The old lady is mad with excitement. Anyone would think she was getting married herself. Of course, she idolises Georgie.'

'I hope she won't spoil her,' said Ellen.

'Spoil her? Of course she spoils her. We are all going to spoil her. She is going to do exactly what she wants to always, aren't you, my sweetest?'

Georgie made a mouth at him and smiled sweetly. 'I shall obey you, dearest, first,' she said, fluttering her lashes.

'H'm,' Ellen thought, as she poured hot water into the teapot, 'you weren't born with that chin for nothing, young woman; don't think you are going to deceive me. I know determination when I see it.' And she handed her future sister-in-law the sugar-bowl with tightened lips.

But it was difficult to be prejudiced against Georgie for long. She was so very young, so extremely pretty, and so bright and funny and amusing that she kept them all in fits of laughter. As for Kicky, he thought she was the loveliest thing he had ever seen. That profile, and that little shapely head – he ached to draw her, and wondered whether he dared sketch her on the table-cloth, when his mother was not looking. How perfectly stunning she was, and how graceful, and how adorably she had smiled at him when she shook hands, and oh, how perfectly ghastly that she was going to marry an old fellow like Uncle George, although he was a dear, and terribly generous and all that, but it could not be right; it could not be natural; it was against all the laws of beauty.

In spite of himself he began to caricature Uncle George on his shirt-cuff – the red cheeks, the swimming eye, the tender, rather foolish expression. Gyggy watched him over his shoulder and snorted in delight. Kicky was ashamed at once, and put away his pencil; and, seeing poor Aunt Louise looking dull and pensive in a corner, he went and sat beside her and told her all about his approaching examination at the Sorbonne.

She seemed grateful for his attention, and smiled at him, and squeezed his hand, and he found himself wondering how bald she was under her wig and whether she slept in it or put it on a dressing-table at night, and he turned away his eyes for fear she should guess what he was thinking, and be offended.

Aunt Georgie's gay laugh kept trilling in his ears – Jove, how pretty she was! – and the more she laughed and talked, the quieter and more pensive became his Aunt Louise. Perhaps her rheumatism was paining her.

Finally she asked for the *fiacre* to be called to take her to Versailles. She was a little tired, she said; she had not been sleeping very well of late; and her departure made a disturbance in the party. Everyone got up and stood about, and when

Kicky took Louise downstairs he heard his mother say something about putting up his new aunt for the night.

'She's very nice, isn't she, Aunt Louise?' he said, as he tucked the rug round her knees, and kissed her good-bye. 'I consider Uncle George an exceedingly lucky man.'

'It is Miss Lewis who is fortunate,' she replied quietly, 'in having won the affection and esteem of such a good and generous man as Captain Clarke.' And with that she went away, sitting very tall and straight, like a poker, the windows of the carriage tightly closed, and Kicky bounded off upstairs to see his new aunt, three steps at a time.

She stayed with them two days, and by the end of her visit they were all her enchanted slaves – even Ellen, who called her 'Georgie dear' and told her she should have some of the good furniture that her mother had given her originally for her wedding present. After all, it was not such a bad match. Georgina's father and mother were well off, and no doubt would see that their daughter received a handsome allowance, which would be very nice for George. He seemed so attached to her, too, and it was really delightful to see the dear fellow so ridiculously happy. Poor Louise, it was certainly unfortunate for her, but she must get over her disappointment. She had her religion, which was one consolation. Ellen could not but feel that, one way and another, things had turned out for the best.

George Clarke and Georgina Lewis were married in May, and Ellen went up to Boulogne for the wedding, taking Isabella with her to be bridesmaid. Louis-Mathurin was still in London. His brother's affairs had been left in a lamentable state, and he fondly imagined he could put them in order. He had plans for continuing the office and settling over in England, speculations being moderately successful, but not a word of this had yet been broached to his wife. The boys remained at school, weddings being scarcely in their line, and Kicky, anyway, had to go up to the Sorbonne for his *bachot*.

He sighed, it is true, as he saw his mother and sister off upon their journey, and asked – with a little blush of embarrassment – to be remembered to his Aunt Georgie. He sighed for half a day as he thought of portly, genial Uncle George leading that vision of loveliness to the altar, but at seventeen, sighs, though deep for three hours, are of short duration, and at five o'clock in the afternoon Kicky had lost his melancholia and was chasing Gyggy round the Passy swimming-bath, forgetting even his examination of the following day.

Posterity is the poorer for Kicky's absence at his uncle's wedding, for he might have got busy with his pencil – the opportunities were numerous – and he could scarcely have missed sketching his sainted grandmother, complete with frills and furbelows and a beribboned bonnet, toasting the bride in a beaker of champagne, and uttering obscenities at seventy-five.

Ellen felt a slight awkwardness in greeting her. She had seen her perhaps three times in the nine years since they had left Boulogne, the little argument about the memoirs and the annuity having successfully put a stop to visits of duration. She was greatly shocked at the appearance of her mother, who had aged considerably, and seemed to have lost all control over her tongue. She chattered like a senile magpie about everything and everyone, in a state of wild excitement: praised Isabella's beauty in extravagant terms, much to the child's embarrassment; said she would obtain a place for Kicky in the Army – chemistry was an idiotic occupation (Ellen was thankful he was not there to hear); suggested with many nods and winks of an objectionable kind that Louis-Mathurin was enjoying himself in London; and told Ellen herself that whether it was harp-playing or not it did not matter, but she was definitely more round-shouldered than ever. She was evidently foolish over Georgie, and kept calling her 'pet' and 'baby', which Ellen thought very tiresome; and Georgie was equally absurd with her, running up to her every minute and kissing her, and the pair of them laughing and talking with excessive loudness. Georgie appeared an entirely different girl here in Boulogne,

166

and said some outrageously immodest things – at least, so Ellen considered – for a young woman about to be married; and she wondered George did not put his foot down. He was so infatuated, however, that his darling could do no wrong. '*It only bears out what I have always said,*' observed Ellen to Louise in a letter, '*that my mother has a pernicious influence, even to-day. I am not at all sure that she has not ruined Georgina already. Even my brother seems to slacken in his high principles when he is in her company, and, though he makes out she must be humoured, she is getting old, I believe in reality he does not mind her prattle. I can truthfully say that, though I lived alone with her all those years before my marriage, she has never had the slightest influence over me. I have too strong a nature. She certainly used to encourage Louis in his extravagance, and I put down many of our present misfortunes to her way of talking and his weakness in listening to her.*

'*I keep Isabella away from her as much as possible, but it is really very difficult. She has loaded her with presents as it is, and the child will have her head turned. I shall be thankful when we are back in Paris again.*'

If Ellen was the wet blanket at her brother's wedding, young Isabella was certainly the brightest ornament. She was twelve now, and very pretty, with long golden curls. She had, too, a lively, affectionate disposition. She was like Gyggy in many ways, without his devilry, and was more than a little spoilt, though Ellen would have denied this in great fury. She was certainly very talented at the piano, and played with remarkable assurance for her years.

Louis-Mathurin talked about having her trained at the Conservatoire, but he did not say where the money would come from. At the moment Ellen scraped enough out of her slender income to provide a master once a week, while she herself sat with Isabella at her practice, insisting on at least three hours a day.

The child performed to the wedding guests, and was loudly applauded, and she really did look very charming, thought her fond mother, as she stepped down from the piano, smiling prettily, dressed in her simple white frock with a sash, her long ringlets falling over her shoulders. Pity she had the same nose as herself and Eugène – Kicky's was the only snub in the family – but no doubt she would grow to it, and, after all, a big nose was a sign of character, inherited as it was from – well – from a Certain Personage.

'There, there, you have done very well,' she said to her daughter proudly. 'I only wish that papa could have heard you. Come and sit beside me.'

'But, mamma, grandmamma says she is going to show me some pretty rings that a gentleman called Lord Folkestone gave her many years ago.'

'I think grandmamma is busy now, dear. Perhaps some other time.'

'I do not think so, mamma. Look, she is waving to me now. And Aunt Georgie said she would show me her new nighties and petticoats.'

'Better rest awhile, child; you look hot. Come, let us see what books are here in the bookcase. This is an old favourite of mine, the *Châteaux of the Loire*. We must make an excursion there some time, with the boys; it would be an education. Your ancestors had property there, you know.'

'But, mamma, I want to go and talk to Aunt Georgie.'

And the child flung herself away, with a little petulant frown, leaving her mother with tightened lips. Ellen was accustomed to implicit obedience, and here was Isabella showing independence and self-assertion after two days at Boulogne. She hoped that this was not a sign of shallowness and superficiality in the child's nature, that she preferred looking at rings and nightdresses rather than at pictures. She watched her out of the tail of her eye.

'Oh, I wish I had a ring like this one,' the child exclaimed. 'Perhaps when I am grown up I shall meet a gentleman like Lord Folkestone, grandmamma.'

Ellen stiffened in her chair at the old lady's cackle of laughter.

'If you are as pretty then as you are now, you certainly will,' she screamed, 'but don't trust him if he has green eyes, that's all I say! He'll want too much in return.'

'What will he want, grandmamma?'

There was another cackle of laughter, and Ellen rose from her chair.

'Isabella,' she called, 'come and look at these funny little donkeys out of the window. They are even smaller than the one you rode on at St Cloud.'

'I don't want to see the donkeys, thank you, mamma. Grandmamma is showing me her rings.'

'Perhaps grandmamma is getting tired,' said Ellen stubbornly.

'Tired? Fiddlesticks. Why should I be tired?' said Mary Anne, waving a hand like a monkey's paw. 'This darling baby is keeping me amused. Don't listen to your mother, precious pet. You ought to come and stay with me here on your own. I'd allow you to stay up all night and eat what you like. Plenty of nice handsome boys for you in Boulogne, too. I wager your brothers' friends make a fuss of you, don't they?'

'Why, yes, some of them do,' said Isabella, with a toss of her head.

'You are a great flirt, I believe, and quite right too. Twiddle 'em round your finger, that's the way. Let 'em see you don't care whether they like you or not, and they'll fasten on to you like flies on a jam-pot. Keep 'em at arm's length, though. None of your sly kissing in corners!'

'Oh, grandmamma, I don't care for kissing or anything like that.'

'Don't you, my pet? Ha! You will one day. That's what pretty girls like you were made for. Georgie likes it, don't you, Georgie?'

Another scream of laughter, and a giggle from the bride. Isabella looked at her in wide curiosity. Ellen stood by, her lips tighter than ever.

'I think it is time that Isabella went to bed,' she said. 'It is past nine o'clock, and at her age she needs plenty of sleep.'

'Sleep? Fiddlesticks!' cried grandmamma. 'There's only one person here who needs sleep, and that's Georgie. She won't get any to-morrow!'

A yell of laughter went up from the assembled guests – the usual Clarke riff-raff – but Ellen was glad to see that her brother had the grace to look ashamed.

'Mother,' he said quietly, 'that's quite enough in front of the child, and, for the matter of that, in front of all of us. Please remember yourself.'

The old lady made a very rude gesture with her fingers and put out her tongue. Ellen took Isabella firmly by the hand and led her away to bed. One thing she was quite decided upon – that this was her last visit to Boulogne.

The ceremony the following day passed off without any unfortunate incident, and, thank heaven, George restrained his mother from making a speech.

The soldier looked handsome and dignified as he stood by the altar steps, even if he did seem every minute of his fifty-five years, and the blushing Georgina was of course a poem. Ellen did not take much to her family – very middle-class and rather mean, giving nothing in the way of a present, and according to George his wife's allowance would be meagre. Ellen suspected that altogether things would not be so easy for them, especially if Georgina was as extravagant over her dresses as she appeared to be.

She returned to Paris in great ill-humour – she scarcely spoke to the unfortunate Isabella, whose eyes had been opened to a new and rather fascinating world – only to be met by a white-faced, trembling Kicky, who told her in despairing tones that he had been 'plucked' at the Sorbonne, having failed for his *bachot* in the written Latin version.

At first his mother refused to believe him. Kicky, her paragon, her darling, her brilliant boy, who had learnt his early lessons at her knee and had shown such promise ever since – it was impossible! What a disgrace! And one of his friends, a dull creature without half Kicky's talent, had actually passed with honours. She took a *fiacre* and went round to the *pension* to question Monsieur Froussard, in case there had been some mistake made over the marks, but he assured her, almost as disappointed as herself, that the news was true, and du Maurier Un, one of his pet pupils, had proved himself a failure after all.

'I don't know what to say to you,' exclaimed Ellen after dinner, when she sat alone with Kicky, who was gazing miserably at the floor, in the little *salon* in the rue du Bac; 'after all the encouragement you have had, both from papa and myself, and no expense spared over your education, to waste your gifts in this way! I insist that your failure is due to idleness and nothing else. The examination was not difficult. It is not only carelessness, it is gross ingratitude. Who is going to employ you now, without a degree? What sort of position do you expect to take up in the scientific world if you cannot pass your *baccalauréat*? I dare say you think it all very amusing.'

'Oh, mamma, how can you say that?' cried poor Kicky. 'I feel like throwing myself into the Seine. It would be a good riddance.'

'Yes, and add to the disgrace. A very fine idea. The trouble is, your papa and I have been too lenient with you from the first. It is the same with Gyggy and Isabella. You are all three of you selfish and inconsiderate, and have never shown the faintest sign of gratitude for all that has been done for you.'

'Dear mamma, I am grateful. Indeed I am. I don't know what I should do without you. I owe everything to you. You surely do not think I wanted to fail in the examination?'

'I don't know what to think. I am too shocked and disappointed. Failing in your Latin, too – one of the subjects most necessary in your future career in chemistry. Of course, I know what it is: it is all this drawing.'

171

'But, mamma, I only sketch for amusement.'

'Exactly. Amusement. You put the matter in a nutshell. Your generation thinks of nothing but amusement. Isabella grumbles at three hours' practice a day, because she has not enough time for amusement. You fail in your *bachot* because you prefer amusing yourself with a pencil – and generally at other people's expense, I have noticed. Don't think I did not catch a glimpse of that caricature of your Uncle George the other day, because I did. He would have been exceedingly flattered, wouldn't he? A nice tribute to a godfather who made you a handsome present of twenty francs when he went away, I must say. As for Gyggy – I have neither the time nor the patience to work myself into a rage about him. His faults are all too obvious. Why I should find myself the possessor of three such selfish, ungrateful children I do not know.'

'Oh, mamma, please, *please*, stop.'

'Well, I am not going to tell your papa. You will have to break the news to him yourself. A fine surprise it will be to him when he greets you in London to hear that his eldest son has been failed in his *baccalauréat* – after all the grief and worry he has had over his poor brother, too.'

'Mamma, wouldn't it be better if I wrote to him, and did not go to London?'

'Certainly not. It was always arranged that you should go on the fifteenth, and on the fifteenth you shall go. What your papa will arrange for you I do not know. It is extremely probable that we shall all live in London in future. His last letter hinted at the possibility. His business prospects appear brighter there than here. It will be a good thing for Isabella, at any rate. I shall take care that she is sent to a good college.'

'But what about Gyggy, mamma?'

'Eugène will have to stay in France. Your Aunt Louise will make herself responsible for him. Now it is time you went to bed. I have had a long and extremely exhausting day, and my head is splitting.'

She kissed him on the forehead and left the room, leaving a little trail of camphor behind her – she had worn her winter furs to Boulogne – and Kicky was left alone. He wandered to the window and leant out, his head in his arms. 'It's beginning,' he thought, 'what I have always dreaded; the start of a new life, the breaking up of the old. To-morrow I shall be a man. This old, careless, irresponsible life is finished. I shall never be happy again. Never more. I don't want to go to London. Oh, God, why must things ever change? Why can't time stand still? Nothing will ever be the same again. Perhaps I shall have to live in London all my life, and years later, when I am old and grey, I shall come back here, and the house will be pulled down, and nobody will recognise me, everyone will be dead. I shall go and buy sweets from Madame Liard, in the rue de la Tour, and she will serve me like a stranger.'

The familiar smells came up to him from the street below, and the dear, familiar cries. There was old Gaston, with the wooden leg, who was the concierge at the house opposite. He always came out about this time to sniff the air. A *fiacre* clopped by over the cobblestones, and the *cocher* drew rein at the end of the street to allow the hourly omnibus to pass. The cafés were lighting up, and Kicky could see a waiter rubbing the tables with a cloth.

The air was warm for May, and it was laden with homely smells – French coffee, and endive, and burnt bread. Someone was laughing in the house next door. In the distance came the muffled rumble of Paris, the sound that Kicky had heard now as far back as he could remember. Sometimes, in the *vacances*, he and Gyggy used to return late, in the last omnibus, and there was something mysterious and compelling in this Paris seen by night – the lamps at the street corners, the twinkling cafés, the gay, inconsequent strolling of the passers-by; there was a sense of buoyancy in the air, a pleasant levity.

You sang for no reason; you laughed because you must.

And now Kicky had to leave it all behind him, and set out

for London, which was dim and murky and unfriendly, so he had always heard. He must say good-bye to Monsieur Froussard and Madame, and the dear funny *pension*, and the boys; walk to-morrow along the quays for the last time, and perhaps snatch a hasty visit to the green, tangled Bois, and the Mare d'Auteuil. If only papa would invent a bottle that would contain all the scents and sounds one loved, so that in London, in his black and lonely moments, he could take off the stopper and release the smells of home! Sniff Paris, for one brief and magical moment, on the still air. But Louis-Mathurin, with all his imagination, had never gone so far as that, and Kicky had to leave Paris without any reminder of the home he loved except the pictures he made for himself in the back of his mind.

He felt like a criminal on his way to prison as he kissed his family good-bye, shaking hands with old Charlotte, who had been with them for years and wept openly at his departure, waving to p'tit Jean-Jean, the son of the *boulanger* next door, glancing for the last time up at his bedroom window, the shutter of which banged a forlorn farewell. And he knew he would never hear it again, or return to the little bedroom he shared with Gyggy.

Dear, brave, comic Gyggy, fighting to keep back his tears, turned a somersault in the street to make Kicky laugh. This was the last Kicky saw of him for six interminable years – for he was a man when they met each other again – and, turning round and looking over the back of the *fiacre*, he waved to him, waved to the long, leggy figure with the shock of chestnut hair, as though he left part of himself behind and was saying good-bye to his own boyhood.

His misery was acute as he drove through the streets of Paris for the last time. It seemed heartless and incredible that that man, standing on the pavement reading his morning paper, would go about his daily life in the usual way, work at his office, lunch at his little restaurant, return in the evening to his pleasant, familiar home and his own bed, and he, Kicky, would be hundreds of miles away in an alien land. If only they could change places. A *chiffonier* padded in the gutter, a stub of cigarette behind his ear, and later in the day he would rest himself under the warm sun, his filthy cap over his face – it would be better to be him, without a care in the world, than Kicky Busson du Maurier, who had failed in his *baccalauréat*.

All the way across the north of France, and again in the steamer that was to take him the whole way to London Bridge, Kicky was wondering what to say to his father when he arrived. Kind, jovial papa, who had never scolded him, and was never angry except once – and that was when he had seen someone ill-treat an animal, and then he had gone straight up to the fellow and knocked him down – papa was so vague he might even forget to meet him. But he had taken such an interest in Kicky's work the last time he had been home, and had said that they must work together in a laboratory and give the greatest scientific discoveries of all time to the world. What agony of disappointment would be his when he learnt the dreadful news! Mamma had so rubbed in the shame of his failure, and the terrible effect it would have upon papa, that Kicky was seasick for the entire voyage, even though the sea was as smooth as the proverbial mill-pond.

And going up the London river, of course, it began to rain – that relentless grey drizzle from a leaden sky so depressing to the newcomer – and what with seasickness, and homesickness, and the sickness born of nerves, Kicky was in the depths of despair as he watched the dirty water, full of wisps of straw and sodden bread and orange-peel, and saw the murky chimneys and the roof-tops of London draw nearer through the evening mist.

The boat drew alongside London Bridge with a groan and a shiver and the clattering of chains, and the air was hideous with rough cockney voices and unfamiliar sounds, Kicky faltered down the gangway, a poor, woebegone fellow with a small portmanteau in either hand, and there was papa waiting for him, a mad, incongruous figure under an enormous scarlet umbrella.

He waved violently – in tremendous spirits, of course – while Kicky's heart drooped to the bottom of his boots. Papa kissed him on each cheek, and then, seeing his reluctant eyes and his miserable little face, he threw back his head and burst into a shout of laughter.

'You have failed,' he said. 'There's no need to tell me. Your expression is enough. Don't worry; it doesn't matter a bit. We'll go and have some dinner and forget all about it.'

And off they went together, arm in arm, Kicky's heart nearly bursting with love and gratitude and relief, while Louis-Mathurin, singing at the top of his voice, charged the surly passers-by, the ragged urchins, and the solemn London policeman with the point of his scarlet umbrella.

Part Four

10

No 44 Wharton Street, Pentonville, was a very different place from the rue du Bac in Paris, and Kicky wondered how existence there was to be endured at all. His mother and Isabella came over in the autumn, and it seemed as though they were to settle in London for good. Kicky ached for Paris, for his old life at the Pension Froussard, and his companions, and Gyggy, but he was condemned instead to become a pupil at the Birkbeck Laboratory in University College.

Quite undaunted by his son's failure to pass his *baccalauréat*, Louis-Mathurin decided that a further study of two years would be profitable to the boy, and, as he happened to know Dr Williams at the college, the matter was easily arranged. Kicky was very disheartened. He thought that papa would realise his total unsuitability for a scientific career, and would permit him to take up music or drawing professionally. Papa never suggested anything of the kind. As for mamma, she insisted with so much emphasis that Kicky was the luckiest person in the world to have so much done for him, possessing a father who not only forgave him for his failure but arranged for him to become a pupil for two years at University College, where he would have the most wonderful opportunities, that he dared not utter the mildest protests, for fear of disturbing the family harmony. It was better to say nothing, and make the best of things, than risk an explosion in the home. Besides, Kicky was far too tender-hearted to bear the thought of hurting papa's feelings.

Papa was exactly like a big, overgrown schoolboy, with his tremendous enthusiasms and his fantastic ideas for improving the world, and he made an excellent companion. Kicky had seen little of him during those last years in Paris; he had been away a great deal, and Kicky always at school, but here in London they were thrown together, taking long walks very often on Sundays, to Hampstead or to Richmond, Louis-Mathurin striding out like a long-distance athlete, his arms waving, his grizzled curls blowing in the air. He talked vaguely of business in the City, which he was supposed to be carrying on in his late brother's name, but what exactly he did in the office Kicky never found out. His speculations were no longer a secret. He simply could not keep the excitement to himself. Ellen, when the first shock of discovery was over, shrugged her shoulders from long habit and awaited the inevitable sequel. Ruination would come one day, sooner or later, and for the children's sake she hoped it would be later.

She supposed there must be a certain fascination in obtaining something for nothing – a hundred pounds from five – and it was very useful of course, when a lucky investment enabled her to send Isabella to an excellent daily school; but she could not approve of the method; it was against her principles.

Besides, it was not always certain. Some days he lost, and then came the little demand upon her income, and a casual enquiry as to when she expected her next dividend from Boulogne.

Kicky, naturally, heard nothing of this. Money matters were not discussed in front of him. He knew that his father was poor – Mamma had insisted upon this from his earliest days, and had impressed upon him that extravagance was the greatest evil in the world – but why he was poor she did not say.

Papa was a genius, of course, a great inventor, but somehow or other nobody seemed to have heard of his inventions. He could not help being aware of this in Paris, amongst his school friends, and so he fell into the habit of not discussing the matter, and hoped sincerely, for his father's sake, that these mysterious inventions were appreciated in some other country – South

America, perhaps, or Australia. Papa was great on philosophy, and had tremendous likes and dislikes in ancient history. Like all atheists, he possessed in full many of the most Christian qualities: great tenderness to children and to animals, a hatred of human suffering, extreme generosity, and an eager willingness to help others in distress. His second brother, Jacques, died suddenly in Hamburg (the Bussons were notoriously short-lived) and left a wife and three children in want. Louis-Mathurin, with an excess of good feeling, sent for the widow and her daughters, even taking apartments for them near by in Pentonville, but, as ill luck had it, their arrival clashed with an unfortunate speculation, and Louis-Mathurin found he could do very little for them.

The widow, who had believed her brother-in-law to be a successful man, was naturally a little annoyed, and poured long tales of woe into Ellen's ears of how she had been deceived and dragged over from Hamburg, where she had kind friends, to apartments in Pentonville and no prospects.

It was all very awkward, and the upshot was a definite estrangement between the two families, Madame Jacques returning to Hamburg after a month or two. Ellen wrote off to Louise indignantly, saying, '*It is all very well, but why we should be expected to take responsibility for your brother's family I do not know. He had certainly never done anything for us. Louis suggests that you write to Palmella, and for the sake of your old friendship he might be able to help them. Personally, I doubt the success of your mission. Beyond a few books at Christmas and birthday time the Duke has not been much of a godfather to Eugène, and as for calling Kicky Palmella after him, we might have spared ourselves the trouble. At any rate, I have forbidden Isabella to correspond with her cousin Josephine, as it is not very pleasant that the girls should write to one another when their parents have quarrelled.*

'*We are all well, but Christmas is not an agreeable time for us, and Louis is very uncertain with his speculations. If only he would make some more money we could put it towards Isabella's education.*

I find it very difficult to keep up her music; it is impossible to be a brilliant player without three hours' practice a day. You would be disappointed in her appearance if you saw her; she certainly was a lovely child, but her beautiful complexion is gone, and her front teeth give her continual pain, and I fear she must lose them in two or three years' time. The dentists all say that the decay comes from the stomach. What a pity that she was not allowed to dine at one o'clock like all other children, but Louis would insist on his fad of dining at five. I am quite in despair, knowing what she must suffer with false teeth. Louis himself feels better since he left off beer, and drinks but rum and water. I am quite distressed at the thought of all you are doing for Eugène and I trust he will repay your goodness by exemplary behaviour.'

Which letter would suggest that the nature of Ellen Busson du Maurier did not exactly mellow with the years. . . .

Louis-Mathurin, on the other hand, sang and joked at fifty-five with greater freedom than he had done at twenty-five, and was as pleased as a child when he visited the Birkbeck Laboratory at University College and was allowed to look at all the bottles and mixtures ranged on the shelves, about which Kicky, even now, knew very little. He would try to evade science as a subject of conversation, and would persuade his father to talk poetry, or music, or sport – anything, in fact, but chemistry – and Louis-Mathurin, easily led, would hold forth for hours at a time while Kicky swung his legs and listened, and thought how pleasant it was not to be doing any work.

Kicky was going through rather a difficult period. He hated his surroundings for one thing – the grey-drab respectability of Pentonville, and the dreary apartment where they lived. He had no pleasure in returning to it after a long and uncongenial day at the Birkbeck Laboratory, where the little work he did was monotonous and his fellow-students were loud-voiced and smutty-minded.

His passion for music increased tenfold; he would beg a few shillings from his mother and stand in the gallery queue for

Covent Garden, and sit perhaps, when he was admitted, somewhere right away at the back with his chin in his hands and his eyes closed, drinking in the sounds that had meant so much to him ever since he had lain as a tiny child in his cot and listened to his father.

Music took him right out of his dissatisfied adolescent self that could find no beauty in chemical bottles, and wafted him, as though by magic, into an enchanted land. These figures who strolled so gallantly in Verona or Seville were real to him, and he moved amongst them, from his bench in the gallery, fighting their duels, wooing their women, singing the songs they sang with the same careless rapture. The world of fantasy was his world; he lived in a dream, and the pale young man with the square shoulders who tramped home to Pentonville was only a shadow.

The National Gallery and the British Museum were other methods of escape. On his free afternoons he would take a scrappy sandwich lunch to one of them, and sit for hours at a time before one particular picture or thing of beauty, drugging himself with the appreciation of colour and line and form, until the attendants looked at him suspiciously, as though he were a lunatic escaped from an asylum, and he would have to get up and walk away in pretended unconcern, humming under his breath.

Sometimes a longing for Paris would come over him, and he would walk down to London Bridge and watch the boat leave for Boulogne, feeling like an exile on an alien shore as the steamer drew away with smoke pouring from her squat funnel. He yearned to break French bread again, tear the burnt brown crust; drink coffee black with chicory; cut a large slice of gruyère cheese. He ached to tread cobblestones once more, idle on the quays, stare up at the white face of Notre-Dame; and, when evening came, listen once more to those elusive Paris murmurs, the stir of life, the little throb of gaiety.

Louis-Mathurin and Ellen began to worry about him. He

was silent these days, heavy-browed and pensive, and began to smoke furiously, far more than was good for him. Ellen tried nagging at him, and he looked up at her with puzzled, wistful eyes and made no answer, so that she was forced to desist, disturbed by his expression, and would go off and scold Isabella at her practice in order to relieve herself.

She was disappointed in her children. They lacked drive and concentration. Here was Kicky, supposed to be training for chemistry, and instead of reading up his subject he would wander to the British Museum and try to discover something about the Busson pedigree. This was a new craze, lately come into his head. He declared that the Bussons belonged to the wild wet soil of Brittany, or further inland into Maine or Sarthe – Ellen did not really know; but at any rate he had discovered something in a book at the Museum about a château, and an old Parc Maurier, and was full of it, according to Isabella. He did not say much to his parents. Louis-Mathurin declared he was wasting his time, and was a little annoyed. There was a château somewhere, but he did not think his father had ever lived in it, and why did not Kicky take more interest in science instead of poring over old books in the British Museum?

Isabella, too, was not as serious-minded as Ellen could have wished. She scraped somehow through her lessons, but was constantly going out to tea with her school friends, and chattering nonsense, and thought a great deal more about the colour of a new dress than of practising her piano.

Very different from herself at that age. *She* had not depended on friends for amusement. Ellen was glad to see that, now Isabella was no longer a little girl, Louis-Mathurin was more severe with her. She was not to go out unaccompanied, and Kicky must take her to and from school. He said he believed in supervision, and strict supervision at that, which Ellen found rather surprising.

She had known, of course, for years that when they were poorer than usual he invariably introduced a little note of

184

pomposity into his relations with everybody. Secretly influenced, perhaps, by Kicky's researches in the British Museum, he dropped the 'Busson' here in Pentonville, and called himself du Maurier.

'I will not have Miss du Maurier walking in a crocodile like a charity orphan,' he said magnificently. 'If Kicky cannot fetch Isabella from school, then I will go myself'; and he would wait sometimes, much to his daughter's confusion, just outside the school gate, a strange figure in a flapping cape, and, more often than not, sheltering beneath his scarlet umbrella.

'And pray who is this?' he would enquire, staring down at a dark, leggy child hanging on to Isabella's arm, and swinging a satchel of books; and Isabella, blushing for her father's memory, for she had introduced the child twenty times already, would stammer in reply, 'Why, papa, this is my great friend Emma Wightwick. Surely you remember?'

'Miss Wightwick must forgive me,' he would answer, with exquisite courtesy. 'In future we will recognise one another.' And, with a flourish of his red umbrella and a toss of his cape, he would stride away down the street, talking to himself perhaps, while Isabella pattered after him in great embarrassment.

Gyggy, of course, was causing his family the usual worry and concern. Louise wrote from Versailles to say that she had had an interview with Monsieur Froussard as to the boy's future, and Monsieur Froussard had been perfectly frank with her and told her that her godson was an incorrigible idler and good-for-nothing and so far as he could see he was not fitted for any career. She did not say that the schoolmaster had also told her that the boy was something of a psychological problem, and that his frivolous disposition was probably the result of misunderstanding by his parents. He had a warm, affectionate nature, and nobody had ever responded to it. A careless super-ficiality was the consequence. Gyggy himself, when questioned, said that there was only one thing he wanted to do, and that was to join the French Army. Neither his father nor his mother cared to have him in England; he quite understood that. They

185

could not afford to keep him, and of course Kicky and Isabella must come first. Therefore let him become a soldier – take service under the Emperor – and he would visit foreign lands and enjoy himself. Louise was very doubtful whether Louis-Mathurin would give his permission, and at first there were violent letters exchanged between London and Versailles.

Louise, with a soft spot in her heart for her godson, was in favour of the scheme. He was fond of horses and the open air, and could join a *régiment de chasseurs*. She could see no disgrace in it at all. Besides, as his master said, he was fitted for nothing else. His father, on the other hand, declared that no Busson du Maurier had ever been a common trooper, and why should his son lower himself by cleaning officers' boots and shovelling horses' dung – which, he insisted, would be Eugène's portion through life if he joined the Army.

Nonsense, Louise replied, with unusual firmness; there was every chance that Eugène would rise from the ranks and get a commission – men were doing it every day – and then he might attain to the highest position. It was a man's life, anyway, and would be the best means of developing the boy. She would undertake to spare him a little dividend from her income, and his father and mother need not worry on that account. This letter certainly calmed and mollified the indignation of Louis-Mathurin, and after a few weeks he gave his consent in the following declaration, signed and sealed at the Mansion House:

'*I, the undersigned Louis-Mathurin Busson du Maurier, of 5 Barge Yard, Bucklersbury, City of London* [this was his office address] *do solemnly and sincerely declare that my son, Alexandre Eugène Busson du Maurier, was born at Brussels, in Belgium, on the ninth of February, 1836, and that he was educated in France at the school of Monsieur Froussard, in Passy. And, giving way to his decided inclination for a military career, I hereby give him my consent and authority to enlist into the service of His Majesty the Emperor of the French Nation.*'

So the cheerful, happy-go-lucky, and sadly neglected Gyggy became a *chasseur du ligne*, for better or worse, and went off to Sarreguemines to join his regiment, his pockets well lined by his considerate godmother, and his new uniform paid for into the bargain.

Ellen sent him two guineas, which she told him she had great difficulty in scraping together, and she said to Louise, in another letter, that she would endeavour to do this from time to time, but he must not depend upon it.

'If he is steady,' she said, *'he will manage very well, and as he now will have to depend entirely on himself, being away from his relations, he will soon leave off his boyish tricks and apply himself earnestly to learning his profession. His first care must be of his health, so that he is strong and fit enough to bear all the hardships that will necessarily come his way. Kicky says that as soon as he makes any money from his chemistry he will make Eugène an allowance, but I very much doubt Kicky ever earning enough to keep himself, let alone his brother.'*

Poor, irritable, disillusioned Ellen, why must every one of her letters bear trace of her own disappointment in life? There is a sting on the tail of each, a certain sourness. Those letters of hers, crossed and over-crossed, almost impossible to decipher, penned with a sharp black nib – they betray, every one of them, a sort of mental indigestion, as though there were annoyances buried inside her that would not pass away, but must come forth, now and again, with stale, unpleasing bitterness.

It was almost as if she had a grudge against mankind, and saw her fellow-beings through dark-tinted spectacles. Louis-Mathurin was impossible, no doubt; he had failed her in a hundred different ways – borrowed her money, spent it, and borrowed again. He had fulfilled no early promise; he had achieved nothing. Yet he was the same man who had loved her over twenty years ago, who had won her with his charm, sung to her, cajoled and amused her. He had been tender to her always, faithless never. Eccentric, perhaps, even a little mad – but, then, she knew that when he had stared at her for the first time with his light-blue eyes and sang Schubert's Serenade as it had never been sung before.

She had been given three children, who were neither more selfish nor more inconsiderate than any other person's children. Yet she must nag at them, worry at them, intrude upon their young lives with infuriating fingers, prodding the soft spots, scratching the tender places. '*If Kicky disappoints me, I shall be in despair*,' she told Louise. '*He has no initiative, no energy. He sits about and dreams. Always a pencil in his hand – and I think of the money wasted on his education*.' But was that perhaps just another excuse on paper? Was a little grain of fear at the back of it all? Kicky was idle; an idle youth became a wasted man, a good-for-nothing, a dilettante. Gyggy had already taken the downward path. Would Kicky go in the same direction? And what about Isabella and her superficial girlish vanities? Would all her children show that same strain of carelessness, that lack of principle, which she had been at such desperate pains to avoid? With a blind, unreasoning fear of heredity she saw her mother as the cause of it all. She looked back to the beginning of the century, back to her own girlhood, and she had only to concentrate a moment on the past and there stood her mother, at the height of her notoriety, smiling her brilliant, superficial smile, throwing morals to the four winds and tearing respectability to shreds. As a child she had perceived the froth and the glamour, but now, a mature woman of fifty-five, she saw nothing but the sordidness, the bargaining, the reckless gamble of her mother's life. And she shuddered and was afraid.

A gay laugh from Isabella, and she would watch her with suspicion. A witty remark from Kicky, scrawled under one of his disgraceful caricatures, and she heard again her mother's voice, the quick repartee, the pointed tongue.

188

You could not fight against heredity; it was too strong for you. Sometimes it strangled you in the end. She thought of Kicky, and Gyggy, and Isabella, and their children, and their children's children, strolling through life with a shrug of the shoulder and a fluttering eyelid, singing all the summer with a yawn and a laugh, like the grasshopper in the fable, forgetting that winter came, when the sun had gone. She saw her mother pointing at her in derision – 'Poor Ellen, so round-shouldered and plain, that's why she has never had a sense of humour' – and she was aware of a sense of frustration, of futile anger, whenever she remembered those swimming brown eyes, that high-pitched cackle of laughter.

When George's letter came at breakfast, in the late autumn of 1852, to say that their mother had died in the night, very suddenly, and was being buried there to-day, in Boulogne, Ellen turned very pale, and said 'Thank God' in a funny strangled voice, hardly aware that she had spoken; then she got up and left the table and went out of the room. The letter lay open on her plate. Kicky and Isabella stared at one another, alarmed and a little uncomfortable, and Isabella said, 'I think mamma cannot be very well,' and looked anxiously at her father. Louis-Mathurin, who had been reading the financial page of *The Times* with deep concentration, glanced up vaguely, and perceived for the first time that Ellen had left the room. 'What is the matter with your mother?' he began, and then, seeing the letter in George's handwriting on her plate, he leant over and read the first page.

'*My dearest Ellen, – It is with a sorrowful heart and many tears I take up my pen to write to you this day, but I am confident you will bear the blow with your usual fortitude. Our dear mother has left us. She passed away very suddenly on Friday night, and to the best of our belief she suffered no pain, but went in her sleep. She had been her usual cheerful self during the day, and had even driven out with Georgie and the baby* in the afternoon. She complained of a little indigestion before retiring, but as this was usual after her glass of porter, we thought nothing of it. "It is high time we had another party," she said, as she kissed Georgie and myself good night, and I have no doubt that these were her last words. When her maid went to her about twelve o'clock, as was her custom, with a cordial, she was lying across her bed, still dressed, and breathing heavily. We were summoned, and I went out myself for the doctor, but all of no avail. She never regained consciousness, and was dead by a quarter past three.

'Georgie is much affected, and has scarcely ceased from crying since the calamity. I fear her grief will affect our little son, as to-day he has refused his food for the first time. By the time this letter reaches you, my dear Ellen, our mother will have been laid to rest, quite quietly and without ceremony, in the English cemetery here. We will, of course, come over to England and discuss the future, once matters are settled here. I am, as you know, provided for, and with my little pension can support my wife and child. Mother's annuity is now yours for your lifetime. But more of this when we meet. . . . I am greatly shocked by what has happened, and can scarcely believe that I shall never hear her laugh again, or hold her dear hand in mine. Memories of our childhood come back to me very forcibly, and it seems but yesterday that you and I stood shoulder to shoulder at the drawing-room window in Tavistock Place, and looked down upon our mother, superbly dressed as usual, stepping into a carriage beside a gentleman – Sir Charles Milner I think it was. And as the carriage bowled away, she looked up at the window, and smiled, and waved her hand to us. Whatever charges have been laid against her, and will continue to be laid, as long as her name is remembered in the pages of old scandals, at least we know, you and I, that she was a good mother, and much of what she did was for our sakes. My regards to Louis and the family, and you may expect to see us soon.

'Your affectionate brother,
'GEORGE NOEL CLARKE.'

Louis-Mathurin laid the letter back upon the table, thought for a moment, and then, clearing his throat, addressed his son and daughter:

'Your grandmother is dead,' he said, and he hesitated, as though he would make a little speech about her suitable for the occasion, but the situation was too much for him; he murmured something in Latin about the swift passage of life, and then took a pair of scissors from his pocket and cut out a long column from the financial news. He glanced at the clock. If he went to his office in the City right away he would be able to get in touch with Hatton at the Stock Exchange and tell him to place that investment after all. . . .

191

11

The annuity certainly did make a little difference. Ellen bought new curtains for the sitting-room, and had the dining-room chairs re-covered. She laid in a couple of dress-lengths for herself and Isabella, and instructed the principal at Isabella's school that in the coming term her daughter would take two lessons in German a week instead of only one. On those days she would also take midday dinner at school. Beyond these small extravagances Ellen did not go. Louis-Mathurin, on the other hand, risked the portion that his wife handed over to him in a wild speculation, that luckily for all of them succeeded to a certain extent. At any rate, it brought in enough ready money for him to install Kicky in a laboratory of his own, close to the office in Barge Yard, Bucklersbury. The laboratory was fitted up in the most expensive style, with water and gas laid on in every possible corner, and bottles, chemical stores, and scales reaching from the floor to the ceiling. Louis-Mathurin was like a child with a new toy. The laboratory was supposed to be a surprise, but from his mysterious hints Kicky suspected what his father was engaged upon, and he would have given anything in the world to be able to say, 'Papa, dear papa, don't think me ungrateful, but please believe me when I tell you that you are wasting the money you need so badly. I shall never make a chemist. Not even after this training at University College. I have not the brains. I have not the concentration. Let me do anything but chemistry – go to Australia, join the Army, like Gyggy, sing in the street and beg for coppers. . . .'

He tried to screw up his courage to make some sort of

declaration, but when he entered the laboratory for the first time, and saw the trouble that had been taken, the care with which everything had been arranged – this was the reason, then, why papa had been home so seldom in the evenings lately – he had not the heart. His father watched him eagerly, his own face wreathed in smiles, and Kicky turned to him, holding out his hand, deeply touched by all that had been done for him, and said, 'Papa, I can never repay you for this.'

He wanted to bury his head in his hands, he wanted to cry. His father looked so pleased, so happy, so unbearably pathetic. What would he have done had he known his son hated the laboratory, hated the bottles and the scales, hated everything to do with chemistry?

But Louis-Mathurin suspected nothing. He walked round the room, touching the fittings with a loving hand, caressing them almost; and he began to talk excitedly, violently almost, about some invention for fertilising the land that he would give to the world very shortly. Kicky would help him; they would do this thing together. He broke off in the middle to show Kicky the prospectus he had had especially printed in his name – 'G. L. P. Busson du Maurier' – which stated that assays of ore and analyses of minerals, etc., would be most carefully conducted, and all business of that kind attended to, with great steadiness and dispatch.

'You wait and see,' he said, patting him on the shoulder. 'Orders will come pouring in. You will have to refuse many, I have no doubt'; and he left Kicky alone in the laboratory and went off to his own office next door, rubbing his hands in tremendous spirits.

So every day Kicky went off to his gorgeous laboratory, and waited for the orders that never came; and while he waited he turned yellow liquids into blue ones to amuse his friends, who came to cheer his solitude, and gave lunch-parties and supper-parties when his father was out on business.

He would have liked to install a piano, but did not dare

commit such sacrilege in a laboratory, so smuggled in a concertina instead, and a guitar, and he gave little impromptu concerts in the afternoon to one or two medical students he had known at University College, and sometimes to Isabella and her school friends when they could escape from supervision.

The long-legged Emma Wightwick gazed at him in admiration, whether he sang to her, or poured fascinating coloured liquids into bottles, or produced strange explosions and even stranger smells, and he thought what a jolly, unaffected child she was, and how handsome she would be in a year or two.

After all, life was not so bad at twenty-one as one might suppose, and he was getting over his adolescent worries to a certain extent. If only he were not so hopelessly unfitted for a scientific career his future outlook would be bright enough. The family had acquired a new and generous friend in George Clarke's late commanding officer, a certain Colonel Greville, who was now retired and living on his estate down at Milford, in Wales. Louis-Mathurin had met him first many years before, and he had shown himself interested in the famous portable lamp, and had even purchased one to use on manoeuvres. They met again during the summer of 1854, and Louis-Mathurin profited by the occasion to explain his new invention for fertilising soil. The Colonel, who was a keen farmer and owned a lot of land, was an easy prey, and even went so far as to put money into the scheme. He was also kind enough to give Kicky his first order. Specimens of soil from the Milford estate were sent up to London for Kicky to analyse, which he did with becoming gravity, and was paid £10 for his pains.

He immediately bought presents for his family, and sent £2 to Gyggy out in France. By the time he had pleased everybody he had about thirty shillings left for himself, which he laid out in paints and brushes, much to his mother's disapproval, but as he had given her a handsome and very expensive shawl, she was scarcely in a position to remonstrate, and wisely said nothing.

Colonel Greville continued to act as good fairy to the family, and in August he introduced Kicky to the chairman of the Victoria Gold and Copper Mine in North Molton, Devon. Everybody in England had gold fever in the summer of 1854, and there was much wild talk of discoveries throughout the country, and fortunes to be made in a night. Strange to say, Louis-Mathurin did not catch the fever, but showed himself superlatively calm throughout the crisis – which, needless to say, was a very lucky thing for the Busson du Mauriers. Kicky had an interview with the directors of the Devon mine, and so much impressed them with his scientific jargon (he had looked up several terms in the dictionary half an hour before-hand) that he was offered a guinea and a half a day to go down and inspect the workings of the mine, and to bring back a report in three or four weeks' time as to the practicability of working it. It was with difficulty that Kicky stopped himself from throwing his arms round the chairman and kissing him, but he managed, by making a supreme effort, to look as though a guinea and a half a day meant nothing in his life, and he said very solemnly that he must think the matter over, and would let the board know his answer the following day. And so out of the building, tripping over the mat as he went.

He returned home to dinner in a great state of excitement, and broke the news to the family, all of whom had palpitations of the heart in consequence. A guinea and a half a day! It was really tremendous.

'If you take long enough over the business, your salary will amount to quite a considerable sum,' said Louis-Mathurin. 'I see by the contract they have drawn out that you are not tied down for time. What an opportunity! Of course you will not find any gold, but that does not affect the issue.'

'I wish I could go and enjoy myself in Devonshire, too,' sighed Isabella, who was finding German and Italian lessons rather excessive during the holidays.

'Kicky does not go to Devon to play, but to earn his living,' reproved Ellen. 'Let us hope that the Victoria Mine does not come to grief before he gets there.'

Such an appalling idea had never entered Kicky's head, and he wrote off his answer at once to the directors, to say that he would be very pleased to undertake the survey. Three days later he travelled down to Devon, and was met by the engineer and about thirty very rough-looking miners.

Kicky felt horribly young and inefficient, and wished he had not come after all.

'You'll have to keep these fellows under your thumb,' said the engineer. 'The first sign of weakness on your part and your life will be one long hell. Show 'em who's master and they'll eat out of your hand.'

Kicky smiled nervously. He had never given an order in his life. . . .

He did not look much like a superintendent of mines, either, with his slim youthful figure, his brown wavy hair, worn rather long, and his thin pale face. To his immense surprise, he agreed with the miners very well, and when they found out that he no more believed in the discovery of gold in Devon than they did, he became more popular than ever.

He immediately established himself on a footing of easy *camaraderie*, which was far more successful than the iron fist advocated by the engineer, and when the work of the day was over he would go back and stand them drinks at the inn, and question them about their lives, and draw their portraits on the backs of envelopes, much to their surprise and delight.

He became friendly, too, with some of the farmers of the neighbourhood and, August and September being particularly pleasant in Devonshire, there were expeditions on Saturdays and Sundays to the local beauty spots with the farmers' pretty sisters, and much consuming of plum cake and cider, and singing of choruses, and chatter and laughter, and returning home by moonlight.

It was little wonder that the time passed happily, and he

wrote long letters home full of praise of the rural life.

He was really very lucky to be made superintendent of a gold-mine that had not any gold, and he wished this particular phase in his existence could last for ever. In duty bound he reported on the absence of gold in North Molton, but the directors replied that he must be mistaken, and would he continue taking his guinea and a half a day until gold was discovered.

Such obliging employers are rarely to be found, and Kicky took full advantage of the situation, spending his mornings in distilling mercury and his evenings in yodelling Tyrolese melodies under a harvest moon.

His sketch-book was black with miners and sunburnt labourers and smiling gypsy-faced maidens, and no doubt he would have continued living amongst them, and might have ended by marrying the prettiest and settling down in Devon, had not the neglected shareholders of the Victoria Mine written an indignant letter to the board of directors demanding an extraordinary general meeting.

So Kicky had to bid farewell to the rustic life, and kiss the farmers' sisters good-bye, and shake hands with the shaggy miners, and return again to London, where he attended the general meeting and infuriated the board of directors by his frank statement as to the barrenness of the gold-mine.

Whether the Victoria Mine came to grief and the shareholders were ruined, history does not relate, but Kicky's association with it terminated from that moment, and he went back to 44 Wharton Street neither a sadder nor a wiser man, as is generally the case, but very brown from the sun, and a little heavier from the Devonshire cream, and gayer than he had been for many months.

He found the family well: Louis-Mathurin in high spirits, Ellen sleeping better (she had suffered from insomnia for many years now), and Isabella looking very pretty, and working hard at her music. The reports of Gyggy were poor, as usual. A curt letter from his Colonel had been forwarded by Louise with many regrets. The boy played practical jokes from morning till night, and took nothing seriously. If he continued in this way there would be no prospect of promotion. Louise did not mention that he was continually getting into debt, and that every time he wrote to her he made some request for money. His letters were funny, no doubt, and full of little sketches of his companions, and she cried over them sometimes, they reminded her so much of the letters Louis-Mathurin had written as a boy; but she shook her head when his reports came in, and the bills from the tradesmen he had neglected to pay.

She sent him five hundred francs, wrapped in a religious book, and, instead of paying the tradesmen, he gave a party to his friends, and they all got tipsy on *vin du pays*. Poor Gyggy was incorrigible. . . .

Ellen wrote him pages of reproaches about the Colonel's letter, and not a word of encouragement, so he tore them in two, and danced a can-can on them, and then wrapped a wet towel round his forehead and composed a letter to his aunt.

'*I need not ask you to accept,*' he said, '*my grateful thanks and real gratitude for all the immeasurable kindness and invaluable services you have rendered me these last years in behaving as the best of mothers towards such an unworthy being as myself. Suffice it to say, that throughout my life I will never forget you, and your disinterested friendship, and that it often gives me great pleasure, during the manifold hardships of my profession, to know that I have at least one kind and affectionate parent thinking of me.*

'*I have more than once reproached myself for the regrets I may have caused you in not following letter for letter your instructions to me as regards religion, not that I mean to say that I have none, but I feel it's too great a subject and much too profound for me, and my only aim for the moment is honesty and manly feelings. Nor need I say that I would never have forgiven myself had I contrived to make myself out better than I really am in affecting more religion than I possess.*'

Gyggy was so moved by his own eloquence that the tears

poured down his cheeks, and he believed himself the most miserable and misunderstood of human beings. He ended by sending individual and affectionate messages to all the sisters at the convent, and added in a postscript that his socks were all in holes and his shirts not fit to be seen, and that the reason his Colonel had a dislike for him was because he was not so well turned out as his companions.

This fabrication, which was calculated to bring a large parcel back by return of post, cheered Gyggy enormously, and, wiping away his tears, he sealed his letter, began to whistle one of papa's songs, and, seeing one of his friends crossing the square below, he leaned out of the window and poured a jug of water over him, by way of passing the time.

There is no doubt that the Busson du Mauriers are born lacking a certain sense of proportion. . . .

Kicky meanwhile had caught the measles, and had lost all his summer brown. He was invited to Milford for Christmas to stay with his Uncle George, who had become, while Kicky was down the mine, estate agent to his old friend Colonel Greville. His income was not a large one, and his pension a mere flea-bite, so the position suited him very well, especially as he had a wife with extravagant tastes, and a young son into the bargain. Whether the fair Georgie would mind being buried down in Wales was another matter.

Colonel Greville was a generous employer, and gave his agent the free run of his house, Castle Hall, and, of course, there was a certain amount of entertaining to do, where, as the Colonel was a bachelor, Georgina might find herself called upon to act as hostess. There was generally a regiment stationed at Pembroke, and this meant balls and parties, so she would be able to wear the lovely dresses bought recklessly for her by her infatuated husband.

She was prettier than ever, and soft-hearted Kicky fell completely under her spell. He was able to draw her at last, a thing he had always longed to do, and during the long evenings

199

by the fireside, when his uncle had gone up to the Castle to discuss some matter relating to the estate with Greville, Georgie posed for her nephew, and looked enticingly at him under her long lashes, and put him into such a state of agitation generally by her merciless flirting that for twopence he would have flung himself at her feet and implored her to run away with him.

Oh, the agony of being twenty-one, and head over heels in love with your own aunt! It was an impossible situation. She sent him on errands, and made him fetch and carry for her, smiling at him like a true divinity one moment, frowning upon him the next. On Christmas Eve at Castle Hall she sat next to him when the waits came to sing carols in the hall, and held his hand under the table in the most confiding, disturbing manner. He felt like an arch-villain when Uncle George wished him a happy Christmas, and could scarcely meet his eyes.

There was a frightful moment, too, when everybody kissed everyone else under the mistletoe, and Georgie advanced upon him with shining eyes and an eager mouth. There was nothing he wanted to do more, but the appalling publicity of it, in front of all the guests – and surely no one could miss seeing the flaming colour in his cheeks, betraying his guilty secret?

He went to bed that night both exalted and miserable, wondering whether he would end by fighting poor Uncle George in a duel, and killing him, and himself being pardoned at the trial because of his youth, and being transported to the colonies for life – Australia or somewhere.

From which it will be seen that Kicky was as romantic and impressionable as all young men at twenty-one, with perhaps an added spark of imagination and a certain rather touching naïveté which was the saving of him.

'*My dear Louise,*' wrote Ellen to her sister-in-law in the spring of 1855, '*I opened your letter of the twentieth as Louis left on Sunday morning for Amsterdam, and I do not expect him back for a fortnight. I need not tell you that your news of*

Eugène gave me the greatest satisfaction, as really I was quite in despair about him during the autumn, from his Colonel's letter. Let us hope that he will continue making an effort and does not go back to his old ways.

'*I am sorry that Louis did not mention in any of his letters to you that he has been borrowing from George, as we have been in much distress here, from an unlucky speculation, and that is the reason we have not been able to send Eugéne any dividend. We have had eighty pounds from George, and I know he has been inconvenienced, as he has not been able to pay his subscriptions at his clubs, and of course cannot enter again. Kicky tells me they have sometimes been without half a crown down at Milford, but of course as much credit as he wishes for. London creditors have been down here twice in the last four months.*

'*I tell you these things, my dear Louise, that you may not think George in any way mean or unjust. The reverse is just the case. Louis must now find the means of sending Eugène what is necessary; we cannot depend on you for everything. In a fortnight he will have a hundred and thirty pounds from Greville – the balance from the fertilising invention. I am sorry I have not been able to spare any of my little dividend, but I assure you it has not covered our debts these last six months by thirty pounds, and as there is a double income tax, and reduced percentage, I lose this year twenty pounds. Everything is very discouraging, and I see by yesterday's paper that the Vienna Conference is a failure and there is now no hope of peace – and so no hope from speculation – not that we ever gained much from it. The office in the City is let, as there is no business worth while to keep it. They have got the laboratory, but I do not think Kicky will make his fortune there. Chemistry is a very precarious profession and discoveries are seldom made but by profound study and research. Kicky would never have made a shilling had not Greville behaved so handsomely with his first job. Since his return from Milford he has been consulting his friends about studying painting, as he certainly draws very well*

201

and has great taste. They tell him it is hard work to make his way as an artist. I don't see what else he can do – as to his ever being a man of business, he has no talent for it, and his father's success that way anything but encouraging. . . .

'When he was down at Milford, Greville asked George to study him and find out what he was capable of, so we think he feels an interest in him and will assist him, when he has fixed on something. Louis thought that he might obtain a place for him under the Government, but Greville lives quite out of that milieu nowadays, and is too proud to ask a favour. I suppose Louis told you that my application to my mother's old friend, Lord Parmoor, was a failure.

'I have no doubt that, had she lived, she would have procured a place for Kicky. It is hard to have a son, one and twenty and no profession. He, poor fellow, is anything but happy, and I know would work hard if there was anything like a certainty of success. He is improved in health and is brown, since his return from Milford, but his prospects have not altered. I am very glad he has got over the measles well – both boys are fortunate to have such kind aunts to take care of them. I am sure Gyggy would have been lost without your continued kindness and assistance. I really am in hopes that he will succeed in his profession, though the very last I should have chosen for my sons; he is the twelfth soldier in my family, and none ever made a fortune. . . .

'I see by your letter that you have been taking Dr Page's Elixir, which surprises me much, as I cannot imagine for what complaint – and three spoonfuls too – what an enormous dose! Louis takes it for palpitations and asthma and certainly if the weather had been warmer he would have benefited much by it. I shall persuade him to take it all this summer. I gave Isabella one dose, as I thought she had worms, and it made her so sick she would not take any more.

'How happy you must be in the convent, and how delightful it would be if I could join you, and bring Isabella. What a lovely quiet life! How noisy and vulgar this place is; there is always

something to take Isabella's attention from her lessons. Fortunately she will learn something this quarter, as I have kept five guineas for her out of our tradespeople's money – they can wait, and she, poor child, has already waited too long; she is only doing now what she ought to have learnt four years ago. It is hard not to have the means of educating one's daughter to be a governess, when one has nothing to leave. . . . She has begun German, and I have got her on pretty well in Italian. She has Walter Scott's novels translated, and reads them very fluently, but I cannot get her to study good Italian authors; she is too young and giddy. I do not perceive much progress in her music, though she has played several of Beethoven's Sonatas at first sight, accompanied with the violin, without missing a note. A first-rate musician, a Mr Price, thinks she has great talent but wants encouragement from a really good master. His wife is an excellent player, but their daughter cannot perform at all. He says clever women never have clever daughters. I suppose he means to say I am very stupid – and I perfectly agree with him – I have had so much disappointment altogether that sometimes I forget everything, and cannot either remember a word of what I have read or what I have said. I have become a great politician and occupy myself with this horrid war to prevent thinking of my own affairs. I learn from to-day's paper that the Emperor is to take the command of the English Army in the Crimea! What do you think of that? Something like an entente cordiale! After all the horrors I read of the sufferings of our Army for want of proper organisation, I am very glad Eugène is in the French one. My paper is coming to an end, I must finish this screed, which I am afraid, my dear Louise, will give you more trouble than it is worth. I have not taken a pen in my hand six times, I think, since I have been in this house, and can scarcely hold it. Kicky is in the laboratory finishing his long journal to his brother; he will write to you in a few days. Isabella sends her love, and pray accept mine, my dear Louise.

'Your affectionate
'ELLEN.'

The summer of 1855 dragged to its close, and Kicky was still without regular employment. His practice in Barge Yard, Bucklersbury, was a farce, and he had not been offered any work since the adventure in the Devon mine a year before.

His Aunt Georgie was always inviting him down to Milford, but the last time he went, just after Easter, he noticed a certain coldness in his uncle's attitude and a little shortness of temper when Georgie was more than usually flirtatious, so he made some absurd excuse, after he had been there a few days, and went back to London. His passionate calf-love of Christmas-tide had spent itself by March, and at Easter he found the attentions of the lovely Georgie much more embarrassing than pleasing. He was so completely cured, in fact, and his conscience so easy on the matter, that he made a joke of the whole affair to his mother, and told her that Uncle George was jealous of him. She was very much amused and agreed with him that it was great nonsense, but said also, with a little sniff, that George must be prepared for such eventualities, and he had only himself to blame for marrying a child of nineteen when he himself was in the middle fifties. She had never really approved of Georgina, and, from what she heard, not only from Kicky but from Colonel Greville as well, that young woman was thoroughly spoilt and selfish, thinking only of dressing-up and silly flirtations, and as for looking after little Bobbie, she apparently never took any notice of him at all. She decided that the marriage had been a great mistake, and her poor brother would have been far more comfortable had he married dear Louise. There would have been no jealousy where she was concerned, that was quite clear. Oh, well, perhaps some day people would listen to *her*, and take notice, and then they would be saved many a bitter disappointment. If Louis-Mathurin had relied upon her judgment with regard to money, they would not be living in the present precarious state.

'If you ever marry,' she said to Kicky, 'I hope you will let me choose your wife for you. A mother is always right about these things.'

'Find me an heiress with ten thousand a year, then,' laughed Kicky, and he stretched out his hand for a piece of paper and a pencil and began to draw his ideal woman, who looked strangely like the Venus de Milo. . . .

Really it was little wonder that poor George Clarke showed signs of shortness of temper. His position as agent at Milford was not entirely congenial to him, and the social side of it was distinctly tiring. He could not for ever accept hospitality without returning it, and entertaining, even on a small scale, meant a large slice out of his salary. Added to this was the care of his sister's finances, and Louis-Mathurin's continual borrowing. Even young Gyggy had the impertinence to write from Sarreguemines and demand a loan, which he said his mother would of course pay back from the next dividend.

He was devoted to Ellen, and fond of her family, but, after all, he had a wife and son of his own, and he could not keep all of them. He knew that Louis-Mathurin had no intention of ever paying back that eighty pounds, and if he started lending money to his son the story would begin all over again. Besides, if what Ellen said was true, the boy was entirely irresponsible, and could not be trusted with a farthing. So the gallant Captain wore something of a frown at Easter for very good reasons, and it was really the last straw when he found his wife flirting with his eldest nephew and namesake. This young fellow, playing cat's cradle over the tea-table in the drawing-room, and both of them laughing and looking so damned intimate at one another – no, by Jove, he wouldn't have it. 'The child is crying up in the nursery,' he had said, sharply too, and made 'em jump to their feet. 'The nurse tells me you have not been near her all to-day, and the boy has been fretful since this morning.'

'There is nothing wrong with Bobbie,' Georgie had answered, with a toss of her head. 'He cries from sheer naughtiness. Nurse should smack him.'

'If you spent a little less time with my nephew and a little more time with my son, life would be very much more agreeable to all of us,' said the Captain. And at that she had had the grace to blush, he was pleased to notice, and Kicky got up and wandered towards the bookcase. Well, he hoped he had made them feel uncomfortable. It was about time. This sort of silliness had gone on long enough. He sat down at the tea-table and opened his newspaper and did not address a word to them for the rest of the evening.

It was after this little episode that Kicky thought up his excuse for returning to London, and small blame to him either.

It was a good thing Grandmamma Clarke was not alive; this would have been a situation after her own heart.

Youth has a short memory for unpleasantness, and in a month's time Kicky was staying up in Norfolk with a friend of his, Tom Jeckell, the son of a dissenting parson, and listening to the exquisite singing in Norwich Cathedral.

'*It's rather tight work, stopping with a parson,*' he told his mother, '*and hungry work too. On Sundays we have an entirely cold dinner, with a quarter of an hour's grace before, and hymns and prayers after. I can't help thinking that something warm, if it was only a hot potato, would give one much more courage for that sort of thing, especially as I do not think that warming a potato is a greater infraction of the fourth commandment than laying the table-cloth. However, I console myself at the cathedral, where the music is splendid, and where there is one boy whose voice gives me more pleasure than anything I have ever heard. Tom introduces me to all his friends, and we drive some twenty miles every day in the gig, at the spanking rate of twelve miles an hour, to call upon the neighbourhood. The people are charming, and we spend the day riding, or boating, or drawing, and the evening in singing and dancing. Went over to Cambridge the other day, some seventy miles, by train of course, and met some of the Collegians — great dandies — and we spent the evening with them — supper, wine and singing.*'

'I hope,' thought Ellen, as she folded his letter, 'that Kicky is not going to become one of these young men, so prevalent nowadays, who think of nothing but amusement. I shall have to talk to him very seriously when he returns.'

Her eldest's dalliance in Norwich was put out of her head by the sudden entrance of Louis-Mathurin, very pale and shaky, saying he had been attacked by violent stomach pains and he was certain he had the cholera.

'My dear Louis, surely cholera is impossible in England,' protested his wife.

'Nothing is impossible,' he moaned. 'I was analysing some germs in the laboratory this morning, and I have no doubt that I have caught the infection. The disease will spread, the whole of Pentonville will be wiped out, and half London contaminated.'

'But let us send for the doctor at once.'

'Doctor? Absurd. I will have no doctor in my house. I know more about illness and medicine than all the doctors put together. Fetch me a pen.'

He really was a ghastly colour, and his lips were blue. Ellen rushed for pen and paper, in a great state of alarm.

'I am writing down the names of certain drugs I have in the laboratory,' he gasped. 'Go as quick as you can, take a cab to the laboratory and ask young Wilkins to fetch them for you. It is my only chance. Wait for nothing here. I am all right. I can get myself to bed.'

Groaning loudly, he climbed the stairs, while Charlotte came out of the kitchen, her hands all over flour.

'Did the fish upset you, too?' she said. 'I thought it was off when I fried it, but it seemed a pity to waste good money.'

'Ignorant woman,' he said sternly, grasping the hand-rail, 'behold me in the grip of cholera. I may not last the night. If Mrs du Maurier is a widow in the morning and Miss Isabella fatherless, I look to you to help them.'

'Good heavens, sir, it's surely not as bad as that,' said the startled servant, rushing towards him to help him to his room.

'Away, away,' he roared, 'touch me at your peril. The deadly germs of cholera will attack you as well. Better one death than a thousand.'

He staggered to his room and slammed the door. She heard a frightful groan, then silence. White to the lips, she went into the kitchen and collapsed. Half an hour later Ellen returned from the laboratory, untidy and out of breath, clutching four sinister little bottles with coloured labels.

Charlotte dragged herself into the hall at the sound of her mistress, breathing heavily, her hand to her side. 'Oh, madam, I think I have the cholera too,' she said. 'The pains shoot through me like a knife. If there's to be an epidemic, don't you think the police should be informed?'

'Nonsense,' snapped Ellen. 'It would cause a panic at once. If you feel ill, go to your room and lie down. The master is going to make up this medicine.'

'If it's like the stuff he gave me for kidney trouble, I'd rather have the cholera, madam,' said the frightened woman.

'You will do just exactly what I tell you,' came the sharp reply.

Ellen went up to the bedroom and found her husband sitting up in bed, his face as grey as his dressing-gown, his teeth chattering.

'I believe I am entering upon the second stage,' he said. 'It is marked by convulsions and contraction of the limbs. Look, my muscles are quite stiff. When my face turns a dull black, then you will know it is the end.'

'For God's sake, Louis, let us have the doctor.'

'These fools know nothing of cholera. I have studied it for years. Have you the drugs? Give me them quickly, and fetch me a saucepan of boiling water.'

She tottered up and downstairs at his bidding, fetching pans, water, towels, and every sort of thing, for Charlotte had entirely collapsed, and was useless. She watched in agony while her husband, looking exactly like a mad wizard incanting, brewed his strange medley of drugs, which gave forth the most appalling smell and was the colour of liquid fire.

'Are you sure you won't poison yourself?' she ventured.

208

He glared at her over the saucepan. 'Am I a fool or a chemist?' he said.

To this she had no possible answer. He poured the mixture into a glass and drank it down, his eyes nearly starting out of his head at the strength of it, and she almost expected fire to come out of his nostrils.

'That's better,' he gasped. 'Now help me lie down. Gently, carefully; it is just possible that we have caught it in time. How is my face? Has it darkened at all?'

'It is rather flushed, dear, if anything. Perhaps the heat of the saucepan.'

'Nonsense. It is fever. High fever. I dare say I have a temperature of forty-three. However, that was to be expected. Fetch some ice.'

'Ice, dear? Where from?'

'How do I know where from? The butcher, the fishmonger, anyone. A great block of ice. Then you must crush it and wrap it in a towel, and place it on my forehead.'

'Yes, Louis, I will go at once.'

He closed his eyes, groaning again, and she rushed from the room and down the stairs into the street. Pray heaven the fishman would have some ice. Perhaps if she told him it was a question of life and death . . . Unfortunate that his book had not been paid for two months.

To her surprise, he looked rather sheepish at the sight of her, and touched his forehead, smiling foolishly.

'I thought you might call in,' he said. 'I'm very sorry, I'm sure. It is rather warm for May, and that must have been it.'

'What on earth do you mean?' she asked, very much out of breath.

'Why, that bit of cod you had for dinner,' he said. 'Mrs Allan, along the road at No 7, had the other end, and she came in to complain twenty minutes ago. Turned her very peculiar. I'm very sorry, madam.'

Ellen breathed a great sigh of relief. The fish. Of course, it

209

had been the fish. She had not fancied any; she had eaten a poached egg instead. But Louis-Mathurin had made a hearty meal, and no doubt Charlotte too, in the kitchen.

'It is quite unforgivable,' she said to the fishmonger, 'to sell yesterday's stale produce and pass it off as fresh to your customers. Don't talk to me about the heat. That fish was off when your boy brought it to the door, and you know it. Please see that such a thing never occurs again. Naturally you will not charge me for it.' And she swept out of the shop, in a great state of indignation, while the fishmonger shuffled with his feet and rubbed his forehead apologetically.

The relief from anxiety put Ellen in a fine temper, and on returning to 44 Wharton Street she went straight in to the kitchen and called for Charlotte.

'Pull yourself together, for heaven's sake,' she said. 'It isn't cholera at all. It was the fish. You had no business to send it in. You must have known it was tainted. And it serves you right if you were upset; you know perfectly well that I ordered a sheep's head for your dinner. Had the fish been all right I was proposing it for to-night in a pie. Now I know why my weekly books are such a figure. Please make tea at once.'

Charlotte, red and uncomfortable, busied herself at the range, and Ellen bustled upstairs, making clicking noises with her tongue.

Louis-Mathurin was lying very still upon the bed with his eyes closed. When Ellen bent over him he opened one eye, and moaned faintly.

'I feel as though I am sinking into a coma,' he whispered. 'I very much fear the last stage is about to begin. You had better send for Isabella.'

'Anyone would be in a coma after swallowing down all those drugs,' snapped his wife. 'A tablespoonful of castor oil is what you need. Frightening everyone to death with your talk of cholera, while a child in arms could tell you it was the fish you ate for dinner. I've just been to the larder, and the smell is atrocious.' She went to the window and threw up the blind with a clatter. 'Charlotte weeping in the kitchen, and no sign of tea, of course,' she said, rattling the door of the medicine cupboard. 'A dose of castor oil for her too. I suppose it doesn't matter that my saucepan is ruined.'

She picked it from the washstand and crashed it down again. 'I only had it renewed last week, and now the bottom has cracked right across. Of course, if you must pour poisonous medicines into it, what else can you expect? Heavens! The heat in this room! Enough to give anyone apoplexy, let alone cure cholera.' She jerked at the window, nearly breaking the sash. 'Whoever built this house knew precious little about his trade, I must say. I've never opened a window yet without wrenching my arms out of their sockets. Well, how are you feeling now?'

Louis-Mathurin looked, if possible, even paler than before.

'I'm very ill,' he said. 'I must have silence − absolute silence. You haven't the remotest idea what I have suffered. And if it is fish poisoning, as you say, then I am not at all sure that the drugs I have consumed are not the very worst things to have taken.'

'In that case it is imperative that you have castor oil.'

'I will not take castor oil. It will tear the delicate tissues of the stomach. Put the bottle away at once.'

'My dear Louis, it is a known thing that castor oil cures any pain.'

'I disagree most violently. It is a foul purge, only fit for dogs. I positively refuse to take it.'

'Then I think you a very great fool.'

'That does not move me in the slightest. I have doctored myself for fifty years, and know more about these things than you do. My pains are definitely easier, and I fancy a glass of rum and water. Pray send Charlotte for a bottle.'

'I cannot believe that rum . . .'

'Must I drag myself from a sick-bed and go for it myself?'

He stared at her reproachfully with his blue eyes, his grey

locks standing up on end. He looked absurdly like Kicky, and her heart softened.

'I am sure it is very bad for you, but, since you insist, I suppose there is no alternative. Do you want me to settle your pillows?'

He winced as she thumped them behind his back, and tucked in his blanket.

'I must say you don't look very bad,' she said.

He smiled meekly, and made no answer. 'If you won't take castor oil, I am quite determined that Charlotte shall,' she said, and with a last jerk at the window, which failed to respond, she hurried from the room.

Louis-Mathurin waited until she had clattered downstairs, and he could hear her voice scolding in the kitchen. Then he crept stealthily from his bed and opened the door of the wardrobe. At the back was a box of thin black cigars. He selected one, and climbed back into bed again, first seeing that the window was tightly closed, as it had been before Ellen's ministration.

He leant back against the pillows, and smiled contentedly, puffing at his reeking cigar. Then he fumbled in his dressing-gown pocket and brought out a rather crumpled late edition of the *Financial News*.

'*Bon gentilhomme n'a jamais honte de la misère,*' he murmured.

12

It was a surprise to everybody, and most of all to himself, when Gyggy passed his promotion examination and became brigadier in the summer of 1855. Although brigadier in the French Army is only equivalent to a corporal in the English Army, it was at least a step in the right direction, and if he continued to do well no doubt he would be promoted again, in a year's time.

The regiment moved to Châlons, and there was talk of Louise leaving Versailles for a time and going there to spend a month or so, to be near him.

There was no doubt that Louise took far more interest in the luckless Gyggy than the rest of the family put together. Louis-Mathurin wrote but seldom to his second son, and Ellen only to scold. Kicky sent cheerful scraps of information when he could be bothered, and smuggled him money too, if he could scrape some together, but four and a half years is a long time to be separated, and Gyggy did not know any of his London acquaintances, so there was really very little to write about. Isabella was the boy's best correspondent. She sent him trim little handkerchiefs she had embroidered herself, and wrote him funny, stilted schoolgirlish letters about her classes at school, and her progress in her lessons, and they were continually planning how and when they should meet again.

'*How I long to see you,*' he would say, '*and are you growing up very pretty and tall? I cannot hear a piano without thinking of you. I tell all these fellows here that none of their sisters are as good-looking or as talented as you.*'

'*Kicky shall make a portrait of me for you for your twentieth*

213

birthday next February,' she replied, 'and then you will judge whether I am pretty or not. He has drawn one of me already, but he says he will make the next "du profile", as I am better that way. He is really very clever with his likenesses. I have now left off going to school and go to a college instead, twice a week, Mondays and Thursdays, from twelve till three o'clock, and learn French and English literature. In the French class we learn a great deal of poetry, and put it into prose, and have lectures too. Mamma pays thirty shillings for three months, and the English class is the same price, which makes but three pounds for the quarter. In the school they charged five pounds a quarter, but there they taught you everything. Mamma says that what with these classes and what she teaches me herself, I shall do very well, and could take a place as governess in a few years – that is, until I find a husband!

'I am learning a very difficult piece of music called "Moses's Prayer in Egypt", by Thalberg. It is very beautiful. And another one consisting of fifty pages. Reassure Aunt Louise, when you write, that Papa did not have cholera. It was fish-poisoning. We have had a letter from her, greatly alarmed.

'At all events, he is quite recovered now, and in his usual spirits, and talks of going over to Paris to see her.'

Louis-Mathurin did go to Paris, in the early spring of 1856, but, as it turned out, the visit was hardly one of pleasure. He went to borow money. During his fifty-eight impecunious years he had been in almost every sort of financial difficulty, but never until this year had he been actively engaged in a lawsuit. The transactions with regard to the portable lamp in 1846 had been tricky enough, but he had scraped out of the business without very much trouble or difficulty. This time he was heavily engaged, and there was no escape. Exactly how and why he was now involved it is impossible to discover. Presumably the invention for fertilising the soil had already been patented by somebody else, and the same somebody had his attention drawn to the similar process invented, and believed to be original, by the unfortunate Louis-Mathurin. The good fairy, Colonel

214

Greville, must either have sold his interest in the invention or come to some arrangement with the inventor, for he does not appear to have been involved in the lawsuit at all. No doubt, generous friend that he was, he lent Louis-Mathurin money, when it came to legal proceedings, and possibly gave him advice as well, but he stood to lose nothing himself.

Brother-in-law George was approached in vain, Georgina was an extravagant wife, and had absolutely no idea of running a house economically, and the natural consequence was that the honest Captain found himself burdened with debts down at Milford – tradesmen she had neglected to pay and arrears of servants' wages, besides enormous milliners' and dressmakers' bills from London.

That original eighty pounds he had lent to Louis-Mathurin had never been repaid, and it had made a large hole in his income. With scrupulous honesty he saw that his sister's dividends were paid in regularly to her account, for he acted as trustee since his mother's death, but never once did he himself take a penny from the annuity. He had been provided for by the Duke of York at the time of the trial in 1809, and, though the income was large enough for a bachelor of simple tastes, it was rather smaller now he had a wife and child to keep in luxury, besides which, the times had changed since the beginning of the century, and a pound went much further in 1809 than it did in 1856.

George wrote a kind and truthful letter to both his sister and his brother-in-law, explaining that in his present circumstances it was quite impossible for him to give any financial assistance.

Quite undaunted, Louis-Mathurin travelled to France and went to Versailles to see Louise. She, of course, would do anything for him. He knew that. And he was not mistaken. She gave him what she could from her income, leaving herself enough for the barest necessities, and, though ill with rheumatism now, and practically crippled from the pain, she accompanied her brother to the various lending-houses in Paris in order to raise the funds.

She even wrote to her old friend the Duke of Palmella, whom she had not seen or heard of for some time, explaining the position, and taking care, of course, to mention his godson's name. A happy allusion to the past, some little incident revolving round his dead wife Eugénie and the little Gyggy's birth in Brussels, must have had the desired effect, for the Duke replied kindly from Lisbon and enclosed a small contribution. Louise wondered, as she sold an antique and very pretty ring that had belonged to her mother, whether her own little hobby of painting flowers could not be turned to profit, for she had considerable talent that way, and, though she made no mention of the fact to Louis, she took a small collection of her paintings to a picture dealer in Versailles and, to her surprise and delight, he bought the lot.

She turned the money over at once to her brother, saying nothing of the bare walls of her room in the convent from which she had stripped her pictures, but made some murmur as to a windfall from an investment that she had forgotten all about.

Louis-Mathurin returned to London with high hopes of winning his *procès*, but, like all legal difficulties, the affair dragged on through the winter and spring, and much of his enthusiasm and optimism were lost before the case was settled.

Day by day through March and April of 1856 his patience went, and his courage too, little by little. Those jovial spirits and consistent gaiety, that had always been so large a part of him, even in adversity, went from him with strange and alarming suddenness, and Ellen and Kicky and Isabella had the pain of watching him droop and wilt, like a poor wounded bird with a broken wing, flying no longer and singing no more, wandering about the house like a lost thing.

His blue eyes were clouded now, and troubled, and his face grew thin and pale. He was short and irritable who had never

216

before known anger. He who had always looked so young and irresponsible, and happy, no matter what ill fortune came to him, was now aged, both mentally and physically.

His world had gone black around him and he did not understand. Ellen, watching him, a pain of anxiety in her heart, kept thinking of his brother Robert and those dark fits of melancholy that had been the prelude to insanity. Robert had sat thus for hours and days at a time, staring before him like a dead man, talking to no one; and she remembered how once Louis and she had called upon him, that year they were in London, just after the birth of Isabella, and they had found him sitting with his head in his hands, talking to himself. Louis had made a joke of it at the time, but Ellen had never forgotten the shock it gave her, this man in the prime of life whispering and murmuring to no one, and when he lifted his head she had seen the terror in his eyes.

Yesterday she had come upon Louis-Mathurin in much the same state, seated in a corner of the parlour, huddled over the little fire, and there was a shadow in his eyes which she had never seen before.

He had not been well the whole of the winter, she knew that. The weather had been exceptionally cold, and suffering as he did from asthma at frequent intervals, the season had been against him and the prolonged and severe frosts prejudiced recovery. But he had endured asthma and chills in other winters without complaint, and had even enjoyed the doctoring of them with his strange medley of drugs. Now he did not even bother to go to the laboratory. He had lost interest even in his toys. '*Je suis si fatigué,*' he would say, '*si fatigué . . .*' and would shake his head without a smile when Kicky brought him a drawing or a caricature that in the old days would have given him pleasure.

Even Isabella and her piano must be silenced, because he could not bear the sound of those rippling, triumphant notes.

Ellen learned to hold her peace these days. She would coax

217

him with a bowl of soup as near as possible to the *soupe à la bonne femme* of Paris days, and she did not fuss or bustle or scold, because of that shadow in his eyes that was a constant reminder of Robert, of that poor dead brother who had lost his reason before he lost his life.

Kicky was his best nurse. He had that gentle, tender quality with suffering people that she herself had never possessed. He was infinitely patient, and this was something she could not be. She was too easily irritated. Although often very tired herself, and maddened by headaches, she seldom complained and never spared herself. It might have been easier for her family if she had. But no. People who stayed in bed were idle; were shamming illness; were not doing their duty. Invalids were a drag upon the community. An effort must always be made. Therefore, though wretched and distressed at the sight of her poor gay Louis so fallen and sick in his corner by the fireside, she was not of much assistance to him mentally. She betrayed her own impatience.

It was Kicky who sat with him, Kicky who read to him, Kicky who made up little stories in an endeavour to amuse him who could now no longer amuse himself. In the middle of April the decision of the court was made known, and Louis-Mathurin had lost. It was like a death-knell to all their hopes.

The laboratory was sold, and the expensive fittings. Isabella's lessons at the college were discontinued. The two top rooms of 44 Wharton Street were let to lodgers. The family existed on Ellen's little income, and even so were deeply in debt. George Clarke invited Isabella down to Milford, and this meant one mouth less to feed. Kicky was still without employment, and it did not look as though he would ever obtain any, especially now, with the laboratory sold.

Sometimes he wondered whether he could earn a shilling or two by singing in the streets, and would have done so but for the shame it would have caused his mother. Ellen determined to do a little plain sewing for her neighbours, but Louis-

Mathurin falling ill again, with another attack of asthma, made this impossible. She had to nurse him. They nursed him together.

It was during these days that Kicky grew up, and little lines of worry, that he would never entirely lose, formed themselves on his forehead. He understood why his father suffered, why he must endure these fits of black despair. The seed of melancholy had lain dormant in his father all these years, showing itself only in the unbearable poignancy of his singing; but now it was dormant no longer, and he could not save himself.

Kicky asked him one day, when he was sitting propped up in bed, gazing at the sky, gazing at nothing, 'What are you thinking about, papa?'

And he turned his pathetic, mournful eyes upon his son and said, 'Life, Kicky, so sad – *si morne*. I've lost everything. Courage and hope. Alone – alone. . . .'

'No, papa. We are with you always, mamma, Isabella, and I. We'll never leave you.'

But he shook his head; he plucked at the sheet with nervous fingers.

'I don't mean that sort of loneliness,' he said, and would say no more.

'If we had stayed in France this would never have happened,' thought Kicky. 'Ever since we came to London there have been difficulties and worries, and nothing has gone well. It has been five years of fighting against odds. We were all so happy in Paris. I shall always hate the memory of this house. It has been unlucky for us from the beginning. No 44. I shall remember that: 44 is an unlucky number. Oh, God, why did we ever leave Paris and come here?'

And then, just at this moment, at the very height of their troubles, Gyggy had to write from Châlons to say that he had got into debt, and would be degraded from his rank unless the money was sent at once.

For the first time Kicky wrote harshly to his brother, cursing him for his thoughtlessness and his dishonesty – for he was dishonest, he said, to use money that did not belong to him. It was theft under another name. And papa was ill, and probably going to die, and Gyggy must solve his problems for himself.

Which Gyggy did by borrowing from a companion and also from his aunt, as his father had done only a few months before.

Louise was staying at Châlons, though due to return to the convent at Versailles within the week, so there was no need for long explanations by letter. She gave in to her godson, as she had always done, and Gyggy was not reduced to the ranks. Louis-Mathurin's illness was now the main concern of both of them, and Gyggy wrote back at once to his brother, saying nothing of his debt, but offering advice and assistance in the present trouble.

It was now June, and Louis-Mathurin had been seriously ill since the end of April.

'*Dear Kicky,*' wrote Eugène, '*I have just received your short letter and am desolated to learn that my father is no better. You have no doubt received a letter from my aunt, who is in Châlons, and in excellent health, although she was slightly indisposed when she first arrived. As for myself, I am very well, as usual. But to return to my father. My aunt is firmly convinced that religious aid would benefit him enormously, not administered as a last consolation – far from that – but to calm his mind. She is persuaded, and so am I, that if only my father would stop worrying ceaselessly, as you say he does, about first one thing and then another, his illness would be nothing more than a light indisposition, and it is a known thing that for mental disorders of any kind medicine is useless, and science can do nothing.*

'*It is a very delicate subject for a son to discuss regarding his father, especially for you and I who know papa's manner of thinking only too well, but in a case like the present it seems to me we must cast prejudice aside and think only of what is best for papa, and how he can be cured.*

'So, dear Kicky, try and arrange this with mamma, if you think papa would not object; but if he flatly refuses anything of the sort (which, between ourselves, would not astonish me) take care to say nothing of it in your letters to my aunt, as she places the utmost confidence in the idea.

'This suggestion must sound very bizarre, coming from a common soldier, but you must understand that my poor aunt has been worried to death at your news, and I would do anything to calm her mind.

'If my father is as ill as you make out, then I think I ought to see him. In two days I could be in London; my aunt has suggested it herself, and would pay my fare. You have only to send the word and I will start immediately. I am sure my father would be glad to see me, and it would not be too great a shock, besides which I have such a longing to see all of you.

'My aunt would come also, but for the journey being too much for her nowadays. Please, Kicky, don't refuse me over this. It will soon be six years since I have seen any of you, and the circumstances are exceptional. Just put "Yes" on a piece of paper, and put it in the letter-box. It will be the easiest thing in the world for me to obtain leave to go to London. When you write be careful what you say regarding my father, as I shall have to show your letter to my aunt, and she is very impressionable, and is easily upset.

'I await your reply, and meanwhile send my sincere sympathy to all of you.

'EUGÈNE.'

The letter was dispatched, and Gyggy passed the next week impatiently, hoping for a reply. None came. He wondered if his father were better, and Kicky did not think it worth while for him to travel to England. No news was good news, so people always said. Aunt Louise returned to Versailles, and Gyggy remained in the barracks at Châlons, promising to write to her as soon as he heard from London. But at 44 Wharton Street

221

no one had time to think of the scapegoat of the family. His letter, if the truth were told, had been hastily read, and then cast aside. There was enough trouble and unhappiness without adding Gyggy to the number. 'No doubt he does want to see us, poor fellow,' thought Kicky, 'but he would be hopelessly in the way, and another responsibility. I don't think mamma would consent for a moment.'

He was perfectly right. The very hint of such a project was enough to put Ellen in a state of agitation. 'Eugène come to London?' she said. 'But we could not possibly afford his board and lodging. And with papa in his present mood I doubt if he would consent to see him even. Depend upon it, Eugène just wants an excuse to come to London to enjoy himself. He does not really want to see us. He has never shown much affection to any of us before.' Which was very unkind, for Gyggy was devoted to his family, careless and irresponsible though he was, and he never wrote without saying how sadly he missed them, and how he longed for their reunion, sooner or later.

But Ellen was prejudiced where her second son was concerned, and the idea of having him in her house now, when her nerves were strained to their limit, was more than she could bear. So Gyggy waited in vain for his summons.

Louis-Mathurin made no improvement. In spite of the warm weather his asthma remained the same, and he had great difficulty in breathing. He was an impossible patient, of course. Doctors he would not tolerate; he had always believed in treating himself, and now he had not even the energy to do this.

Ellen and Kicky smuggled a physician into the house, and consulted him downstairs, for Louis-Mathurin would never have permitted his entrance into the bedroom, and the perplexed doctor did his best to prescribe medicines and the necessary treatment, but it was an impossible task when he was never allowed to see his patient. He ventured the suggestion that a mind specialist was what Mr du Maurier really needed, for from his wife's description his physical state did not sound so very desperate; and when he dragged the truth from her about her husband's brother, and his last years, he looked very grave indeed and shook his head. 'There is probably a hereditary tendency to severe melancholia,' he said, 'and I should advise you to see a specialist as soon as possible. I can arrange a consultation, if you like. Of course – and I must prepare you for this – it would almost certainly be necessary for your husband to be removed to a quiet nursing-home, where he would have the proper care and attention due to his state.'

'Do you mean a mental home?' whispered Ellen, going very white.

He made a vague gesture with his hands. 'That is rather a severe name for it,' he said kindly. 'I am not suggesting that your husband is insane; far from it. But if there is, as I suspect, this hereditary weakness in his family, it would be far better for him, and for all of you, if he was under observation. The place I have in mind is exactly like any good nursing-home, but the nurses and doctors are very carefully trained, and are used to dealing with mental disorders of every kind. However, there is no great urgency for a week or so, at any rate. Think it over in the meanwhile, and let me know your decision as soon as you come to one. As regards the immediate present, if you can get your husband to take this medicine – it is a harmless sedative – it may do some good, and I suggest humouring him as much as possible.'

And the good man took his leave, having contributed little to the comfort of the household, and leaving behind him a great black shadow of fear.

When he had gone, Ellen broke down for the first time in her life, and Kicky knelt beside her and held her in his arms.

'We can't send your papa away,' she said. 'He is like a child, Kicky, a poor puzzled child, sitting up there in bed, staring at the sky. He has always been a child, from the very beginning of our married life. Even as a baby you had a far larger sense of responsibility than he ever had.'

'Darling mamma, of course we won't send him away,' said Kicky. 'If he gets worse, I can look after him. I am very strong; I can be his nurse. And he is so gentle and quiet, he would never be any trouble to us.'

'From the way that doctor talked anyone would think he was violent,' she continued, 'your papa, the gentlest of creatures, who has always hated cruelty in any form. I shall never forget his anger once, long ago, when he saw a man ill-treating a dog. I can see him now, after he had beaten the fellow and sent him away, taking the dog in his arms and holding it. He took it back and bandaged the poor broken paw, and the tears were running down his cheeks, and I remember that all the time he was doing so he blasphemed most terribly, and said all sorts of dreadful things. It seemed so incongruous, to be doing a Christian act and swearing at the same time. But that is your papa all over.'

'He will get better, mamma, I am certain he will get better.'

She would not listen to him, though; she kept going over little incidents in the past. 'He was always so generous, so heedless and reckless with his money. How well I remember his hiring a carriage to drive out to St Cloud, soon after we were married, and he had no money to pay for it afterwards. He gave money to beggars in the streets, and was always so courteous to them, bowing and taking off his hat. I used to get quite annoyed sometimes. If only he had not been so thoughtless we would not be living here now.'

'Were none of his inventions successful, then?'

'The portable lamp brought in a little money, but the partner died, and your father sold his interest. I've rather forgotten now, it seems so long ago.'

'How happy we were in Paris, weren't we, mamma? And the old house with the green shutters, and the drawing-room looking down on the rue de la Pompe. Do you remember how we used to walk in the Bois on Sundays, and fish for tadpoles in the Mare d'Auteuil, and papa would set us to running races, and Gyggy always won? Do you remember when old Annette broke her leg and went to hospital, and you had to cook the dinner?'

'Did she? I don't remember, Kicky. I have had so many worries in my life, and so much anxiety. There was always this endless struggle against poverty. . . .'

'It never seemed to me that we were poor. We always had plenty to eat, and oh, such good food too. I have only to shut my eyes and I am sitting at the table again, and you are at the head, with your hair done in the old way, mamma, in ringlets, and Isabella is beside you in her high chair, and Gyggy is standing in the corner, because he has been naughty. You are helping us to *soupe à la bonne femme* out of a large tureen, and suddenly papa comes in with his cape flung over his shoulder like a cavalier, and his silk hat on his head, and he starts singing Schubert's Serenade. And it is so beautiful that I burst into tears and rush from the table, and everybody laughs, but none so loudly as papa! If only we could go back and live again in the rue de Passy, and everything be as it was before. . . .'

'Did all that happen, Kicky? I have forgotten. I have no memory left. You have all the imagination in the family. I don't believe Isabella remembers her childhood as you do.'

'Isabella was such a baby in the rue du Passy, but Gyggy would remember. Oh, mamma, we were happy then, whatever you like to say. Those were the good times. We shall never be so happy again.'

And they clung to one another, and cried a little, and Kicky felt he understood his mother for the first time; and then she pulled herself together and blew her nose, and said how ashamed she was to behave in such away, and he sighed and let her go, and she went into the kitchen to scold Charlotte, while he stayed on the little stool beside her empty chair, dreaming of the days that were no more. Upstairs in his dreary bedroom that looked over the grey chimney-pots of Pentonville, Louis-Mathurin lay dreaming too, but what were his thoughts and his fears, what were his dreams, no one ever knew.

Perhaps he too regretted the past, and, when he closed his eyes, saw himself young and ardent again, full of high endeavour, the inventor who was to startle the world. Perhaps he felt again the lost enthusiasm, and the glory of creation. It may be that he retraced his steps into the past, and walked once more the cobbled streets of Paris, the old quarter round the rue de la Lune, and was a boy again, laughing and fiery-headed, hot on a new discovery, talking of a journey to the moon.

The following day, the eighth of June, his breathing seemed a little easier, and he swallowed some vegetables and broth that Charlotte cooked for him at dinner-time. Ellen took the tray up to him herself, and stayed with him a little while, and though he did not speak he smiled at her now and again, which was something he had not done for many weeks. He had been silent now so long, with that ceaseless gaze towards the window, that the smallest change in his expression was something to be caught and treasured. After his midday meal he slept, and he was still sleeping in the late afternoon when Ellen peeped in at the door.

'I find it very warm in the house,' she said to Kicky, 'and I think I must go out for a little while. I may call in to see Dr Harvey, and explain to him that at present, at any rate, we cannot bear the idea of your father going to a home. Besides, even if it were imperative, we could not afford it. Will you stay here and listen for papa?'

Kicky nodded. He was very busy copying his own sketch of Isabella, which he had promised to send to Aunt Louise at Versailles, as she had professed herself enchanted with the one he had sent to Gyggy.

Poor Gyggy! He felt rather heartless not having answered his letter, but what could he have said? Mamma would not hear of his coming to London.

He went on with his drawing, sketching in the lace round Isabella's throat with meticulous care. It was very quiet in the sitting-room – the parlour, as Charlotte always called it. The clock ticked on the mantelpiece, and there was no other sound. Presently it began to rain, the thin drizzle that he was to connect all his life with Pentonville, and with this day in particular.

Perhaps there would be a storm later, and this was the prelude to it. It was very hot and airless. He hoped mamma had taken her umbrella. She would never permit herself the luxury of a cab, he knew that. He stood up, and looked out of the window, and wondered whether he ought to go round to the doctor's house to fetch her. Charlotte might go; she would be glad of the walk. He went into the kitchen, but it was empty, and seeing the supper-things laid ready on a tray reminded him of the day of the week. Of course, it was Charlotte's evening out. They were to wait on themselves. In that case he could not leave the house, as it would mean there would be no one to listen for papa. He went back into the sitting-room and sat down to his drawing. Mamma would have to take a cab for once, or perhaps the doctor would see her home. He yawned, and stretched his hands above his head. It was sleepy work, concentrating on this head of Isabella, on a hot June evening. Nearly seven o'clock. He rested his head on his hands and closed his eyes. A jumble of nonsense went through his head, as it always did if he fell asleep at the wrong time and in an uncomfortable position, but presently the nonsense straightened itself, and he dreamed he was a boy in Paris again, sitting in his little bed, and papa was singing in the drawing-room after dinner. The same poignancy returned, the same unbearable note of tragedy, and in his sleep he felt the tears running down his cheeks, as they had often done unbidden in those old days, and he heard himself call out, between the bars of his bed, 'Sing something happy, papa, sing something gay. . . .'

The voice continued, as though his father had not heard, and he sat up with a sudden jerk and a throb of anxiety, and he was sitting in the little room at 44 Wharton Street, and upstairs in the bedroom Louis-Mathurin was singing in reality

– Louis-Mathurin had not sung all these long, weary months.

There was something strange and uncanny about it, this voice like an angel calling through the silent house. Kicky crept upstairs, and crouched outside his father's door. The notes came sweet and pure and strong, as they had always done, as though his father was standing, as he had done so often, his head thrown back, his hands clasped behind him. Kicky turned the handle and went into the room. Louis-Mathurin was sitting up in bed, looking towards the open window. He did not turn his head when Kicky came into the room, but went on as though he had not heard. He was singing 'Der Nussbaum', Louise's favourite song. Kicky crossed the room and came and knelt down by the bed, and Louis-Mathurin paused an instant, and glanced down at him and smiled.

He was very pale, and his eyes looked larger than ever. His grey dressing-gown was like a cloak around his shoulders. His curls clung to his forehead, dank and sticky.

'*Es stehet ein Nussbaum vor dem Haus*,' he whispered, and the whisper became a murmur, and the murmur became a song, and the song was a volume of praise, a blessing, and a prayer. It was a last tribute to the God he had denied, a last offering to the world in which he had failed.

His voice grew louder and stronger as the time quickened, and it was like a triumph suddenly, like a cry of exaltation.

Then it sank again to a whisper, it trembled an instant and was gone. The song vanished and was no more.

And Louis-Mathurin died then, with Kicky's arms round him.

Part Five

13

Their one desire was to get away from 44 Wharton Street as soon as possible. There was nothing to keep them in Pentonville now, no pathetic pretence of business. They sat in the little parlour after the funeral, dry-eyed and tense in their sombre black, and discussed the immediate future.

George Clarke was there, of course, suitably grave and a little more pompous than usual, for he felt that Ellen looked up to him for advice as head of the family. After all, she had no one else. His nephew Kicky was still hardly more than a boy, in spite of his two-and-twenty years.

He looked absurdly young and frail to shoulder the family burdens. George very much doubted if he would ever make anything of his life. He was too much of a dreamer. But George was astonished to find that his nephew was not quite as diffident and inexperienced as he looked. During the discussion it was Kicky who talked, and not Ellen. It was Kicky who said the house must be let, and the lease disposed of for good. It was Kicky who said Isabella should continue her education for a year at least, and then possibly seek a situation as governess. It was Kicky who said he had no intention of remaining in London, hoping for employment as an analytical chemist, but was determined to go to Paris and study art.

'My dear fellow,' said his uncle drily, 'you may have a certain talent with your pencil. I will not deny it. You have made some very pretty sketches of all of us from time to time. But to make it your profession is another matter. It will be years before you make any money.'

'I can't help that,' said Kicky, his jaw square. 'It's the only

231

thing I care about and the only thing I can do. If my voice were only stronger I would have taken up singing, but that is out of the question. No, even if I starve in a garret I'll learn my trade in Paris at the best possible studio.'

'And may I ask what you propose to do about your mother?'

'Mamma will come and live with me. Those old rooms of papa's in the Faubourg Poissonnière are still available. He had not succeeded in letting them when he was over there in the spring. Mamma's little income will be enough to keep us, and as soon as I earn a sou I shall pay for my board, of course.'

'Ellen, does this idea meet with your approval?' said her brother.

'I really do not see what else we can do,' said Ellen, looking more sallow and pinched than ever in her widow's dress. 'Kicky is perfectly right about himself. He is not fitted for chemistry, in spite of all the money and patience poor Louis and I have spent on him. He can draw, we know that, and if he has perseverance he may make something of it. I could not possibly let him go and live in Paris by himself, and, as you know yourself, George, we can live for next to nothing over there.'

'And Isabella?'

'Kicky has suggested that she should go as paying guest to the parents of her great friend, Emma Wightwick. They are a very good sort of people. Of course, he is in trade and is rather vulgar, but that cannot be helped. They are exceedingly kind, and I know Isabella would be well looked after. Emma is a very nice-mannered, well-brought-up sort of girl, and I should have the utmost confidence in her as a companion to Isabella.'

'That, of course, is as you think best. We are rather isolated down at Milford, from the point of view of education, but she will always be welcome there for her holidays. Has anyone heard from Eugène?'

'He has not yet had time to reply to Kicky's letter. We imagine he will continue at Châlons as before, though no doubt we shall see something of him if we go to Paris. Of course,

232

there is another alternative: that Isabella should come to France too, and she and I make a home with Louise. She, poor dear, would be very pleased to have us, and we could live very cheaply in Versailles.'

'That, as you say, is an alternative. How is Madame Wallace? Please give my humble respects when you see her.'

'Oh, certainly. She will be very gratified at your asking after her. She suffers very much from rheumatism these days, you know.'

'I do not think I approve of Isabella living in the convent at Versailles,' said Kicky. 'Those nuns would be trying to convert her all the time. They would have no success with mamma, I know that, but a young girl is a very different thing. Papa always hated that convent. I am sure it would be the last thing he would have liked. Isabella will be much better in London, with Emma Wightwick as a companion.'

'I'm not at all sure I shall like to be parted from Isabella for so long,' said Ellen, surprised and a little aggrieved at this show of determination on the part of her usually amenable Kicky. 'If Louise can have us at Versailles it would be much the best arrangement.'

'I disagree with you,' said Kicky. 'It would be a very good plan if you and Isabella were parted for a time. You get on each other's nerves. You, mamma, nag at her continually, with the result that she becomes impertinent, and she pretends to be giddy and foolish just to annoy you. I don't dream all the time, you know; I observe people sometimes.'

'Hardly the way to talk to your mother, all the same,' said his uncle.

'Uncle George, papa is dead now, and as his eldest son I step into his place. You have been extremely considerate and generous to all of us over a number of years, and I can't thank you enough. But in future, if there is any decision to be made regarding my family the final word will be with me.'

They all stared at him in amazement. Was this pale young

233

man with the floppy hair and the square shoulders the same gentle, brooding Kicky who always took the least line of resistance, and dared not speak for fear of hurting someone's feelings?

'My dear boy, I am sure I have not the slightest desire to interfere,' said George Clarke, going very red in the face, and rising to his feet. 'Naturally your mother consults me, as her legal representative. Your father has left a number of debts, as you are probably aware, and until they are settled you can't any of you have a penny. I suppose you understand that your only source of income comes from the annuity made over from my mother to yours, and which, incidentally, stops on your mother's death. So I hope, for your sake, you make yourself independent with your paint-brush as soon as possible. Ellen, my dear, I have a train to catch. You and Isabella will, of course, make Milford your home until you come to a settled decision regarding the future. Georgie and myself and young Bobbie will be delighted to have you.'

He kissed his sister and niece, nodded solemnly to his nephew, and, planting his silk hat firmly on his white head, walked with great dignity from the room. If only one did not know for certain that George Noel Clarke was born in the year seventeen hundred and ninety-four, before his mother had turned her brazen eyes upon a Certain Personage, one would have said the family likeness was unmistakable. . . . Perhaps Captain Clarke suffered under the same delusion as his sister, and let his imagination run away with him.

'I am afraid your uncle has never quite got over that silly little jealousy of you and Georgina,' said Ellen, looking at Kicky afterwards. 'It was rather pointed that he did not invite *you* to Milford as well as us.'

Kicky did not answer. He was dreaming again. He was looking into the future this time, and not back into the past. He even forgot his father, who would never sing again, but must lie to eternity in the sad little grave where they had buried

234

him this afternoon in Abney Park Cemetery, Stoke Newington.

He was dreaming that in a month's time perhaps, or even less, he would be in Paris again, treading the cobblestones, breathing the familiar air. In a few days' time he heard from Gyggy, whose letter, strangely enough, bore out many of his own opinions regarding Isabella and her future.

'*I have just received your letter,*' he said, '*and there is no need to tell you the effect it has had on me, although in a sense I was prepared.*

'*I can't help being glad that I am not in the midst of the grief, as you are, not from any feeling of selfishness but because I am not particularly brave, morally speaking. I always had a faint hope, as one clings to a straw, that the fine weather and your good nursing would bring back his strength, if not his complete recovery. I have written immediately to the Mother Superior at the convent begging her to break the news to my aunt, either at once or gently by degrees, whichever she thinks best. What are your plans, my dear Kicky? I am overcome with joy, in spite of my sorrow, that I may be seeing you all again. Isabella's future must, of course, be our main concern, though these are rather early days to discuss it, I suppose. Poor mamma can hardly continue living in London, with its gloomy associations. What about Versailles? Mamma and Isabella could live there very well on her income, and as for you, you would be in Paris, on your own ground.*

'*As for me, don't worry in the slightest. Here to-day, to-morrow somewhere else — that is a soldier's life. It is quite possible I may be sent out to Africa. I do nothing but get into debt where I am, and would be far better out of the way. Don't say a word of this to mamma, though, and anyway I should see you before I went. If mamma and Isabella should go to Versailles, I trust they will live in lodgings, away from my aunt. I do not think it would be a good plan for them to live together, and anyway I should hate to think of Isabella in the hands of all* those Jesuits in the convent. If my aunt had stayed a month longer here in Châlons, she would have driven me mad, and, though I am grateful for all she has done for me, that hypocritical piety is impossible to live with for long.

'And you, old boy, do you think you will be able to exist in Paris on your own legs? I am sure you will be able to, but what exactly will you do? If you want to sell pictures, must not you begin in a certain style, by painting portraits in oil, for instance, or by doing miniatures?

'By the way, my aunt can obtain any amount of credit at Versailles, as much as she wants, she is so well known, but between ourselves she will be much more selfish with her money in future, because everything she has done for us in the past – everything, I tell you – was for the sake of my poor father.

'My mother could get a nice little furnished apartment for four or five hundred francs, with a garden for Isabella, and they would not find the living too dear, but, whatever happens, I beg of you, see that they live in one place and my aunt in another. I have often heard my aunt gossiping with that Mother Superior, and, though I have no right to talk, I could not bear Isabella to become a Catholic, after the fashion of those women. However, I am sure whatever you do will be for the best. Poor fellow, what a terrible responsibility! Look after my poor mother and sister, and may you be given courage to deal with it all. I have always thought of you as being superior to anyone I have ever known.

'EUGÈNE.

'P.S. –For God's sake never let my aunt know that papa died without the last rites of the Catholic Church, or she will never get over it.

'I have written this on ordinary paper – it isn't with crape and black edges that I mourn my father.'

When it is remembered what Louise had done for Gyggy from his earliest childhood, certain phrases in his letter seem very ungrateful; but, after all, he was barely twenty, he had taken everything for granted, and an intensely religious maiden lady of sixty-one is hardly the ideal companion for a careless, irresponsible young soldier. No doubt poor Louise was bigoted, and the artificial, narrow life of the convent at Versailles had not broadened her outlook. At any rate, Gyggy's letter confirmed Kicky's private opinion that Versailles was not the place for his sister, and it was decided that she should remain in London, at any rate for the present. Mr and Mrs Wightwick professed themselves delighted with the idea of looking after her, and the matter was arranged.

The lease of 44 Wharton Street was disposed of successfully. Ellen and Isabella went down to Milford for July and August, and Kicky caught the Boulogne steamer at London Bridge, as he had longed to do so often during those six long years of exile in Pentonville. His mother had given him enough money to live on until she joined him in September, and he was to go to his father's old rooms in the Faubourg Poissonnière. They were small and cramped, on the third floor, over a cheap hatter's, but comfort meant very little to Kicky, and the joy of returning to Paris was so tremendous that he would have slept on a slab at the Morgue had he been asked to do so. The smell of France invaded his nostrils as soon as he stepped ashore at Boulogne – chicory and cheese, the white dust of cobblestones, tobacco and burnt bread, and the porter who trundled his luggage seemed an old friend, almost a relative, in his faded blue blouse and his peaked cap. Kicky wanted to shake him by the hand, and ask after his family, and how many children did he possess, he was so carried away by the excitement of coming home.

And then, when the smoky, smelling train drew in to the platform in Paris, and there was the same old noise, the same old incredible confusion – everyone shouting at the top of their voices and engines puffing and snorting steam, and the same fat *vendeuse* selling fruit that nobody wanted to buy – Kicky could have burst into tears. The *fiacres* were drawn up on the cobbled square outside, the horses with their absurd *chapeaux de paille* perched on their heads, for all the world like a row of preposterous dairymaids, and the fat, red-cheeked *cochers* asleep on their boxes, pieces of newspaper protecting them from the sun. Kicky left his luggage at the cloak-room, to be called for, and jumped on to an omnibus at the corner of the street.

It was the *heure de l'apéritif*, and all the little bourgeoisie were taking their evening walk along the boulevards, or sitting down on the terraces of the cafés. Kicky felt he knew them all and loved them too – that round-faced *père de famille* with a child on either knee, feeding both of them with indigestible macaroons, and the large-bosomed mother, talking volubly to a neighbour about nothing at all, gesticulating with a fat finger. The thin black-frocked priest glancing up furtively from his breviary; the bearded patriarch reading his evening paper from cover to cover, nodding solemnly to an acquaintance; the group of jolly fellows in the corner arguing over a game of dominoes – Kicky had seen them or their counterparts a thousand times. They belonged to every street and every café, and he wondered how it had been possible to exist in London so long, away from this friendly, familiar atmosphere, and why he had not fallen ill, or gone into a decline, or jumped into the Thames.

He spent his first few days visiting all his old haunts, some of which had changed already in the six years he had been absent. The Pension Froussard, for instance, was now a girls' school, and was to be pulled down to make room for a larger building later in the year. Monsieur Froussard himself was down in the Midi somewhere. Kicky wrote to him, and had no reply. They were building, too, in the enchanted garden next door to their old house with the green shutters in the rue de Passy, and Kicky could scarcely recognise it.

These changes made him sad, and rather depressed, and, once the first excitement of arriving had worn off, he began to feel lonely. Living alone in Paris was very different from living in his own home with his family. In the old days there had been the familiar routine of day by day – meals at regular hours, the companionship of his schoolfellows, all the normal bustle of a happy, monotonous existence. Now he was a friendless young man, with no money and no profession, and he realised, with a little stab of disappointment, that he did not know what to do with himself. His school friends were grown up and scattered over France; even the concierge at the apartment in the rue du Bac was dead, and the grocer at the end of the street did not remember him.

'Am I the only person in the world with a long memory?' thought Kicky bitterly; and he walked through the Bois and out to St Cloud, and every tree, every blade of grass, was a reminder of the past that was gone for ever. There was the long avenue where papa had set them to run races – the protruding root was still there to trip the unwary, as it had tripped him when he was eight years old; perhaps other boys ran races there now. There was the glade where they had had a picnic on mamma's birthday, and Isabella had been stung by a bee. He could see her round baby face now, puckered up to cry; and Gyggy had turned ten somersaults running to make her laugh instead. He had been sick afterwards, behind that tree; too much plum cake, mamma said severely, but Kicky knew it was the gallant somersaults. As he strode along well-remembered paths, a pale, thin young man with his hands in his pockets, his square shoulders hunched, he wondered what had happened to that other self who had existed then, and it seemed to him that the boy Kicky ran beside him like a little ghost.

Of course he paid his duty visit to Aunt Louise at Versailles, and she wept over him, and kissed him and said he was his papa all over again in many ways; and she looked much older and rather pathetic; it struck him for the first time what a lonely life hers had been. She was very bent and crippled with rheumatism, and her wig was more obvious than ever. He asked her advice about painting, and what was the best way to begin, for he knew all about her talent with flowers, and she suggested that he should obtain permission to copy good pictures at the Louvre. So he went off and bought an immense canvas, and obtained a student's pass, and put himself before one of the most difficult subjects in the whole of the Louvre – a crowd of angels bearing a saint to heaven – and of course he made the most atrocious copy of it, like nothing on earth, while people came and breathed over his shoulder and made insulting remarks.

Greatly discouraged, he left the building, and went out to a café and had a drink, smoking innumerable cigarettes; and when he got home to his lonely rooms in the Faubourg Poissonnière, who was lying on his bed, boots and spurs and all, but the incomparable Gyggy, just arrived from Châlons *en permission*!

Kicky forgot all about painting at once, and off they went together, arm in arm, dining superbly for a franc apiece, with a gallery seat at the Opéra Comique thrown in as an after-thought. It was so good to see Gyggy again, and, Jove! how he had grown, and what a dear, fine, handsome fellow he was too, a regular heart-breaker in his uniform, all the girls in the place looking at him. He was as full of fun and frolic as ever, and made Kicky laugh until his sides nearly split, but his expres-sions were incredible and his conversation so full of slang that Kicky had difficulty in following it, for they talked in French, of course.

Gyggy had forgotten nearly all his English, and had become the complete *troupier*. Kicky was afraid his mother would be more ashamed of him than ever. It was a very good thing he had not come over for the funeral, for no doubt he would have left his uniform behind him for the occasion, if it was permitted, and put on a top-hat and frock-coat and looked – terrible thought – exactly like a shopwalker or the undertaker himself, and not at all like a gentleman.

Poor, careless, happy-go-lucky Gyggy, it is very difficult to be a corporal in the French Army and not smell a little bit of straw, and stables, and the barrack square. At any rate, he made the most amusing companion, and there was so much to say and to remember after six years.

He said it would be an easy matter to get *permission* from Châlons to come to Paris, and now Kicky was settled there, and mamma coming out next month, they would see a lot of one another and it would be like old times.

When Gyggy returned to Châlons, after spending three days in Paris, Kicky had lost all his feeling of loneliness, was cheerful and happy, and ready to start painting in earnest. At this very opportune moment he met someone he had known at University College, London, and who was now over in Paris with the same idea as himself – to study art – and this friend took him along to Gleyre's studio, in the rue Notre-Dame des Potirons St Michel. Here Kicky became a pupil, with some thirty or forty others, paying ten francs a month to the senior student for the freedom of the studio and the use of the model, added to which was a nominal sum of thirty or forty francs to be spent on 'treats' – cake and rum punch – the whole to be pooled for the benefit of the community.

Monsieur Gleyre himself came once a week, and spent a few minutes with each pupil – sometimes ten or twelve with the more promising ones – and these Friday mornings were the great moments of the week, every student on tip-toe with nerves and excitement, hoping that the great man would single him out for praise.

Gleyre had been a pupil of Delaroche, and the studio was in classical tradition, line and form being of paramount importance, colour taking second place to accuracy of drawing. Kicky worked most diligently, being generally the first to arrive and the last to leave, and when his mother arrived at the end of September she found him bursting with enthusiasm for his new occupation, and his rooms plastered with nudes and torsos in every conceivable position.

He had grown a small moustache, and his hair was rather long, and he was paler and thinner than ever, smoking, too, much more than was good for him – thin black cigars that dropped white ash down his velvet jacket.

He had made numerous companions of every nationality, all of whom seemed very affectionate and familiar with him, calling him 'Kicky,' and begging him to sing, or sketch caricatures, or box with them, or swim in the Seine. Ellen was really quite surprised to see him surrounded by all these young men; he had never shown himself particularly sociable in London. However, it was gratifying to maternal pride to see him so popular, and he looked so happy and contented too, having quite lost that worried, vague expression that he used to wear in Pentonville and that had made her despair of his future. There was no doubt but that he had found his vocation at last; it was only to be regretted that so much money had been wasted on his chemical education.

Kicky used to go off every morning after breakfast to the studio, and work until twelve o'clock. Every sort of type studied at Gleyre's, from greybeards of sixty who had been copying the Old Masters all their lives with extreme care and precision, and never got any farther, to young rapscallions of eighteen who came just for the fun of messing with paints. Many, of course, were serious, and worked really hard, and afterwards became famous both in England and France. At twelve there was a break for cakes and rum punch, and this was always the moment for ragging of any kind, for fun and chaff. The noise would be terrific, and there was sure to be a scrap of some sort between two fellows, ending up by everyone joining in, and paints and brushes and easels were hurled through the air, and chairs broken, while the model's 'throne' was generally the vantage-point, to be won with blood and tears.

A newcomer to the studio would be teased unmercifully, and made to perform in some respect; otherwise he was carried to the courtyard and put under a pump. Luckily for Kicky, on his first appearance he was requested to sing a song, which he did with so much grace and charm that he was loudly applauded and encored, and was treated with infinite respect ever after-wards.

Kicky felt as though his London existence belonged to someone else: the gloomy rain of Pentonville, and dingy 44 Wharton Street, and the laboratory in Barge Yard.

How remote was Milford, and Uncle George, and the beautiful Georgie. He listened with a laugh and a shrug of his shoulders when mamma talked about them, which she often did; and she told him his uncle was still jealous of him; he looked very stern and disapproving when his name was mentioned. As for Georgie, she neglected her little boy disgracefully. Ellen did not remember seeing her go to the nursery in all the three months she and Isabella were at Milford. The poor child used to put his hand in hers, said Ellen, and ask her to play with him, because 'my mamma never will.' And such luxury there, too; she was certain George could not afford it. There was a ball at Pembroke while they were there, and Georgie, it appeared, was the best-dressed woman in the room, and there were eight hundred people! Mamma chatted and scolded, criticising everything and everyone, just like a witch, with her sharp chin jutting into the air, while Kicky drew heads of lovely young women in his sketch-book, all imaginary, and covered the carpet with white ash from his cigar.

Most of Kicky's friends lodged in the Hôtel Corneille, by the Odéon Theatre, a large, dilapidated house with about eighty apartments; and, when his mother went off to visit Aunt Louise at Versailles, Kicky would join his companions and hold revel until the early hours of the morning.

His best friends were Tom Armstrong, who was two years older than himself and had been painting now for several years, and a Scotsman, Lamont, with a dry sense of humour and a twinkling eye. There was Rowley, too, a giant of wonderful physique and the tender heart of a child, moved to tremendous rage if anyone insulted his friends; Poynter, and Aleco Ionides, and the sinister, slightly crazy Jimmy Whistler, who wore his dark curls long and was a great *poseur*, even in those days.

These joyous, care-free Quartier Latin days were described by Kicky over thirty years later in *Trilby*. Rowley was Taffy in the book, and Lamont was the Laird. Tom Armstrong, Kicky's greatest friend, was not characterised at all, and when the book appeared he pretended to be very offended. The hero, Little Billee, possessed many of Kicky's own sensitive qualities, but it was not a portrait of him in any way, and the actual likeness was taken from the artist Fred Walker, who was never one of the Paris group, but met Kicky many years afterwards in London. The famous studio in *Trilby*, shared by the three friends – Taffy, the Laird, and Little Billee – really existed in the rue Notre-Dame des Champs, and was No. 53. Tom Armstrong, Poynter, Lamont, and Kicky took possession of it on New Year's Day, 1857. Kicky and Lamont used to study at Gleyre's in the morning and go on in the afternoon to their own studio, where they would find their friends already installed. Armstrong and Lamont slept there, but Kicky, of course, lodged with his mother in the Faubourg Poissonnière.

Madame Vinot, the concierge, appears in *Trilby* as Madame Vinard. Kicky took very little trouble to disguise names, and he made a great character out of her in the book. The adorable Trilby herself was always said to be the pure creation of Kicky's imagination, and certainly Armstrong and Lamont, when questioned in after years, had no recollection of any artist's model who answered to her description. Félix Moscheles, however, a later friend of Kicky's, with whom he became very intimate in Antwerp a year or so after the Quartier Latin days, had very vivid memories of a bewitching and charming tobacconist's daughter, Carry, of Malines, of whom both he and Kicky were devoted slaves. She certainly seems to have had a Trilby touch about her. And it is more than likely that a picture of her hid itself at the back of Kicky's mind, and, when he came to write *Trilby* all those years afterwards, he brought her out and polished her, and beautified her, and breathed a little of his own charm upon her, and Trilby, the freckled Irish giantess, was born, with her clubbed hair and fringe, her military coat, her exquisite feet thrust into a pair of men's slippers.

Whether Carry of Malines modelled as Trilby did, and smoked cigarettes, and sang like a goddess, Félix Moscheles never said, but at any rate both he and Kicky practised mesmerism at that time, which must have put the conception of Svengali into Kicky's mind.

In the rue Notre-Dame des Champs, however, it can be safely assumed that no Trilby or her counterpart ever entered the studio, which was superlatively male, and full of fencing-foils and boxing-gloves. Rowley would come over from his rooms on the north side of the Seine and do dumbbell exercises, silently, on tiptoe, while the others worked, and after four or five o'clock paint-brushes and easels were cast aside, and one or two would box and fence, while Kicky generally made for the hired piano, and, although he could only play with one finger, he would sing in his sweet tenor voice, so like his father's, until the others became weary of their boxing and grouped round him to listen.

Other friends would wander in and out, and smoke, and drink, and sit about the floor, and when Kicky had sung enough for one evening, somebody else would take his place, and Kicky would reach for his sketch-book and quickly draw a likeness of them, with their heads thrown back and their mouths open, and he would sigh a little at the popularity of these nonsensical sketches, and wish that he could be as successful with his oil-paintings as he was at his caricatures.

The friends called themselves 'Ye Societie of our Ladye in the Fields,' and Kicky did a minute drawing of them all, in pen and ink, which was pinned up on the wall beside the foils and the boxing-gloves. Lamont – or 'Tammie,' as he was always called – is represented asleep in bed, a heap of pillows under his head, and Tom Armstrong is walking with a stick, rather

245

bent and crippled, having just recovered from a bout of rheumatic fever. The bearded Poynter is at the piano, swaying to 'Ah! che la morte' from *Trovatore*, and Aleco Ionides is intent on colouring a pipe. Jimmy Whistler, of the greasy locks and sardonic tongue, smiles in cynical fashion to himself, and props his feet up on the mantelpiece.

As for Kicky, he put himself on a high stool at an easel – a position he rarely occupied, according to his friends; his light-brown hair is flopping over his face, and instead of smoking the usual cigar he has taken to a pipe instead. It was all very idle and pleasant and amusing, and very little work seems to have been done. Sometimes they cooked their own dinner in the studio – rather an effort, this, with chops in a frying-pan fitted into the top of the stove – and if it were Kicky who was sent to buy the chops he always forgot something, or dropped the potatoes in the street, or broke the bottle of wine.

So generally they dined at a little café in the rue de Vaugirard, not far from the Odéon Theatre, where the proprietor did not mind how much noise they made. They drank *vin à seize* (sixteen sous a litre) and sang more songs, and laughed a lot, and finally yawned home to bed any time after midnight, supremely happy about nothing at all. The wonderful Christmas dinner in the studio was described at length in *Trilby*, with hardly any embellishments – how the friends sent to England for a hamper of good fare, and the package did not turn up until nine o'clock on Christmas evening, when everyone was nearly fainting from want of food. There was hardly a square inch of room on the studio floor; the room was packed with students from wall to wall, and Gyggy was there, of course, *en permission*, and was, as usual, the life and soul of the party.

What a party it was, too! Turkey, and ham, and sausage, and *pâté de foie gras*, and jellies, and *pâtisseries*, and, best of all, and most expensive, English bottled beer. After supper everyone performed in some way or other, Rowley doing dumb-bell exercises, and Tammie Lamont a sword dance, and the irrepressible Gyggy brought the house down by performing the can-can. The noise was deafening, especially when they took to playing at cockfighting, and a *sergent de ville* came in and protested, saying they could be heard from the other side of the river, and no one could get any sleep. He was persuaded to have a drink, and a strong one too, and before he knew what had happened the fellow was as tipsy as the rest of them, and sitting down on the floor cock-fighting with Gyggy.

The party went on until eight o'clock in the morning, and Kicky was so tired he fell asleep in the Champ-de-Mars on the way home, having lost his collar and tie, and with his hat on the back of his head.

How lucky it was that mamma was spending Christmas with Aunt Louise at Versailles! Her welcome would surely have been a little cold had she opened the door to her quiet and dutiful Kicky and found him flushed and dishevelled, rocking on his feet. He had enjoyed himself more than he had ever done in his life before, and he was still singing, as he flung himself face downward on the bed:

> '*Fi! de ces vins d'Espagne,*
> *Ils ne sont pas faits pour nous.*
> *C'est le vin à quatre sous*
> *Qui, nous sert de Champagne. . . .*'

14

K icky worked hard at Gleyre's studio during the winter and spring, but at the same time he found he was not making the progress he should.

Existence in Paris was sweet – too sweet, in fact, for consci-entious labour – and those long, happy afternoons and evenings in the studio he shared with his friends were scarcely conducive to serious study. There was too much singing and playing, too much fencing and boxing and idle, pleasant chatter, and Kicky knew that if he wanted to make anything of his life he must wean himself from the easy, lazy atmosphere. There were too many fellows in the Quartier who had begun earnestly, as he had done, and were now no more advanced than they had been four or five years ago, for the simple reason that the atmos-phere of the Quartier had enveloped them. They wore their hair rather longer than was necessary, and were not particular about washing or cleaning their finger-nails, and their velvet jackets had a scrubby, dusty air. They went about in groups of four or five, and spent much more time in the cafés than they did in the studio, and, though they were always talking 'art,' nobody ever saw their work, other than messy sketches on the café table-cloths.

It was so easy to become like one of them, and Kicky pulled himself together at the end of April and decided to make a change.

Someone had told him about the Academy at Antwerp, which was at that time under the direction of De Keyser, while Van Lerius, well known to many English and American art-lovers, was professor of the painting class. The teaching there was sound and practical, and, unlike the Atelier Gleyre, colour was considered to be more important than form. Kicky had become a little tired of the Gleyre tradition, and by the sound of it De Keyser's Academy seemed just the place for him. He discussed the idea with his mother, who showed no objection to a change of quarters. One could live just as cheaply in Antwerp as in Paris – cheaper if anything – and there were many things in the latter town to interest her – pictures, and buildings, and churches. Poor Louis-Mathurin had been there several times on business in the old days, and had always sung its praises. She suggested that Kicky should go off on his own to start with, to see whether he liked the place and felt like settling, and in the meantime she would go to England and stay down at Milford, where she would see George about money affairs, and also be in touch with Isabella.

She might even stay for three months or so; it was always very delightful at Milford in the summer. So Kicky went off to Antwerp at the beginning of May, and became a student at the Academy. He worked much harder than he had done in Paris, rising early in the morning and painting from six until eight. He then breakfasted on a roll and a cup of coffee, and worked again from nine till twelve. A cheap dinner in one of the little restaurants, and work again all the afternoon, generally copying Old Masters at the gallery.

In the evening he went for a walk along the quays or the ramparts, smoked a great many thin black cigars, and went to bed, where he read himself to sleep.

At first he missed his friends in the rue Notre-Dame des Champs, and was inclined to be lonely, but he soon became a close friend of one of the students in the Academy, who, incidentally, was an old pupil of Gleyre's. His name was Félix Moscheles. He was half German, half Russian – a true cosmopolitan – and besides being a painter was an excellent musician. His unruly black locks were generally tied up in a band of crochet work; and he wore an enormous workman's blouse,

249

painted every colour of the rainbow, and on the back of which he had scribbled all sorts of strange words. His appearance fascinated the susceptible Kicky, whose pencil was always too ready to caricature, and during their first conversation Moscheles noticed the look of appreciation in the newcomer's eye, and saw him scribble something on the back of an envelope. He snatched it from him and saw it was a likeness of himself, grossly exaggerated and very funny, and the pair became fast friends from that moment.

This caricaturing, of course, was only an amusement, and oil-painting was his serious occupation. Kicky, inclined to impatience, started vigorously with a life-sized group − a peasant mother with a child in her arms − which showed a certain amount of talent. He became fired with the ambition to paint masterpieces, subjects that required huge canvases, and was a little disheartened when his progress was not as rapid as one or two of the other students − a fellow called Alma Tadema, for instance, and another Heyermans.

He was certain that if he worked hard enough, however, his industry would be rewarded, and he got up even earlier and went to bed later, never sparing himself at all.

He grew paler and thinner than ever, eating very little and smoking much too much. Living alone as he did, in a stuffy little room above a market-place, of course he had no idea of looking after himself, ate the wrong sort of food at the wrong sort of hours, and, when he did get to bed at some late hour, long after midnight, would be kept awake by chimes that rang a tune every quarter of an hour. The summer was exceptionally hot, and Antwerp in August was never a good place to be at any time.

If he had taken a holiday, or his mother had been with him, it is possible that the tragedy of his life might never have happened. He would have avoided excessive fatigue, and in that way been spared the blow that was to fall upon him with alarming swiftness.

He was not aware that he was tired and run-down, not aware that he had tried himself too high, and that August morning when he set off for the Academy as usual he was, perhaps, happier than he had ever been in his life.

He had no worries, enough money from his mother to live without privation; he enjoyed the company of many friends, and he adored his work.

He was as full of confidence as his father had been, nearly thirty years before, when on the track of an invention. He had the same faith in himself, the same belief in a power that did not call itself God, but was a mixture of truth and justice. Like Louis-Mathurin, he was without religion. A church was a beautiful building, interesting as museums were interesting, but not a place for worship.

Prayer was something he could not understand. There was something servile and supremely unintelligent in bending the knee and asking for favours. The only permissible prayer was one for courage, or resignation, for that was a prayer turned inward, an appeal to the best in oneself.

Aunt Louise had tried to make him say grace before meals as a little boy, and he had refused, saying that such an act was wrong when there were so many boys who did not have a meal at all. The only real grace was to give half of his meal away, which he admitted he was too selfish to do.

Cruelty was the only sin, kindness and truth-telling the supreme virtues. And with this simple creed he was prepared to live and die.

A passionate unbeliever like Kicky needs to be very brave and strong and self-reliant when trouble comes, and he was none of these things; he was tremulous, and sensitive, and young. Therefore he was without armour when the sword struck him.

He sat with the other students that morning, painting the head of an old man from the life, and he found suddenly that he could not focus properly; the man's head dwindled to the size of a pin. He clapped his hand over his left eye, and the

251

head returned to normal, but when he shut his right eye and looked towards the model with his left eye only, he could not see anything at all, not even his companions on either side of him.

He sat quite still for five minutes, feeling very sick. The perspiration gathered on his forehead, and the palms of his hands were wet. The lassitude of the last few weeks, those headaches that had attacked him in the night, banishing sleep – he understood now what they meant, and what would happen. He was going blind. His left eye was useless to him already.

He must have turned very white, and looked helpless, for Van Lerius, the master, came up to him and asked him what was the matter, had he been taken ill?

Kicky muttered an excuse, and, collecting his things together, he got up, and went out of the studio. He walked for hours along the quays, in the stifling heat of the day, seeing nothing and no one, and staring before him, one thought only running through his head – 'I am going blind. I shall never paint again.' It was five o'clock before he returned to his rooms, worn out and utterly wretched. He had promised to meet Moscheles and one or two others at a café, but he had not the heart to go. He sat on his bed instead, looking before him at the blank wall. Then he made up his mind to go and see Van Lerius, and ask for his advice, and, throwing away his cigar, he got up, and went out again, and called upon the master at his private address.

Van Lerius showed great sympathy and understanding, and told him the name of the best oculist in Belgium, and suggested that he should write at once and ask for an appointment. There might be some trifling little thing the matter – nothing serious at all – and meanwhile he must not worry; he must rest his eyes, and no doubt in a week or so he would be back again at the Academy.

Kicky left him, cheered a little by the interview, and he went and found his friends in the café, and they crowded around him, like the dear good fellows they were, patting his shoulder, and pouring out drinks for him, until he nearly burst into tears, thinking that, whatever happened to his sight, friendship was the only thing that mattered.

In three days he heard from the oculist, who gave him an appointment, and he went up to Louvain to see him, very nervous, and shaking at the knees.

The great man made all sorts of tests with mysterious instruments, and finally told him there was very little wrong, merely a congestion of the retina, and gave him some drops for use every night and morning, and told him to go away for a few weeks to the sea, and he would be well by the end of the month.

He pocketed a large fee – poor Kicky's savings for the last month – and wished him good-bye. Greatly relieved, Kicky went to the nearest shop and bought a pair of blue glasses, and had his prescription made up, and took a ticket to Blankenberghe, a village by the sea not far from Ostend.

He stayed there a month, mooning about by himself and talking to no one, watching the happy bourgeois families taking their annual holiday, and, though he bathed his eye night and morning as the oculist told him, and wore his blue glasses, his eye did not seem to improve; it felt, if anything, a little worse.

He returned to Antwerp at the end of the month, in exceedingly low spirits, and consulted the doctor again. This time the man confessed that there was slight detachment of the retina, and that Kicky must give up all thought of working for several months, and devote himself to the cure.

He must have treatment at least once a week, continue with the ordinary bathing and poulticing at home, and put himself on a diet. He must, in fact, resign himself to being more or less of an invalid for the immediate future.

Kicky wrote off at once to his mother at Milford and broke the news, and she crossed to Belgium in a day or two after she had received his letter.

She was horrified at the sight of him. She had left him in

April happy and contented, in excellent health and looking forward to the Academy at Antwerp, where he was confident of doing well; and here it was September, barely five months later, and he was thin as a ghost, pale and haggard, a bundle of nerves, and, worst of all, almost totally blind in one eye.

Of course, she blamed herself. This would never have happened had she stayed to look after him. The whole wretched business had come about through neglect. She chattered, and stormed, and fussed, and he bore her scolding with a wan smile, for he was too disheartened to protest. She set to at once to find lodgings within reasonable distance of the oculist, and not too far from Antwerp, and she succeeded in finding rooms in the sleepy, rather dreary little town of Malines, an hour's run from Antwerp by train.

The lodgings consisted of a sitting-room, a bedroom for herself and Isabella should she come out later, and a bedroom for Kicky, and for these she arranged to pay thirty-seven francs a month. A *femme-de-ménage*, who lived opposite, was to come in every day and 'do for them,' Ellen paying her six francs a month, and no food, though no doubt she would eat up anything left over, said Ellen in a letter to Louise; these women were all alike, and robbed you right and left. However, it was much cheaper all round than anywhere in Antwerp, and the air was good, and Kicky would be able to have his friends out whenever he liked.

'He has not been to the oculist since I wrote to you last,' she said to her sister-in-law, 'as there has been no improvement in his eye, but go next Friday he must, whether it is better or not, and I shall go with him and protest against him taking all this medicine – better to lose his eye, I keep telling him, than to ruin his constitution, which he is steadily doing. As for his work, I have given up all idea of his ever painting again.'

She did not say this to Kicky, but he guessed it all the same, and read the pity, too, in the voices and the expressions of his friends, however cheerfully they spoke, making jokes and plans about his return to the Academy.

Sympathy was what he dreaded most at this particular time; he wanted to be treated as though nothing had happened. Whatever his inward despair, he showed none of it to his companions, and when Félix Moscheles and one or two others came out to Malines on Saturdays or Sundays they would find him in excellent spirits, full of chatter and fun and nonsense, making light of his tragedy with pencil and paper, scribbling a caricature of himself as an *aveugle*, with eye-shade and stick, limping along in the gutter hunting for scraps.

He was pathetically glad to see them, of course, and eager for all the news of the Academy. When it was time for them to catch the train back to Antwerp, he would walk with them past the level crossing to the station, and would stand there, with his back to the barrier, watching the last of them as the train disappeared. How lost he looked, and forlorn, with his square shoulders hunched slightly, the dark glasses hiding his eyes; and his friends cursed and blasphemed for very pity, guessing the extent of his suffering, impotent to help. And Kicky walked home alone through the dull, quiet streets of Malines, where the grass forced itself through the cobblestones, and all the inhabitants were priests with long faces. Malines was a town of churches – Kicky was certain there was a church in every street – and he never passed one without seeing a draped hearse outside, and two black horses with nodding plumes. The few cafés wore an apologetic air, and tempted no one. The countryside was uninteresting and flat. He walked for miles and not even a bird rose in the sky to stretch his wings. The roads were bordered with poplars on either side, and led interminably to nowhere. The sky was generally clouded, and the wind was in the east.

If Ellen had scoured the map of Europe she could not have found a more depressing place to harbour and succour her poor blinded son.

In the evenings, after their frugal supper, he lay down in a darkened corner of the dreary little sitting-room, and Ellen read to him.

The books were mostly novels by Mr Thackeray and George Eliot, in the Tauchnitz edition, and, while she read, Kicky smoked his black cigars, and drew a mental picture of the lovely Beatrix coming down the stairs in *Esmond*, holding a lighted candle above her head.

The long winter months dragged past. Isabella came out for Christmas, very pretty and slim, and rather shy, not entirely at her ease with the students from Antwerp who came to visit her brother; but when she played the piano she forgot to be self-conscious, and Tom Armstrong, who was paying them a flying visit from Paris, was very much impressed, and most reluctant to leave.

He was very young, though, and only an art student, and Ellen did not attach much importance to his little exhibition of calf-love. Nor did Isabella show any signs of responding to it.

'*I wish she were not so shy and awkward with the opposite sex,*' sighed her mother. '*She has no money, and, with only her charm to rely upon, I'm afraid she will have difficulty in finding a husband.*' This to Louise, in a letter, when Isabella had returned to England again. By the end of the year she would have finished her studies, and there would be time enough then to decide about her future. The Wightwicks were being very kind, and she was safe for the present.

Existence at Malines continued as before. Kicky's eye was poulticed and bandaged, and pained him considerably. He tried another oculist, who told him the first one was a quack and knew nothing at all, and he alone could cure him; and for a few weeks Kicky believed this, and thought he was improving, but soon he was worse than ever, and in a fit of despair he returned to the first one again. The east winds were at their coldest during the spring, and the only people in Malines were old ladies and priests. Kicky drew the heads of imaginary young women on the backs of envelopes, and longed for the flesh-and-blood reality, for someone with soft hands and a gentle voice.

The nearest approach to this was Octavie, whom he and Moscheles had nicknamed Carry. She sold tobacco in a little shop close to one of the churches. Her father had been an organist, and had left her mother with very little money. She was eighteen or twenty, had a mop of brown hair, and blue, inquisitive eyes, and both Kicky and Félix Moscheles swore an oath of fealty to her.

When he had nothing better to do – and there was little he could do during that miserable year of 1858 – Kicky would go along to the tobacconist's shop and sit on the counter, swinging his legs, and he would draw Carry. Sometimes he sang to her, and sometimes he only talked, and whichever he did she opened her eyes very big, and smiled at him, and was familiar and unreserved and detached in a delightfully Bohemian way. Moscheles would come down for the week-end, and Kicky and he had fierce arguments as to which of them she preferred, but never came to a decision.

Moscheles had taken up mesmerism with sudden violence and enthusiasm, and was for ever making passes before people's eyes, and muttering strange incantations, and staging experiments. He succeeded once in making a stupid little Flemish boy believe that he was eating a pudding when it was really the key of the door – this in the back-parlour of the tobacconist's shop, while the charming Carry was selling cigars to a nobleman of Malines over the counter a few yards away – and Kicky was much impressed, and wanted to learn the magic, but Moscheles said it was a gift from the devil and he could not pass it on.

They tried to mesmerise Carry, without any success; she only laughed at them and looked more alluring than ever.

Kicky's sketch-books were full of Carry at this time, and he wrote scraps of verse, too – complete nonsense – about himself and Moscheles fighting for her favours; and how she would marry one of them and love the other.

Carry must have been the germ that produced the ultimate Trilby, there can be no two opinions about it; she had the same *camaraderie*, the same boyish attraction, the same funny shy reserve. Kicky absorbed her, without realising it, and absorbed the game of mesmerising at the same time, so that the two things combined and became one at the back of his mind. He forgot all about them for nearly forty years – and then he wrote *Trilby* and made a fortune at sixty.

Carry and Félix Moscheles were the only people who made bearable that black year of 1858, which Kicky looked upon in after years as the most miserable of his life. Even the dull days of Pentonville were bright in comparison. At least he had his health then, and the clear sight of both eyes. He realised now that there was no hope for his left eye; detachment of the retina was complete; and just before Christmas came again the oculist told him that there was a chance his right eye would also become affected. The shock was terrible. Kicky knew he was not strong enough to bear it. He saw himself helpless, his hands outstretched, being led about like a little child. He might live to a great age, a burden upon his relatives and friends. He wondered who would look after him when his mother died. Isabella, perhaps, spoiling her own life for his sake, becoming a poor, embittered spinster, finding religion like Aunt Louise. They would continue to live in a little dead town like Malines, because they would be unable to afford living anywhere else.

And the years would go on and on, and release would come never.

It seemed to him then that the only possible thing to do was to kill himself now, before he suffered any more, and before he became a burden. All the way back to Malines in the slow jogging train he made his plans. He knew where he could get some cyanide of potassium – one of the lodgers in the house was an amateur photographer, and kept the stuff for removing stains – and if he melted some of this down in a little water it would be quite simple. It would be clean, too, not like jumping off a roof or throwing himself under a train.

One or two people would be sorry – Moscheles perhaps, and Tom Armstrong, and poor Carry. His mother would be heart-broken at first, but she would soon get over it. She had had such hopes of him, that he would be a success, become a great painter, and here he was nothing but a blinded, useless thing, who could not even earn a penny, but was dependent upon her for his very steps from room to room. He felt very bitter when he got out of the train, very bitter and very old. Much older than twenty-four. He walked up the dreary Malines street to the lodgings, making a mental farewell without regrets.

Only a little longer and he would not be conscious of it any more. Total annihilation did not worry him. It meant there would be no more pain. He came to the lodgings and let himself in at the door. He hoped to creep up to his bedroom unobserved, but his mother heard his step and called him into the sitting-room.

'Such good news from Isabella,' she cried. 'I really believe there may be something in what she says. It would be worth trying, at any rate.'

She was sitting in front of the fire, reading a letter, with the lamp just lit, and Kicky waited in half darkness by the doorway.

'Listen to this,' she continued. 'Isabella says that Mrs Wightwick was in the train the other day – returning from Folkestone, I think – and entered into conversation with a lady who had just come back from consulting a celebrated German oculist in a little village near Düsseldorf, on the Rhine. This lady was saying that the oculist was the first in the world, and people come from India, America, London, Paris, everywhere, to consult him. Rothschild was under him, and the late Bishop of London. She herself was completely cured by his treatment, though she did not say what was the matter with her eyes. There were two thousand patients there this summer, she said, and a great many of them English. Half a day's journey from Düsseldorf only, and, what is more, there is an excellent school for painting in Düsseldorf itself. Now, what do you think of that!'

She looked up at Kicky in triumph. He came into the room and knelt beside her on the floor. He fingered Isabella's letter as though it was something infinitely precious, a last-minute reprieve from death and desolation.

'Of course, we could not undertake a journey of that kind without first consulting your Uncle George,' she went on, 'and I really do not think he would refuse to advance us the money in a case such as this. He has surely got over his silly jealousy by now.' A miniature dropped from her lap on to the floor.

'What is it?' said Kicky, picking it up and turning it over in his hand.

'Why, that is Emma Wightwick's likeness, that Isabella enclosed with one of her own. It is remarkably like, so she says, and I must say that Emma has grown into a very handsome young woman, very superior-looking to her parents.'

Kicky held the miniature in the palm of his hand. A lovely face stared up at him from the rounded frame, delicate and narrow, with a little pointed chin. Two enormous dark eyes looked at him with a very wise expression, grave and calm, but so sweet and gentle were they at the same time that the wisdom was forgotten and only the tenderness remembered. They looked almost black in contrast to her pale complexion, and the whole was framed in a great plait of dark hair, wound above her head, showing her small ears.

Kicky thought of the long-legged schoolgirl, swinging her satchel of books, and how tall and straight she had stood, like a boy, with a boy's friendly curiosity, too, about his bottles and mixtures in the laboratory, touching them all with a slim brown hand. What age was she then? Twelve or so, he supposed. And now she must be nearly eighteen. Quite grown-up, with probably many admirers sitting round her mother's drawing-room. He put the miniature back on the chair, but the eyes followed him, inquisitive and staring. It was as though they reproached him in some way, reproved him for his mental cowardice.

He had come into that room with the firm resolve of killing himself that very night, and so ridding the world of a very useless person.

And now his determination was shaken, not by Isabella's letter, not by the discovery of a magic oculist who lived at Düsseldorf – for he had little faith in any doctor now – but by that face that stared up at him with so much confidence and grace. It shamed him with its dignity. And he remembered that she had always been at the back of his mind, somewhere, in lovely privacy, since she was a little girl of twelve years old.

15

In the spring of 1859 there were several changes in the du Maurier family. The first to make a move was Gyggy, who went to the cavalry school at Saumur on a two-year course. This was considered an honour, and it was hoped he would begin to take things seriously at last. At any rate, he had not written for money just lately, though there was little doubt that the purse of his Aunt Louise was in constant demand. There had been one period, very soon after Kicky's left eye had failed him at Antwerp, when Gyggy, with his usual lack of tact in choosing inopportune moments, had declared himself to be in debt again, and had even written to his mother for help.

The letter he received in return was no encouragement. In fact, it had scared him so much he had not written again for months. The only news he had of Kicky and his sudden misfortune was through his Aunt Louise.

However, being chosen for Saumur restored him slightly to grace, and his mother even went so far as to bring him into conversation nowadays, mentioning with a slight carelessness that her second boy was doing very well in the French cavalry. It was not necessary to add that he was still only a corporal, and had lost his rank once or twice for misdemeanours.

Isabella had also made a change of address, and had obtained a position as governess to a large family of children in the country near Windsor.

Her employer was a rich building contractor, and according to Isabella he had not an 'h' to his name. They were very kind, and treated her with immense respect, which was probably something to do with the length of her name. Miss Isabella

Busson du Maurier was a mouthful for a governess.

It was rather too much for anyone, and the owner dropped the Busson and shortened her Christian name to Isobel, much to the annoyance of her family. It was not half so original, but, as she had to possess the name and her brothers did not, it was really her own affair. Isobel she became, and Isobel she must remain from henceforward. The Wightwicks were miserable at losing her, and Emma became so dull without her company that her parents had to send her away on a visit.

The last year had been very enjoyable for both girls. Their schooling was over, and Mr Wightwick was a jovial creature, and fond of entertaining. He took the two girls to balls and concerts and parties, and they had a very good time indeed. Much too good, thought Ellen, when she read about the parties in Isobel's letters. It looked as though the Wightwicks never passed an evening at home. Not at all a good example for young girls. She was very relieved when this situation of governess was found for her. All through Colonel Greville's kindness, too. He had been a true friend to the family, and even if George did find things a little difficult down at Milford, Ellen was sure it was not the fault of Colonel Greville. At any rate, Isobel went down to Windsor in the early spring, and wrote a most amusing account of her first evening to Kicky.

Her employer fetched her from the Wightwicks' in a smart phaeton, drawn by two splendid horses, and Emma could not have been more upset, said Isobel, if he had come for her in a hearse. However, in she got, and was tucked up comfortably behind, and was driven away at a rapid pace, to the lamentations of the Wightwick family. The building contractor's h's were certainly a little misapplied, for he expressed his "ope that Miss Demury did not feel the heasterly wind', which came rather as a shock to the prospective governess, and he also said that he heard she spoke 'Henglish without a haccent'.

He talked a lot about her future home, which gloried in the name of 'White Hall', and Isobel expected something in

263

the nature of a palace. As a matter of fact, it turned out to be a very small, whitewashed villa, and shockingly furnished into the bargain. Isobel, cramped and stiff from her drive, was taken inside and introduced to her mistress, a kind, downright, motherly sort of woman, also overwhelmed with the importance of having a 'Miss Buson De Mure' as governess. Isobel's charges – Milly, a girl of seventeen, and Tom, a boy of nine – seemed nice and friendly, but the governess was a little disturbed to find that the two other children, girls of eleven and seven, were invalids – consumptive, both of them – and did no lessons at all.

After an enormous tea of ''am and heggs', Isobel was requested to play and sing, and was pronounced perfect in both by her employers.

They continued to treat her with infinite respect, which was rather astonishing, and while he kept getting up from his armchair and offering it to her, his wife begged her to wash her face in buttermilk, rather than spoil her lovely complexion, the water being so hard.

'*They are both of them mad about me,*' said Isobel to Kicky, '*and I find all this washing in milk rather a business. Their kindness is overwhelming, but she makes me a terrible victim to conversation, she is such a chatterbox, and talks all the time during Milly's music-lesson.*

'*She told me they knew "all the swells" in England, not to mention a number of foreign royalties. It's rather peculiar that their drawing-room is not as nice as our front parlour at 44 Wharton Street! The children, I forgot to tell you, all adore me, and never leave me alone. Milly is almost as fond of me as Emma. I dare say I shall get fat here, with all the things they give me to eat, not to mention my glass of stout at luncheon and dinner!*

'*But I can't help being rather disappointed in everything, the people and the style of house, although I console myself with the fact that I am making a guinea a week.*'

Ellen frowned when Kicky showed her the letter. She was

not at all sure that she liked the tone of it. So frivolous and so ill-written. It was hardly the letter for a sensible, steady young woman to write. She was relieved the people were so kind to her, but it did not sound as though she would have the chance of making very good connections, the employers being what they were. It was unfortunate they proved to be tradespeople. Colonel Greville should have been more careful. Of course, Mr Wightwick kept a shop in Bond Street, they all knew that, and it was rather disconcerting to think of Isobel being so extremely friendly with Emma, but, then, nowadays things were all so different, and one really did not know who were gentlepeople and who were not.

'I don't like to think of Isobel in a house where there is consumption,' she said. 'Her health has never been her strongest point. I wonder at Colonel Greville recommending such a situation.'

'Beggars can't be choosers, mamma,' said Kicky.

'I am sure we are not reduced as low as that,' replied Ellen, rather displeased. 'Isobel can always make a home with me until she marries. And if the worst should happen, and she should not find a husband, she could make a living by her playing. I discussed it once with your Aunt Louise. She was a little shocked, and said that a public player was not so respectable as a governess, but I said she need not necessarily perform; she could give lessons. However, we shall see. If she does not care for being with these people, I shall endeavour to have her out to us. There might be some prospect of finding a husband for her if we go to Düsseldorf.'

Kicky was not so sure. From what he had heard of Düsseldorf it was full of impecunious art students, like himself and his friends, with a smattering of German princes who spent their time in eating and drinking and amusing themselves, and were not at all likely to propose to young penniless English ladies.

There had been no great change in his eyes, for the better or for the worse, since Christmas, and so many people talked about this wonderful oculist in Germany that he really began to have hopes in him.

Uncle George had been consulted, and had the kindness to advance Ellen her quarterly dividend. Dear Aunt Louise, too, with unfailing generosity, sent them 'a little something' for the journey.

In the late spring, therefore, Kicky and his mother said good-bye to sleepy, dreary Malines, with the line of dusty poplars and the sad-faced priests, and set forth for Düsseldorf and the Rhine.

As soon as he stepped out of the train, Kicky felt he was going to be happy in Düsseldorf. There was a bright gaiety in the atmosphere that went to his head immediately; there were funny little restaurants in every street, as original in their own way and as friendly as the French cafés, and there were beer-gardens where people danced and sang. There were hills and woods, and, best of all, the silver Rhine gleaming through the trees. They put up for the night at a cheap little hotel, and the next day Kicky went to Grafrath, some distance away, to consult the famous oculist, while Ellen looked for rooms in Düsseldorf.

Grafrath was an attractive little village, owing its prosperity entirely to the world-famous eye specialist who had made his headquarters there, and Kicky found the place full of English and Americans, who had either seen, or were about to see, the great man. Kicky arrived at ten o'clock, but the oculist did not examine him until four in the afternoon. Kicky was impressed by him at once – by his quick hands, his direct manner, his air of complete efficiency.

He told Kicky straight away that his left eye was gone for ever. There was no hope that the sight would come back. The inflammation would go down, however, and the pain would not return. As to his right eye, there was no reason why it should not last him for the rest of his life, provided he took care of it. Six or nine months under his treatment at Grafrath and he would be a different man.

Best of all, he could start painting again. There was nothing to prevent him. As long as the light was good and the hours not too long, it would be far better for him to be employed. There was a good school of painting in Düsseldorf. 'And I myself will commission a portrait from you,' said the delightful little man.

Kicky went back to Düsseldorf treading on air.

His mother had found rooms at No 84 Schadowstrasse, on the second floor, quite neat and clean, but the price seemed enormous after Malines, even if attendance was included. The meals were to be sent in by a restaurant round the corner. The landlady was English, the widow of a naval officer, and there were other English people boarding in the house. This was rather a disadvantage, Ellen thought, as she had wanted to rub up her German, and now, with English around her continually, she would not have the chance. However, after the first little complaints which were inevitable with every move, she settled down; as for Kicky, he was delighted with everything. The season was just beginning in Düsseldorf, and it seemed so bright and gay and amusing after Malines. The oculist had given him confidence, too, and he was no longer haunted by the fear that his right eye would become blinded, as his left. He became friendly with the other patients who went to Grafrath, most of them English, and somehow, without knowing how it happened, he was plunged into the little Düsseldorf society, hobnobbing with the German princes of the blood, and dubious counts, and so-called barons, and down-at-heel captains living on pensions, and retired admirals, and colonels of sorts. Some of them came for treatment at Grafrath, and others because Düsseldorf was considered fashionable at the moment, but nearly all of them considered Kicky a very charming, delightful young fellow, and most talented with his pencil.

Their sisters and their daughters thought him charming, too; there was something rather romantic about a thin, pale young man, who was nearly blind, and drew such flattering likenesses,

267

and spoke English and French equally well, and, best of all, sang so charmingly and with such feeling.

It was really very agreeable passing the summer in Düsseldorf: so many excursions in the forests, and on the Rhine, and then, what with the picnics, and the drives by moonlight, and one thing and another, it was a wonder that anybody kept his head at all.

Kicky wrote such glowing accounts of Düsseldorf society to his sister that she began to think the life of a governess to a building contractor was a very slow life indeed. So slow, in fact, that she feared her health would break down completely. The house was low and the air damp, and if two of the children had consumption, she was certain she would contract it. She wrote to Düsseldorf with such emphasis on the subject that Ellen ordered her instant removal from the building contractor's villa, on the understanding that she passed the remainder of the summer with her Uncle George at Milford, and came out to Düsseldorf in the autumn. This, of course, was exactly what Isobel wanted to do, and she said good-bye to her employers without the smallest pricking of her conscience.

By the end of the summer, Kicky was well enough to start painting again, and he shared with a Swiss named Hunziken a studio with a fine view over the Spertzen Garten. He had to come home to lunch every day at one o'clock, which rather broke his day, but Ellen insisted on his being properly nourished, and rather than argue the point he obeyed. The studio existence was very jolly, though, and reminded him of the happy days in Paris. The Swiss and he were capital friends, and, according to Kicky, they worked, sang, smoked, and quarrelled from dawn till dusk. When it became too dark to work, a few *intimes* wandered in, as they had done in the rue Notre-Dame des Champs, and, after arguing and criticising the efforts of Kicky and the Swiss, the whole party would move out to dinner at a restaurant and begin the conversation over again.

Models were inexpensive, and very often a friend with

nothing better to do would volunteer to sit, so that Kicky had plenty of subjects to work upon, and even hoped to have something in the exhibition in the winter.

If he were successful in this, he might get an order for a portrait, and one order would lead to another. If he could only make ten pounds it would be something, and he would be able to contribute towards the expenses of life in Düsseldorf. It was a wretched business depending on his mother's slender income entirely, as he had to do, and for his medical treatment as well.

What would they do without that blessed annuity, Ellen dared not even think. It was their sole means of support. However disgraceful the origin of the income, said Ellen to herself with tightened lips, at least it had been, and must continue to be, the saving of herself and her family from complete poverty and starvation. George's finances were at a low ebb again – there was so much entertaining to do at Milford, apparently – and he had been seriously ill into the bargain – seven weeks in bed with inflammation of the lungs – so that when Isobel was ready to come to Düsseldorf in the autumn he could not offer to pay her fare.

Ellen had bargained on him paying that, at least, but no, he could not afford it, and she was obliged to send Isobel fifteen pounds out of her October dividend for the journey. She rather wondered Colonel Greville had not offered to advance the sum. He knew their circumstances so well, but he never made any allusion to the journey, according to Isobel, and calmly went off to Brighton himself a few days before she left for Germany. He could have well afforded it, and, being a bachelor, and always so charming to Isobel, Ellen had sometimes wondered . . . However, it was no use thinking of that now. Had such an idea been in his mind he would have spoken before this.

'*Isobel is at last come,*' wrote Ellen to Louise in the middle of October, '*and I am glad to announce her great improvement in every way, since she was with us last. Just think of it, nearly two years*

269

absent. Her complexion is very much improved, and she has grown quite stout — too stout, I think, for her height.

'Her health will always be delicate, though, and from the observations I have made I can plainly see that she will never be able to sustain the fatigues of a governess's life. Besides, she is not educated for it. No, her existence, if she must depend on her own exertions, must come from music. Her playing has quite astonished me. Her execution is really wonderful, and she is out of practice too. I am fully sure there is no master here in Düsseldorf who could teach her better than she does herself. She played me a very difficult piece of fifteen pages, and this at sight. I have subscribed to a music library for her, and she will have two new pieces a day. She has been a great deal in society lately, at Milford and elsewhere, which has been of advantage to her, her manners are so easy and ladylike, and last, but not least, my dear Louise, her mind is just as pure as when she first left her mother's side. I could now trust her anywhere. Even if she were surrounded by all these officers, and they are the worst flirts in the world, I should not have the slightest uneasiness. So after all there is much to be thankful for. She has good health and good principles, and what more can a mother expect?'

What indeed! Except the ability to find a husband. Time would show whether Isobel succeeded in this. Her mother feared otherwise. Her front teeth spoilt her expression. She was afraid she would have to lose them, and it was difficult enough to find a husband if you possessed good teeth, let alone false ones.

Isobel plunged into the gay young society of Düsseldorf without a thought of the future, and was soon the toast of the gallant German princes and the impecunious counts, none of whom seemed to notice that her teeth and Isobel must soon be parted. Kicky continued to work hard, four or five hours a day, without fatigue, and his eye improved slowly. His left eye, as the oculist had told him, was gone for ever. Félix Moscheles paid him a flying visit from Paris, and they sat up very late drinking Rhine wine out of slender green glasses, and smoking cigars, and talked of poor Carry, left behind in dreary Malines.

Kicky said he had started a novel about her, but had no time to go on with it. Perhaps this was an embryo *Trilby*, and exists to-day in a bottom drawer of a lodging-house room in Düsseldorf. . . .

Carry had changed, Félix said, with a shake of his head; he was afraid she had taken the downward path, and all because she had been in love with one of them, and which it was they would never discover. Kicky suggested he should make a series of drawings, in which he and Félix would be represented helping Carry along the thorny path of life, and he even started one or two of these, to Félix's great delight, but, like the embryo Trilby novel, they were begun and never finished. There were too many distractions in Düsseldorf altogether for poor Carry to be long remembered. Isobel had become very thick with two Miss Lewises, the daughters of a General Lewis, and it soon was very evident that the elder Miss Lewis found Kicky's company more than usually agreeable.

Kicky was always weak where a handsome face was concerned, and Miss Lewis was undeniably good-looking. She was very tall, too, another point of admiration. So, when the working day was over, and paints and brushes were laid aside, he would wander round to the Lewises' lodgings with his mother and sister, and there would be a little singing, and a little refreshment, and perhaps little glances of understanding between the elder Miss Lewis and himself.

It was rather naughty of Kicky, for he was not in the least in love with her, and she, poor girl, took it all *au sérieux* and expected a proposal any minute. Christmas was quite a riotous affair, the happiest he had spent since that unique Christmas in the Quartier Latin, and the German princes joined their party in the evening, paying court to Isobel, which was all very gratifying to Ellen, her two children so popular and well liked, but rather a pity, all the same, that the German princes were not the marrying kind.

271

Another New Year – 1860 – and Kicky, walking home from singing duets with the elder Miss Lewis, realised that he would be twenty-six in March and was still no nearer to fame and fortune than he had been six years ago.

What of the future? Was not it time to begin thinking seriously at last? The oculist had told him that his right eye would last, with care, and that there was not very much more he could do for him in Grafrath. Therefore he must get away from Düsseldorf, before he became as idle and as flirtatious as the German princes, and start earning his daily bread as a draughtsman. He was beginning to realise that he would never make a painter. He made no progress in oils at all. He talked the whole matter over with Tom Armstrong, who had returned from a visit to Algiers, and who proposed spending a few months in Düsseldorf before proceeding to London.

'My dear old fellow,' said Kicky, 'the fact of the matter is that the first study I ever painted in Antwerp is a Titian compared to the oily abominations I perpetrate to-day. I'll go on for three months longer, and *si ça ne va pas – fini alors*! Is it that with one eye I can't see the effect of the colour, on the same principle that I can't knock the cork off the top of a bottle, or what?'

'You ought to go in for illustrating,' argued his friend. 'I'm convinced that is your true *métier*. Have a look at this.' And he threw over a copy of *Punch's Almanack*. 'See what you think of the work of Charles Keene and John Leech,' continued Armstrong. 'They are both on the *Punch* staff. Isn't that sort of thing much more in your line than what you are doing now?'

Kicky did not answer. He was turning over the pages of *Punch* in fascination.

'Why has nobody ever told me about this paper before?' he said at length in great excitement. 'It's the best thing I've ever seen. Jove, these chaps can draw! What I'd give, Tom, old man, to be as good as them.'

'I believe you could be, if you'd only try that instead of

going on with your painting. Come back to London with me in the spring, Kicky, and we'll take the plunge together. You're wasting yourself in Düsseldorf.'

'I should never be able to follow in the footsteps of these fellows, Keene and Leech,' sighed Kicky. 'I'm not a bit funny. I'd only make a fool of myself. Swells, and snobs, and flunkeys – all these figures they caricature in *Punch* here – are absolutely unknown to me. I've never moved in that sort of world, as you know.'

'Yes, but you soon would, if you went to London. I can get you introductions, old man. In three months you'd be in the swim of society!'

'Can you see me? No, the only society I know anything about is the Bohemian-Continental-artistic-cosmopolitan freemasonry, and the English public wouldn't care much about them. You and I and the rest of us here like smoking and drinking coffee in the evenings in the cafés, and talking eternal shop, but who the hell cares about that but ourselves? I'm incorrigibly lazy, Tom, and always have been. I enjoy loafing here, with pretty English girls as idle as myself; it's all damned easy, and doesn't require any effort.'

'Rot, Kicky. I don't believe you. You are itching to get away and do some real work. Pull yourself together, old boy, and cut yourself loose from all this.'

'Shall I? I don't know. I can't make up my mind. Let's go along to the café and meet the other fellows.' He got up, and smiled, and stretched himself, and laughed at Tom's straight face – silly old Tom shouldn't have such a high opinion of him – and off they went to the coffee-house at the corner, arm in arm, Kicky singing 'Vin à Quatre Sous', and wondering why he wasn't so happy as usual.

There were six or seven of the 'fellows' already there, who gave a shout of welcome when Kicky appeared. There was Best, a new and intimate friend; and young Bancroft, the son of the American historian, to whom Kicky had taken a tremendous fancy – he was so clever, and deep, and earnest, and so unlike himself. There was singing, and talking, and laughing, and fierce arguments, too, about the merits of English writers, of Kingsley and Carlyle – this more sober part of the proceedings being checked by the boisterous arrival of the red haired Swiss with whom Kicky shared a studio, and whose entrance was heralded by a general turning-over of tables and chairs, a smashing of glass, and a screaming of girls being kissed. He cared for nothing and for no one, and would seize upon some harmless, respectable little worm drinking his beer in the corner and throw him over his shoulder, to the roars of joy of everybody else in the café.

'The noisiest, merriest, genialist devil that ever lived,' said Kicky, laughing, pulling the Swiss to a chair beside him; and the Swiss, who had already had one or two drinks, insisted on standing treat to everyone in the room.

'All very fine and jolly,' thought Tom Armstrong, 'and no doubt it is amusing doing this night after night, but it's not getting Kicky anywhere.'

He thought of all the sketches and drawings he had seen in the studio, all of them possessing talent to an uncommon degree, and none of them finished.

'Have you ever known me finish anything but a cigar?' Kicky had said, and had wandered to the piano and strummed on it with one finger.

He was drifting, and if he allowed himself to drift much longer he would never be able to do anything else. He needed some of his mother's force and determination, thought Tom Armstrong. What a Tartar the old lady was! Nose in everything and an eye like a hawk. She never let him have five minutes with Isobel. . . .

The winter and spring passed, and still Kicky had not achieved anything much in the way of work. He had begun a series of illustrations for *Idylls of the King*, but, as he said himself, where on earth in Düsseldorf was he to find models for Lancelot and Guinevere?

Armstrong was still urging him to go to England, where he himself was bound in May, and still Kicky could not make up his mind.

It was as though he was waiting for someone to make the decision for him; he had no initiative of his own. He had not even consulted his mother yet; the scheme was too much in the air. He was sure she would not want to return to London; she and Isobel could live so much more economically on the Continent.

And then, just after Easter, he decided to go to England, for better or worse, which decision coincided rather curiously with the fact that Isobel's friends, the Wightwicks, had arrived on a visit to Düsseldorf, and would be returning again to England at the beginning of May.

Kicky was a little shy of Emma at first. She was even lovelier than her miniature, which he still kept, unknown to anybody, in his waistcoat pocket, like a talisman. She was very tall and grown-up, and he could not tease her like he had done when she was a pigtailed schoolgirl, but she was so grave and gentle and charming that he soon forgot to be shy, and began showing her his sketches, and even talking of his ambitions – a thing he did to no one except to Tom Armstrong.

Miss Lewis was quite forgotten; she was thrust away without as much as a thought. It made things just a little embarrassing for Isobel and Ellen, who saw the Lewises every day, and they were obliged to make excuses for Kicky, saying he was working very hard, only to be confounded, of course, by coming upon him later in the afternoon promenading Emma and her mother in the Düsseldorf gardens. Miss Lewis turned bright pink and made an excuse to go home almost immediately. It was really very noticeable. Ellen began to wonder whether Kicky had actually committed himself in any way. She and Isobel felt most uncomfortable. No doubt it was exceedingly kind of Kicky to show the Wightwicks the beauties of Düsseldorf, but why go off on his own to do it? Why not make a big party of all of them, the Lewises included?

Isobel suggested that he was attracted by Emma, which was absurd, of course. Emma was hardly more than a child. A dear, good-natured child, but not at all the type to attract Kicky. A stupid idea of Isobel's. No, Kicky was tactless and thoughtless; he should have consulted her before tearing off with the Wightwicks in that strange manner. She would speak to him about it.

She did so, and found him oddly unresponsive. He shrugged his shoulders when she taxed him about Miss Lewis, and said he had never thought twice about her, far less given her any encouragement. And, if there was going to be any awkwardness about it, surely it would be better if he cleared out of Düsseldorf.

He had been talking very seriously to Tom, and Tom thought there were excellent chances for him in London. If he could get an introduction to a paper as illustrator, it would be the beginning of a future. He might even be asked to contribute to a paper like *Punch*. If mamma lent him ten pounds he would guarantee to pay it back to her within three months. He would find cheap lodgings in London and work like a black. As a matter of fact, the Wightwicks had offered to put him up – he had been discussing the project with them – and this he had refused, but at any rate Mrs Wightwick very kindly promised to ask him in to meals and to keep an eye on him generally.

Ellen did not know what to say at first. She was not sure that she approved of his going off to London without her to look after him. Mrs Wightwick was a kind creature, no doubt, but she could not possibly take the place of his mother. On the other hand, she quite saw that Kicky was making no progress in Düsseldorf, and now that his eyes did not need such close attention it was really rather a waste of time and valuable money. As soon as he could make enough to keep himself it would be a great relief to her, and she would be able to give poor Isobel a better time. After all, the poor child must dress nicely

276

if she was to go about, and if she did not go about how was she to find a husband?

As for Gyggy, no use expecting any help from him. He could barely keep himself at Saumur. He was never likely to contribute to his sister's future. But if Kicky got on, and became successful in England, no doubt he would contribute something towards his family's upkeep. That was, if he did not get married. He would be extremely foolish if he did, without a settled future. He said he cared nothing for the eldest Miss Lewis, but he had certainly paid her a considerable amount of attention. The girl was looking very unwell these last few weeks – ever since Kicky had so taken up with the Wightwicks. Nothing in that, of course, but still . . . Oh, dear, it was all very worrying to be the mother of a family. Nothing but anxiety from morning till night. Louise was better off single, even if she was lonely.

'You must really decide for yourself,' said Ellen at last, after she had frowned, and scolded, and clicked her tongue. 'I will let you have ten pounds to go to London, and you must be as close with it as possible. As for Isobel and myself, we can live as cheaply here as anywhere, I suppose – at any rate for the present, until we know whether you are going to be successful or not.'

Kicky was aware of a great sense of relief, now that his decision was taken. He was stagnating in Düsseldorf, and going to London meant that he would have either to do or die. If he died, it did not matter so very much perhaps; if he did – well, that was another matter! The first thing he would do then would be to pay back the ten pounds he had borrowed from his mother.

He was wildly impatient to be gone. It was May already, and Düsseldorf and Grafrath were filling up for the season. The same familiar faces were to be seen in the gardens and in the restaurants and at the concerts. Last year he had found them amusing, but this year there was something stale in the atmosphere, a certain futile sense of sameness. It was all rather forced, and shallow, and insincere. He wondered how he had ever been able to tolerate those German princes or find them the slightest bit amusing. They were fat and grossly over-fed. How tawdry were the women beside Emma Wightwick; even if she were callow and still in her teens, nobody else in Düsseldorf could hold a candle to her for looks or charm – Miss Lewis wasn't in the same street. He wished Miss Lewis wouldn't look at him so reproachfully these days; it made a fellow feel such a cad. Damn it, he'd never said anything to her. Anyone would think they had been engaged or something. Deuced awkward. Tom agreed with him. Make a graceful exit, Tom murmured; only thing to do under the circumstances. Jolly good friends and all that, and hope to see you in London some time, and what a delightful winter it has been in Düsseldorf, and then just grace-fully fade out of the picture. So good-byes were said – rather embarrassing this, the final call the evening before – and even more embarrassing when the younger Miss Lewis met him and Tom with a slightly constrained manner, and said that her sister had retired to bed with a headache and could not come down-stairs. It made the good-byes easier in a way, but the whole thing looked a little obvious. Kicky wondered whether he ought to demand to see her there and then, and propose to her on the spot out of common politeness. He could not bear to hurt anyone's feelings.

'Carrying tact rather too far, old man,' objected Tom, and bore him off for a last drink in the café.

His mother, of course, kept him up half the night with last-minute advice as to his health, and his manner of living, and what he would be able to do, and what he must avoid at all costs. She could not have been more thorough and explicit if he had been a bride on her wedding-eve.

He smiled, and said 'Yes' and 'No,' and kissed her on the cheek. It made everything so much easier to agree, and he wondered if it was very ungrateful of him to feel glad that he was going to be alone in London, alone and independent, without the eternal cross-questioning that was so large a part of family life.

He would not be lonely; old Tom would be there, and some of the fellows who had worked with them in Paris – Tammie, and Poynter, and Jimmy Whistler among others. They were all of them crossing to England now, all those who meant to do anything in the world. They realised, as he did, that Paris and Antwerp were all very well for study, but, if you wanted to make a name for yourself and become anyone at all, you had to go to London.

Morning came; good-byes were over; Isobel was bidden not to flirt too shamefully with the German princes, and the old lady was scolded for having a tear in the corner of her eye; and then on to the little Rhine steamboat that was to take them to Rotterdam – Kicky, Tom Armstrong, Mrs Wightwick, and Emma.

The air was warm and fresh, and smelt of summer. There was a sort of promise about it, a feeling of expectation. Kicky was light of heart. He took off his dark glasses that he had worn now for over two years, and put them away in a pocket. Safe in an envelope were the ten pounds that his mother had given him – ten pounds from her annuity. His whole future depended on the use he made of them. He took them out and counted them over very carefully.

Emma watched him from her corner of the deck. He was much too thin, she thought, shaking her head, much too thin and too pale. He had no colour at all.

She was sure he had no idea of looking after himself. All those cigars he smoked, she was certain they were not good for him. She sighed and looked out upon the changing scenery of the river. It was not her business of course, but she wished he had someone to take care of him – bathe his eyes, and mend his socks, and give him medicine when he needed it. . . .

Kicky put the ten pounds back in the envelope. It was really very good of mamma. All she had in the world was that rather

279

inadequate but so eagerly expected little dividend every quarter. He was not even sure where it came from – something to do with his grandmother who had died at Boulogne.

What a disgraceful old woman she must have been! Mamma hardly ever mentioned her name. But if she had not lived as she had done, if she had not combined brains with beauty, he would not be standing on the deck of the Rhine steamboat now with her ten pounds in his pocket. He was going to make his fortune, all through her. He laughed, and felt in his waist-coat pocket for the inevitable pencil.

The future would hold no fears for him; he was going to succeed. Papa had failed because papa had let his dreams run away with him. He was not going to fail; he set his lean jaw with a sense of determination that Louis-Mathurin had never possessed. His energy came from another source, flowed in his veins as it had run before in the bloodstream of a woman, seventy, eighty years ago, a woman with a tip-tilted nose and a fluttering eyelid.

At twenty-six she had held her little world between her ruthless, exquisite fingers, and here was her grandson, at the same age, launching himself into the problematical future, in which he was to win fame by satirising the same society she had led by the ears at the beginning of the century.

Kicky began to draw swiftly on the back of the precious envelope, but for once it was not a caricature. It was the face of Emma Wightwick who stood with unselfconscious profile turned upward to the sky.

Part Six

16

The first thing Kicky did on arriving in London was to look up the old Paris crowd who were now working in England. Jimmy Whistler offered him a share in his dilapidated studio at No 70 Newman Street, and Kicky gladly accepted.

The room was long and narrow, with a window at one end looking out to the back, and in the middle of the room a curtain was hung which was supposed to divide the apartment into two. The smaller side was called the bedroom.

Quarters more cramped and uncomfortable it would be hard to find, but Kicky cared little for luxury at any time, and Jimmy was a most amusing companion. He was an indefatigable talker, of course, and would keep Kicky awake until the small hours of the morning, telling him all his romantic adventures, which were no doubt very funny and witty from ten until midnight, but became a little boring when they were continued until three or four.

Jimmy Whistler was doing very well already, and had a picture in the Academy, much to the envy of his friends, most of whom were still hawking round portfolios under their arms and seeking interviews with influential dealers. The studio in Newman Street soon became a happy hunting ground for the crowd, with Poynter, and Ionides, and Lamont, and the rest, coming in to smoke and talk and fence. Charles Keene of *Punch* was introduced to the circle by Tom Armstrong, and was at home from the first moment, smoking a particularly evil clay pipe and roaring with laughter at the wit of the immortal Jimmy, who could talk easily while he painted.

They all used to dine at a little restaurant in Castle Street, near Cavendish Square, which was more of an eating-house than anything else, and was frequented by footmen and lacqueys on their half-days, but on Sundays Aleco Ionides used to invite most of them out to his parents' house on Tulse Hill, where very good parties were given, and most of the 'coming young people' were to be seen – poets, painters, musicians, and the rest. Tom Jeckell, Kicky's friend of Pentonville days, was now a budding architect, and resumed his former friendship, and Kicky began to consider himself one of the luckiest fellows in the world to possess so many affectionate friends.

Work came to him slowly but increasingly, and he would illustrate the serial stories of various periodicals of the day. Tom Armstrong, through Keene, was able to give him an introduction to Mark Lemon, the editor of *Punch*, and the great man was condescending enough to commission a few initial letters as a trial. These appeared to be successful, and from time to time Kicky sent up little contributions to *Punch* which were gracefully accepted.

A new paper was started about this time called *Once A Week*, and Kicky was one of the first artists to contribute to it. The *Cornhill* magazine also accepted his work now and again, and he was seldom without employment of some kind. He was soon able to pay back the ten pounds he had borrowed from his mother, but, even so, he was obliged to live very carefully, for he could not be certain that work would always be forth-coming, and on several occasions he ran so short that he was unable to buy lotion to bathe his eyes.

He had his moments of despair, like every struggling young artist, as when the editor of *Once A Week* suddenly refused a drawing which Kicky himself thought a very good piece of work; and this unexpected reverse melted the small swelling of his head which had grown a trifle during the last months, chiefly owing to the praise and compliments of his friends. His spirits rose, however, when Jimmy Whistler raved over a block he was making for *Punch* – a study of Emma, incidentally, sitting in a garden – by saying, 'My d-d-d-dear Kicky, why, why, this is simply s-s-s-stunning. It's as fine as one of my dry-points, d-d-d-dash it!' Which was exceedingly great praise indeed. Later on, when they were dining in a restaurant in Pall Mall, Jimmy went on about the drawing again, and even began to compare Kicky to Leech and Millais. 'You know, Kicky, all your first talented drawing for *Punch* and *Once A Week* were very c-c-clever, no doubt, and I expected them to be so from such a t-t-talented fellow; but this drawing is a different thing altogether, and has a v-v-value which I recognise as a work of art.'

Kicky was so encouraged that he wrote off to mamma and Isobel in Düsseldorf and told them all about it. '*If my sight continues as good as it is,*' he said, '*one day I shall be a great artist. I haven't quite found my particular vein yet, you know, and I don't want to draw for 'Punch' in the usual way. I'm not a broad-comedy man, and of course Leech is unapproachable in his own style. But when I do find it, then I shall be unapproachable, too!*'

To Isobel he was a little more explicit with regard to his private affairs.

'*You ask me about the state of my fickle mind,*' he said. '*Well, I adore Emma, who sat for my block, but what's the use, you know, pas le sou, hein? and then her relatives – what?! I wonder how much she likes me, the dear prude. She is quite converted to all the pictures and books and music that I admire, and the contemptuous way she speaks of those who have not the same refined taste* (qu'elle n'a que depuis trois mois) *is very amusing.*

'*Who do you think is coming to town and wants to be taken the rounds by her promising young nephew? Aunt Georgie! I don't think I shall introduce her to Emma. . . .*'

Georgie did come to London, and no business to either, as her poor husband was very ill down at Milford. She made for Newman Street like a streak of lightning, and was as fair, fluffy, and flirtatious as ever. Kicky gave a party for her, but none of his friends thought much of her; indeed, she seemed exceedingly provincial these days, and was shockingly overdressed, and as they went in to supper she apologised for not having her gloves on.

Jimmy gave her one look, and never addressed another word to her for the rest of the evening.

Happily for Georgie, she was far too pleased with herself to notice an insult, and she imagined she was a *succès fou* in Bohemian circles, glancing at Kicky's friends under her long lashes and talking sixteen to the dozen. Her manners and poses were throwing them all into convulsions, did she but know it, and would be a source of mimicry for weeks to come. Kicky, invariably kind of heart, put himself to infinite trouble to entertain her, but, though he had a sort of cousinly affection for her, he almost blushed to think of his calf passion of six years ago, and how he had very nearly lost his head over her altogether. He was aware of a feeling of relief when she took herself back to Milford again to her sick husband, and he could dine in peace once more with the Wightwicks and watch Emma's profile across the dining-room table. The Wightwicks themselves were rather a strain, and always squabbling at each other. The old man had only to open his mouth for his wife to contradict flatly whatever he said, but Emma, cool and calm between them, was a gifted peacemaker, and knew how to soothe them both and restore the atmosphere to normal.

After dinner old Wightwick would fall asleep over his glass of port, and his wife would nod in her chair, so that Kicky and Emma had a corner of the drawing-room to themselves and could talk without interruption. Sometimes Emma read aloud to him, if he was tired from a long working day; and it came to him then how pleasant and restful it would be if this was their own house, and he and Emma were married, and if in an hour's time he had not got to get up and put on his coat and go back through the cold streets to his bare little room in Newman Street. It was good to have friends, and Jimmy was an amusing fellow, but oh, Lord, how utterly different it must be to have a home of your own, however small, and a quiet, methodical routine that never varied, and someone angelic like Emma to kneel beside you and put her cheek against yours when you were tired and out of spirits.

He loved the rustle of her dress, and her soft low voice, and that sweet smell of lavender that was not a scent at all, but merely an intangible part of her. Dash it, what was the use, though, of thinking about it at all? He could barely keep himself, let alone a wife. If only he could be certain of always getting work, of never being in debt, and of his right eye staying faithful to him! One day everything would go well. He would take a block up to *Punch* and Mark Lemon would make him feel a hell of a fellow, telling him that if he continued as he was doing he would be fit for the *Punch* staff in a number of years, and he would come out of the office with half a dozen orders and nearly dance the can-can in the middle of the street. And then, perhaps, a week later would come a reverse. *Once A Week* cutting down the number of their illustrations, the *Cornhill* requiring no work for the present, and the new paper, *London Society*, already engaged with that brilliant young draughtsman Fred Walker, whose style was very much Kicky's own but infinitely better, feared Kicky. Walker was a dear little chap, as trim and natty as a pin, and Kicky liked him immensely, but perhaps Walker did not depend on orders to keep him from starvation, and perhaps he did not dream of marriage with the best girl in the world.

Kicky had been in London nearly a year now, and had done extremely well in the time, but he was still a long way from calling himself a successful artist. In the spring of 1861 a series of misfortunes occurred all round. The first to suffer were the Wightwick family, whose business suddenly failed after many years, and the old people were left in considerably reduced circumstances and were obliged to move into a small house and give up entertaining.

This put the idea of marriage further off than ever. Then

Ellen wrote from Düsseldorf to say that Gyggy was in trouble again – the usual question of debt – and if his debts were not paid the creditor would inform his Colonel. Kicky sent a precious five pounds he could ill afford and had a rollicking letter from his brother in return, never mentioning the debt at all.

In April, poor George Clarke died down at Milford, leaving a helpless and distracted Georgie with a small son barely eight years old, and very little money in the bargain. His death was a great blow to Ellen in Düsseldorf, and she wrote off at once to Louise to tell her the sad news, for, as she said in her letter, '*I know what your feelings must still be, on such a painful subject. My poor brother suffered terribly, with swelling of the legs and difficulty in breathing, but he died calmly, I am glad to say, and with religious feelings, and almost his last words were, "Tell Ellen I am very happy". His mental sufferings, as well as his physical ones, are now over, for I know his situation preyed upon his mind, although it was an excellent one, and honourable too. But he felt buried alive down at Milford, he told me so when we were there, and had it not been for his wife and child he would have taken service in some foreign country – he could always have kept his rank of Captain. What will become of Georgie and Bobbie I do not know. Her father is in India, but I believe her mother lives in Brighton. It is certain they will do very little for her: they are notoriously mean from what I hear, and, though her mother will spend a hundred guineas on a ball dress, she will not pay her daughter's fare up from Milford, so we know what to expect. I believe Georgie would like to join Isobel and myself in Düsseldorf, but I don't know about that. I do not think it would be good for her son's education, and I am not sure of her as a companion for Isobel, besides which I can well believe that in the long run the expense would fall upon me, and that you know I cannot afford. It's as much as I can manage to keep Isobel well clothed – she goes about so much and is quite the best-liked girl in Düsseldorf. These German princes are all wild about her; unfortunately they have no money. Of course we cannot do much in the way of entertaining, but the Prince*

Holstein sometimes comes in to tea – he came the other day and found me with Isobel's dressmaker, enveloped in clouds of white muslin and the room strewed with shreds and patches. However, he is so well bred I was not in the least put out of my way. He told us there was every chance of his brother's daughter (heir to the throne of Denmark) marrying the Prince of Wales. She is only seventeen and beautiful, it appears. If only Isobel had a little money she might marry easily enough – that is, if she knew any rich English, but, alas! no rich English ever come to Düsseldorf. I am so afraid she will lose her good looks and then will have no chance at all. Kicky is spoken of in the papers, and the other day a gentleman asked if Isobel was the sister of the rising young artist in "Punch." All that looks well. It sounds as though he were becoming attached to Emma Wightwick. She is an excellent girl, but I can't say I should like such a connection, and now her family have lost so much money they could not do much for her, so it would not suit at all. Anyway, he is as fickle as the wind. This time last year it was all Miss Lewis, I believe she still thinks of him. However, all this chat will not bring back my poor brother. I keep thinking of him, and his home broken up. If anything happens to me what will become of Isobel now? I am in constant anxiety at the thought. Do write and advise me, dear Louise, and perhaps you can settle this little debt of Eugène's, for really I can spare nothing at the moment. We are giving up sugar in our tea now, and I never touch wine; in fact I look like an old skeleton, and so weak. . . .'

Louise, who had long denied herself every luxury for Eugène's sake, and had not tasted sugar for ten years, sent him the money at once, and, although she was crippled with rheumatism and scarcely left her room these days, she managed to crawl downstairs and to church to burn a candle for George Clarke, whom she had ever thought of in the tender light of might-have-been.

Meanwhile the widowed Georgie was a source of great anxiety to the du Mauriers. Ellen's letters to Kicky were full of her, and would he find out what her people would do for her? Kicky, very much occupied with a series of drawings for

Punch, found himself dragged into the discussion much against his will, and had to go down to Brighton to see his unfortunate aunt.

He found her thinner, and draped in black (her bonnet definitely becoming), and not so broken-hearted as he had expected, although she kept twisting an absurd lace handkerchief in her hand. She was violent against her parents, who would not give her enough to live on in London, and she was quite determined to go out to India again, where she had a brother. Bobbie, she said carelessly, could be left at a military school. Bobbie, a cowed, rather furtive-looking child of eight, looked at his cousin slyly under his lashes and said nothing.

Kicky felt rather helpless to advise, and in a rash moment suggested that his Aunt Georgie and young Bobbie should spend a few months in Düsseldorf with the family before finally deciding upon India. Georgie leapt at the idea. It would be just the thing, she said, to restore her shattered nerves. And Kicky must take them out, she declared, making play with her lashes. Kicky said at once that he could not afford the journey. Nonsense, his aunt insisted, she would pay his fare. If an aunt could not do that, what could she do? Kicky blushed and looked uncomfortable. It was true that Georgie could not very well travel alone and unprotected, and it was equally true that he would like to see his mother and sister again after twelve months' absence.

'We will see what mamma says,' he hedged, and Georgie gave him a brilliant smile, and then, remembering she was a widow, she drooped a little, and put her handkerchief to her eye, and looked so frail and pathetic that Kicky would have taken her to the Antipodes had she demanded it of him.

He went back to London, wondering how far he had committed himself to the Düsseldorf plan, and remembered, with added discomfort, that the Lewis family were still there in full force, and, according to Isobel, the eldest Miss Lewis had not yet mended a broken heart and was still hoping for a proposal.

Frightful embarrassment! He could not possibly go to Düsseldorf until they had gone. To forget his troubles he went to luncheon with the Wightwicks, and took Emma afterwards to an afternoon performance of *Ruy Blas*.

It was a fine day, and after the performance they decided to walk home up Regent Street. Emma was looking more handsome than ever, and was so full of sympathy for Kicky and his worries that his heart melted entirely and his knees turned to water when he looked at her. She was, in fact, so utterly adorable that he could contain himself no longer, and opposite Peter Robinson's he asked her to marry him.

'Are you sure you will not change your mind?' she asked gravely, and he answered, 'Never, never,' ready to throw himself down on the pavement in front of her. 'Very well,' she said, 'then I will.' And at that moment a hansom cab came by and splashed them both with mud from head to foot.

Kicky wondered whether he ought to have chosen a more romantic spot for his declaration, but Emma was laughing at him, and he knew then that nothing mattered in the world any more. They walked back hand in hand to announce their news to Emma's parents, both of whom fell upon their daughter's neck and wept, saying it was the one thing they desired. Of course, they all agreed, the engagement must be a long one. Kicky could not possibly afford a wife at the moment. At least two years must go by before they could begin to think of it. The dismal prospect of waiting all that time could not daunt the happy pair as yet. They were too delighted in their status of being engaged to worry about the future.

The next day Kicky wrote to his mother to break the news. To his surprise, she took it astoundingly well. *'Naturally you will not think of marrying for many years,'* she said in her letter, *'but as to the engagement, it has my approval. You have known each other now for seven years, and I remember your poor father considered her very sensible at fourteen. I do not think you could have chosen better; so obedient to her parents, so good and kind to her mother when ill,* so full of feeling for their losses and privations, instead of thinking of her own. The good daughter makes the good wife. She appears to dote on you, and I, with maternal vanity, say, "No wonder" – to have the chance of marrying such a man, who fascinates wherever he goes, and is in such a much superior position to any of her own connections and relations, is a very lucky thing for her. I hope Mr Wightwick will behave generously when the time comes. By rights he should allow her at least forty pounds a year, and her clothes, and furnish an apartment for you. But English people are very fond of making the husband do all, I know very well. However, sufficient unto the day is the evil thereof.'

This was a good deal better than Kicky had expected. A stream of reproaches would not have astonished him. The old lady had such devilish strong opinions. If she had taken a dislike to Emma there would have been no restraining her. Of course, she was never going to swallow the connections, he could see that. The Wightwicks would be flung in his face for evermore. Poor old W., he was such a harmless fellow, too, and, even if he was not quite out of the top drawer, well, did it matter so very much? Dash it all, a lot of people were in trade these days. And, when all was said and done, who were the du Mauriers? Of course, he knew what it was. Mamma had this bee in her bonnet about having royal blood in her veins. She just couldn't forget it. Kicky could not see it was anything much to be proud of. The wrong side of the blanket and all that. Besides, there was no real proof to go on. He had ventured a question to Uncle George once, and Uncle George had shut up like an oyster.

Mamma was being rather optimistic about the Wightwicks making Emma an allowance. He did not expect anything from them, knowing their present circumstances. That was why he would have to work harder than he had ever done in his life, so that he could support her. Luckily, *Punch* took most of his things now, and the *Cornhill* and *Once A Week* were accepting work again.

The last paper had just accepted a piece of writing into the bargain. In an idle moment he had written an account of his adventures in the Devon mine as an analytical chemist, with illustrations, and *Once A Week* paid him twenty quid for it. If his eye should ever fail him, he might be able to support himself by writing. He hunted up his old MS. about Carry and Malines, but could only find a few scattered pages. The rest must have been lost in Düsseldorf. He remembered what he could of it, altering it considerably, and changed the scene to Paris, bringing in some of the old Bohemian crowd. It was really a sketch of Paris days, and made about twenty-four pages of foolscap.

He sent it round to the *Cornhill*, but they would not take it, and, as it was too long for *Once A Week*, he gave up the idea of publishing it altogether, and put it away in a drawer with some unfinished sketches.

One day, perhaps, he would make a novel out of it. . . .

A letter from Isobel, assuring him that the Lewis family had taken their departure, with old Lewis seriously ill, reconciled him to a flying visit to Düsseldorf, and in July Kicky escorted his Aunt Georgina and young Bobbie into Germany. Ellen found him looking pale but well, and there was no doubt that the English food agreed with him and suited his constitution.

After two days he began to look tired; there had been so much to discuss and gossip about after a year's absence that she had kept him up late, talking until three in the morning, and, what with the wretched food she was obliged to give him in Düsseldorf, she could see that the visit was doing him no good. England had certainly improved him, and he seemed so much steadier in every way, and talked of his work with enthusiasm. He seemed devoted to Emma, and fond of her family. Ellen hoped he would not belong to them entirely now.

She could not help feeling it was rather a mistake to have got himself engaged so soon. Apparently Mr Wightwick would not be able to afford Emma an allowance after all, and that would mean all the expense falling upon Kicky. Ellen said afterwards to Isobel that Kicky might have considered his family first. He knew that his mother and sister lived in extreme poverty where they were, affording no luxuries at all, and yet he proposed to get married some time in the future and support a wife, when he might have supported them. If he made any money, no doubt it would all go to Emma, and to their children. His mother and sister would not benefit. She said none of this to him, of course, but he could not help being aware that there was a slight tightening of her lips when marriage was mentioned, and a sniff from her long nose, so after all it was better not to say too much about it, but to talk about his work instead, and go back to London and the faithful Emma at the end of the week. He was a little dubious about Aunt Georgie and mamma living in double harness, and was decidedly relieved that he was not to be embroiled. The tittle-tattle of Düsseldorf sounded absurdly unimportant to him these days, and mamma and Isobel could talk nothing else.

What a narrow, cramped atmosphere it was, compared to the life he led in London; and he was thankful to be free of it. He felt a different man in London, and started dumb-bell exercises again and eating a mutton chop for breakfast.

By now he had a very large circle of friends, and besides the Ionides family at Tulse Hill, who gave such interesting parties, he had been introduced to another patron of art and letters, a certain Arthur Lewis (no relation to the Lewises of Düsseldorf), whose social and musical evenings were the talk of artistic London.

Arthur Lewis afterwards married the actress Kate Terry, sister of Ellen Terry, but in the early sixties he was still a bachelor. He took a tremendous fancy to Kicky, and gave him *carte blanche* to bring any of his friends to the parties. It was here that Kicky met Frederic Sandys, and Val Prinsep – both of whom became intimate friends of his – and little Fred Walker, his rival draughtsman, and Millais, handsome as a young Greek god, and the great Watts.

Kicky liked them all, and was liked in return, but he was wise enough not to become involved in the numerous little cliques that clung together and were thicker than the proverbial thieves. Jimmy Whistler, for example, had become rather an exacting companion, and Kicky took himself off to another studio, in Berners Street, and left Jimmy to the ministrations of two new companions, Fantin Latour and Legros. This trio made a little circle with the poets Rossetti, Swinburne, and George Meredith.

'They are all very well, old fellow,' confided Kicky to Tom Armstrong, 'but between you and me and the door-post they are best left to themselves. Like all societies of mutual admiration, they have a noble contempt for anyone outside their particular circle. I'm convinced that a chap's best chance of doing his finest work is by sticking very much to himself, and of course working very hard, and, most important of all, by talking very little about it.'

With which sentiment Tom Armstrong heartily agreed, and was thankful, for his friend's sake, that Kicky was wearing his hair rather shorter than before, and had given up velvet jackets, and looked with his tongue in his cheek at some of these fellows who wandered about with lilies in their hands and other people's wives. Emma was his good angel, there was no doubt about that. If it had not been for her influence he might have become a very different person. As it was, he worked like a black because he wanted to settle down and be married, and this kept him out of any possible entanglement.

Rubbing shoulders with the lions of the artistic world had not gone to his head at all; on the contrary, it developed his sense of humour and brought out his capacity for satire. They thought such a lot of themselves, Leighton, and Millais, and the rest – quite rightly, too, for they were big men, and their names would go down to posterity – but, Jove! did they never have a quiet laugh to themselves and say, 'What the hell do any of us matter after all?'

Val Prinsep was good fun, of course, and a stunning companion; a great bull of a fellow, sixteen stone and six foot one in his stockinged feet; Kicky had a weakness for giants. Watts was a romantic devil, too. He asked Kicky to dine at Little Holland House, and Kicky, dressing himself in evening clothes, found his host in an old painting-jacket and carpet-slippers and without a collar and tie.

He gave a good dinner, but ate nothing himself but toast and butter.

Burne-Jones was there, and Kicky took to him immediately. An angel of a fellow, so gentle and good-mannered, and, gosh! what a colourist!

Millais and his wife were the guests of honour. Millais was almost too good-looking to be true, and rather showed himself to be the darling of society, which made Kicky a little shy. His wife, who had once been Ruskin's, was disappointing – quite *passée*, said Kicky afterwards to Tom, and wondered why Millais had run away with her. 'Somebody told me Ruskin was deuced grateful to Millais for taking her off his hands, and I shouldn't wonder,' he said.

At all these parties Kicky was in great request as an amateur singer, and he was always called upon to perform some time during the evening.

This never worried him in the slightest; he sang naturally and with the greatest ease, like his father before him, and probably gave more pleasure to his audience in consequence than the serious throaty professional would have done in similar circumstances. They were good evenings, and he enjoyed them, and only wished that he were married and could take Emma, instead of having to creep home about four o'clock to his room in Berners Street, sharing a cab with the red-haired Swinburne on the way, who was too disgustingly drunk to be amusing.

It was after one of these parties that he returned to his lodgings to find a mad letter from Gyggy, written post haste from

Compiègne, where he had gone after Saumur, saying a friend was going to buy him out of the Army; he was fed up with life, and what about coming to London and living with Kicky?

Really, the incorrigible Gyggy went too far! Soldiering was the only profession he knew anything about, and no doubt that was precious little, and here he was suggesting that he threw his chances away and entered a civil life without a penny in his pocket. The next day brought a hectic postcard from Isobel. She also had heard from Gyggy, telling the same tale, and threatening them with his presence in Düsseldorf, mamma nearly having a stroke in consequence.

'*The only way to prevent him is to see him personally,*' said Isobel, '*and I am going by train from here to-morrow. Mamma very agitated, but as she is not very well it is better for me to go. I shall only be away a few days.*'

What a fuss and commotion! Silly, tactless old fellow Gyggy was. What on earth would he do if he left the Army? 'Wish he were your brother,' Kicky said to Emma. 'I believe you would know how to keep him in order.'

He was showing her some pictures in the National Gallery at the time, and Emma did not reply immediately.

'Why,' she said suddenly, 'I have just seen Miss Lewis from Düsseldorf, who looked at me and then looked another way, and hurried from the room. How very odd.'

'Are you sure?' said Kicky, going rather red in the face. 'You must have been mistaken.'

'Oh, I am certain it was she,' Emma insisted, 'but what I don't understand is why she did not want to see us.'

Deuced awkward, thought Kicky, knowing Miss Lewis to have remarkably good sight and a long memory. It was obviously a cut direct. How wretchedly embarrassing!

'I thought you were all such good friends,' said Emma.

'I don't understand it at all,' lied Kicky. 'Let's go and look at the Van Dycks.' What on earth would happen if they met again? He was not comfortable until the doors of the National

Gallery were behind them and they were in the omnibus going home.

'Do you think Miss Lewis does not like me?' said Emma, returning to the fatal subject, and looking Kicky straight in the eyes.

'My dear love, what an absurd idea,' said Kicky, and he yawned − a sure sign of embarrassment.

'Perhaps she had a slight *penchant* for you in Düsseldorf,' said Emma.

'Ridiculous,' said Kicky. 'We never had anything in common.'

'She is very good-looking,' said Emma.

'Some people may consider her so; I certainly don't,' said Kicky heartily. 'In fact, I have never seen anything to admire in her at all. She is too thin in my opinion, and her complexion does not compare with yours. Miss Lewis can go to the devil for all I care.'

His outburst was a little suspicious. Emma was silent. She remained silent all the way home. She pleaded a headache and retired early to bed, leaving Kicky to drink port alone with old Wightwick.

Kicky cursed the National Gallery and all its works. Why, oh, why had he not two thousand a year as income, and a settled job, and two good eyes, so that he could ask Emma to marry him to-morrow and end this present life of uncertainty?

There started for him that night a period of sleeplessness and worry.

17

Ellen du Maurier was in a shocking temper. She felt ill, for one thing; the wretched German food did not suit her, and she had taken some pork a few days ago that had given her a most disagreeable complaint. Their new lodgings in Düsseldorf were uncomfortable, and the landlady robbed them continually.

The Lewis family had returned to England – poor old Lewis had died – and she did not care at all for the other English people in the place.

Now Eugène had given them this fright about leaving the Army, and, though Isobel had travelled to reason with him – a great expense, too; a cross-country journey – and he had been persuaded by her to stay out his time, Ellen knew he was far too unreliable to keep a promise, and might descend upon them at any moment. As for Georgie – she was quite disgusted with her. If this was the way modern young widows behaved, she was exceedingly glad that she herself had been born at the end of the last century. She was a shocking companion for Isobel, and the two did nothing but giggle from morning till night and talk about young officers and German princes. Georgie was making quite an exhibition of herself. She had spent thirty guineas already on evening dresses, although she kept saying she could afford nothing for her son's education, and even had the audacity to suggest that Colonel Greville from Milford ought to provide for her. Absolute nonsense, said Ellen. The Colonel was most liberal to them when George was living, but that was no reason why he should be saddled with his widow. It was not very likely that her present style of living

– evening dresses and trinkets – would gain any sympathy from Colonel Greville either.

Ellen knew what it was; Georgie kept hinting that she should have a share in the annuity. 'Darling Mrs Clarke said I was never to want for anything,' she said one day. 'Was that annuity really settled on you alone, or on you and George?'

Did anyone ever hear of such a thing? Ellen trembled with rage. Such ingratitude, too, when she had given up all her plate and valuables that her mother had given her, and had sent them to Georgina as a wedding present in 1851.

If she was so poor, why did she not go to her own relatives? She had a rich old grandfather and lots of aunts, and no doubt one of them would pay for the child's schooling. Not only was Georgie vain, calculating, and thoroughly selfish, but Bobbie had turned out to be a thief and an incorrigible little liar. A sweeter child at three it would have been difficult to find, and here he was at eight on the high road to being a criminal. The landlady had come and complained to Ellen that money was missing from her purse, and Bobbie was found to be the culprit. What an appalling disgrace! The child was punished, of course, but Georgie had the coolness to say that he had always stolen, even as a little child, and she did not know how to prevent him. Ellen spoke to her of the misery and disgrace she would bring upon herself if the child was not corrected, but it was of no avail. All she did was to send him as a daily scholar to a cheap German school, where he probably learned habits even worse than his present ones. Ellen knew what Georgina was scheming at the back of her mind: simply to leave the boy in her charge and then go off on her own somewhere – to India, perhaps – and have no more responsibility. Well, her fine plan would come to nothing. Ellen would leave Düsseldorf and live in some miserable little village rather than have the worry of looking after Bobbie. And Georgina so cunning and deceitful over it all. Pulling a poor mouth to the German princes about the way her sister-in-law treated her.

Ellen knew only too well. The last time Prince Holstein had come to tea he had scarcely addressed a word to her at all, but sat in Georgina's pocket the entire time. Very different from his usual behaviour. No, ever since Georgina's arrival, Düsseldorf had seemed a different place. Even Isobel had changed, and was becoming silly and frivolous. She was only happy when she was surrounded with people. Ellen tried to make her read to improve her mind, and told her that education for everyone in this life continued until the tomb, but Isobel would not listen. She could not bear being by herself, and found pleasure only in talking and living in a crowd. When Ellen was quite young she contracted the habit of sufficing unto herself, and never knew the meaning of *ennui*. Isobel's nature was very different, more the pity. *Heureux ceux qui aiment s'instruire*.

Unless Isobel married, she would lay up a very empty, lonely life for herself. London, her mother was sure, was the only chance of her finding a husband. Men there did sometimes marry without money, but in Germany they could not. However, as they could not afford to live in London and Kicky had no home as yet to offer her, she supposed they must drag on with this scrappy, uncomfortable existence and hope for the best. It was certain that Georgina would never introduce Isobel to anyone worth knowing; she kept all the most interesting men to herself. It was a wonder to Ellen that Isobel cared for her aunt. The pair were inseparable, though, and there was no parting them. All these parties were not good for Isobel's health, either. She was anæmic and thin, and nothing like as pretty as she had been. Her front teeth, too, were decaying rapidly, and one might as well look for a needle in a haystack as a good dentist in Düsseldorf. All these Germans had bad teeth; no doubt it was the water.

Ellen felt she had the Sword of Damocles hanging over her head continually, what with Kicky in London depending for his existence on his one eye, and Eugène in Compiègne committing some monstrosity for all she knew, and Isobel here in Düsseldorf with bad teeth and no husband. Really, her life was one long anxiety from morning till night!

Poor Kicky in England had his own troubles. He was working far too hard for one thing, in a desperate attempt to make enough money to support Emma, and in the spring of 1862 he became so nervy and ill that he was forced to consult a doctor. It seemed that his brain had become affected by his liver in some odd way, which resulted in sleeplessness and acute depression. He could not eat, and his work appeared trivial to him and valueless. He felt that he would never be a success, never earn enough money to keep a wife, and that his future was doomed to inevitable failure.

Letters came frequently from Düsseldorf, always full of the same complaints about the family standard of living, and when was Kicky likely to make things more comfortable for them? While at home, Emma was looking thin and worried, and, when he questioned her, she confessed that things were very difficult between her father and mother; they bickered at one another from morning till night, and she longed for Kicky to marry her and take her away from it all. The accumulation of worry nearly drove him to despair. The doctor prescribed strong tonics that only made him worse, and finally he escaped from the physician's clutches and went down to Brighton for a change of air.

'*The agonies and tortures I have endured are beyond all parallel in my experience,*' he wrote to Tom Armstrong, '*and it has all been brought on apparently by overwork, anxiety, lack of air and exercise, insufficient food, and the admirable purity of my morals, my boy. I am now taking cod-liver oil, fifteen grains of quinine per day, and have exchanged my fearful state of mind for the delightful* ennui *of a boil on my ankle and a cold in the head. All this accounts for your not having seen anything of mine in the papers; indeed, this last month has been disastrous; no work at all and a lot of expense.* Enfin! Tout est pour le mieux dans le meilleur des mondes. *When I am thoroughly myself again I think my work will have improved a good deal.*

Marriage, says the doctor, would be the best cure. Emma has been dreadfully shaken by this wretched state of things, and I came down to Brighton to spare her the pain of seeing me in this condition. On Good Friday I tried to do a block for the "London News", and it was all done but for a few hands when I felt such a rush of misery and madness come over me that I gave it up and spoilt the whole thing, and went off to see Hendon, the specialist. I believe I fell down on my knees to him or something and cried, Why the devil have we got livers and things? He assured me my brain was quite sound, but I was on the verge of a breakdown. "Punch" and "Once A Week" enquire tenderly after my health, and show great consideration in not over-working me in my present delicate state. Everyone getting on except me. Jimmy Whistler and Fred Walker and the rest, and Leighton has done some glorious things. Would I could marry − I could work more and better, and should be rid of ennuis, beaupaters, and belle-maters, and live with the dearest, goodest, kindest creature God ever made, who, if she knew I was writing, would send you her love. . . .'

In the early summer Kicky was sufficiently recovered to pay a flying visit to Düsseldorf, but he was still very nervy, and Ellen was shocked at his appearance. Her darling boy, so pale and thin, and working nine hours a day in order to marry Emma and take her away from that unhappy home. Ellen had been going to ask him for some contribution towards their expenses in Düsseldorf, but at the sight of him she was determined never to ask for another penny. She really had not the heart to add to his troubles. She could not help complaining, of course, about Georgie and her tiresome ways, and here was Bobbie now down with the small-pox, and Isobel meeting no one and missing her chances. She had bottled it up for so long that she could not contain herself any longer.

'Isabella shall come and stay with us when we are married,' said Kicky. 'Perhaps she will meet someone in London.' But his mother pursed her lips and shrugged her shoulders: she did not see how Kicky could afford to keep his sister as well as his wife.

'Oh, mamma dearest, don't let's look for the clouds till they are on us,' he said in despair. 'Things must come all right for us in the end. As long as my eye does not fail me we need none of us starve.'

'I've had another letter from Eugène,' she persisted, 'wanting to borrow five thousand francs. I haven't five thousand francs in the world.'

'I sent him three quid last week,' said Kicky wearily. 'He wrote back saying we none of us do anything for him and he is going out to Mexico or somewhere. What he thinks he is going to do in Mexico the Lord only knows.'

'He has brought everything on himself by his carelessness and folly,' said his mother. 'Had he worked at his profession he might be a lieutenant by now. It's too late now; he will never make anything of himself.'

'If only I were rich . . .' began Kicky.

'If you were rich you would see that your mother lived in comfort before anyone else,' said Ellen.

Kicky was silent, and thought of the patient Emma waiting for him in London.

'Even the smallest sum would be a help to us these days,' she went on. 'We eat such wretched dinners, and never touch wine, as you know, though I long for it often, and Isobel has been so weak from the want of it and the bad nourishment that she cannot study the piano properly – to say nothing of her never having had the means to have a master since she was twelve years old.

'As to our linen, I have none at all, and we owe several unpleasant bills in Düsseldorf. However, dear boy, I don't want to think of anything but your future happiness, and if marriage is to restore your spirits, why, marry you must. All I hope is that the position will not be too much for you.'

'Emma is very careful; she will spend nothing,' said Kicky swiftly.

'No, but you must remember she is an only daughter, and

is accustomed to think of her little comforts, and if she does not, why, her mamma will see that she gets them. Has Mr Wightwick made up his mind what to give her yet?'

'I think it's enough if he gives me his daughter, mamma.'

'My dear Kicky, I have nothing to say against Emma; she is an excellent girl, though, as to intellect, no companion at all to you, I should say; but to think old Mr Wightwick generous when the generosity is all on your side! You who could have married so well! Take the eldest Miss Lewis, for example. And when I think of the thousands of gentlemen's daughters, beautiful and accomplished, who can't find husbands, it makes me rather indignant, to say the least of it, that the Wightwicks should be favoured, and then not give a sou in return.'

'Look here, old lady, do you know what the clergyman in those rooms on the ground floor said about you to me last night?'

'Something impudent, I'll be bound.'

'He said, "Mrs du Maurier can't swallow the idea of her son's marriage, but I never knew the mother who could!"'

'That clergyman is an exceptionally disagreeable man, and has had his knife into me ever since Isobel refused to take tea with him, but went to a concert with Georgina and two of the young princes instead. He thinks it was all my doing.'

'And wasn't it?'

'All I said to Isobel was that tea with a penniless young clergyman who had no prospect of a living in England led nowhere. But, at a concert with a German prince, you never knew . . .'

Kicky laughed, and patted her hand. 'You're an incorrigible old matchmaker where Isobel is concerned. I only wish you'd be the same with me. Never mind, mamma; when you hold your first grandchild on your knee you will be reconciled.'

'When I was young, such subjects were never discussed before marriage,' said Ellen.

'Why, I've drawn pictures of 'em already,' said Kicky, 'all with big blue eyes and curly heads like angels.'

'I trust you have not shown them to Emma.'

'Indeed I have. She has them framed in her room.'

'Then the sooner you get married the better,' said Ellen, clicking her tongue.

Kicky returned to London in better spirits, and went down to Ramsgate for a fortnight with Emma and her parents. They seemed on better terms than usual – perhaps the sea air had a good effect on their tempers – and the atmosphere was without the usual strain. Emma was looking lovely, and had recovered her lost weight, Kicky was determined to be married early the following year without fail, if he strained every nerve in the attempt to make money. The Wightwicks insisted that he must have two hundred pounds in the bank before they let Emma go to him, and with luck he should have this sum by the spring. *Punch* was giving him plenty of work; in one week he had seven initial letters to do, and two social studies to illustrate, and he wondered whether he could pluck up the courage to ask Mark Lemon, the editor, whether he would definitely give him an order every week, as he wanted to be married. Two initials and one social would bring in enough money to pay the rent of an apartment and keep Emma and himself in the bargain; besides, there was what he might get from other papers – *Once A Week*, and the *Cornhill*, and *London Society*.

Mark Lemon was human, and he was fond of this hard-working young fellow who produced such talented work with one eye, and he agreed to do what he could for Kicky. He even hinted that if Kicky's work continued to improve as fast as it did at the moment, he should join the staff of *Punch* on the next vacancy. Such an ideal was beyond Kicky's wildest dreams. He stammered his thanks and stumbled from the room with his brain on fire.

He went straight to the Wightwicks' house and told them what Mark Lemon had said. There was surely no reason now why he and Emma should not be married in the New Year. Old Wightwick blew his nose loudly and his wife looked tearful, but Emma took Kicky's arm calmly and firmly and said he was perfectly right; neither of them could bear to wait any longer; she at any rate was not afraid of the future, and he had only to name the day.

The Wightwicks could not stand up against the determination of the young people, and the wedding was looked upon as fixed.

The next few months passed rapidly, with Kicky hard at work saving for his future home, and Emma taking lessons in book-keeping.

They found rooms in Great Russell Street, just opposite the British Museum, on a second floor and partly furnished, with an extra room as a studio for Kicky. The third of January was tentatively fixed upon as the date of the wedding. As the time drew nearer, Kicky began to feel almost like a criminal in taking away an only daughter from her parents. From the expression on their faces they might be preparing for a funeral. The atmosphere of the house was heavy with gloom, and Emma and Kicky padded through the tears in goloshes and carrying umbrellas.

'I swear I'll be a most dutiful son-in-law,' Kicky told Tom Armstrong. 'But as *maman belle-mère* and I have not one point of sympathy together, the task won't be quite so easy and delightful as it might have been. However, when we all see a little less of each other we shall get on very well.'

His mother and Isobel would not be able to get over to England for the ceremony – the expense was too great – but Kicky hoped to take his bride over to see them in the spring. Perhaps if he worked hard, and things went well, he could afford in a few years to have them in London.

The wedding was to be a very quiet affair, with one or two personal friends. Tom Armstrong was to be best man, of course, and Poynter would be there, Tom Jeckell, and Bill Henley, with whom Kicky had been sharing rooms ever since he left the Whistler ménage. The old Wightwicks would represent Emma's side of the church, with a couple of cousins and two Miss Levies.

The wedding would be in the morning, with lunch afterwards at the Wightwicks', and then Kicky and Emma would catch the boat to Boulogne for a week's honeymoon. 'Only a week to go,' said Kicky at Christmas, 'and I'm so damned excited that I can't draw a stroke.'

The presents came rolling in: a dinner service, a tea service, and a dessert service; plate and linen; silver teapots, and a substantial sofa. The *pièce de résistance*, perhaps, was the piano, on which Kicky would be able to strum with one finger and sing 'Vin à Quatre Sous' when his friends came to dinner.

Old Wightwick would allow his daughter forty pounds a year for dress after all, but, as she said to Kicky, 'Of course I shan't spend it on myself.'

Her father gave her the bedroom furniture into the bargain, besides curtains and carpets, so that Ellen in Germany could not complain of his generosity.

The great day dawned at last, but with the disappointment that Tom Armstrong was unable to be present, through illness, and an erstwhile admirer of Isobel's, Douglas Fisher, took his place as best man.

There were seventeen people altogether in the church, and the sobs of Mrs Wightwick resounded to the rafters. It was just as well, perhaps, that Ellen was not there to keep her company. Kicky had eyes for no one but Emma, and when he took her hand and held it, and she looked up at him gravely from behind her veil, he knew that the twenty-nine years that lay behind him counted as nothing in his life; they were buried and forgotten, and this was the beginning.

He would never know loneliness or poverty again. The bad days were over and he had cast his troubles to the four winds. Sometimes he would be baffled and perplexed; little spiritual problems would vex his mind; and the whys and wherefores of existence would be a knot he would never unravel; but, however despondent he might become, and however fearful, she would be there to stand by his side and hold his hand, as she was doing now.

This was a companionship that would continue until death; they would never be separated, nor pass one night away from one another.

The work he had done until now was trivial and counted as nothing. He knew that success would begin with his marriage. He would never be a painter now – that much he understood; he would never create great masterpieces for posterity. He would depict the humbler life of day by day. He would reflect the spirit of the Victorian age in which he lived.

They would be laughed over and loved, those drawings of his that were to decorate the pages of *Punch* until his death. How he would satirise society – kindly, quizzically, with his tongue in his cheek! The hostess and her social bloomers, the snob and his atrocious pomposities, the poet and his artistic extravagance. His men and women were so frail, so human, and because of their failings more lovable. The children, with their blundering *faux pas* and exquisite nonsense, were all the children that have ever been. For over thirty years Kicky was to delight his little world with his talent. The seed of genius, that had struggled in vain in his father Louis-Mathurin, awoke to maturity in him and found expression.

In Emma he found the perfect companion, the just balance to his nature. Whatever carelessness had been in him, whatever bitterness or lack of strength, went from him on his marriage and never returned. He had no enemy in the world, which was perhaps the greatest tribute to his character.

When success came to him in full measure, he remained unspoilt, and received it with humility. He was even a little puzzled. 'Why make such a deuce of a fuss over a fellow like me?' he would say, and shake his head, and frown, and hum a tune under his breath. The hysterical praise awarded to his novel *Trilby* even alarmed him. It was rather vulgar. Not very good form. He was certain the book did not deserve it, either. It was kind of people to write letters by every post, but they really should not have taken the trouble. Extremely gracious of everyone to ask him out to dinner, but he would much rather dine quietly at home with his family and a few boon companions.

The happy thing about success was that it meant he could provide for his children and his grandchildren, and they would none of them know want and dire poverty as he had done. He would take care that there would be enough for all of them when he died – enough for distant cousins and little grand-nephews and the straggling remnants of the Busson clan.

Funny that the fortune he would build up, and which would embrace so many of them, sprang from that first ten pounds his mother gave him – ten pounds from her annuity, the annuity that Mary Anne won with her determination and her wit. A stroke of a pen in 1809 decided the fate of so many little unborn men and women. A crude and rather sordid bargain between a prince and a prostitute started a cluster of threads that stretched their way across the world and set so many puppets dancing, some happily, some wearily, but all with an infinitesimal shrug of the shoulder and the ghost of a smile.

The du Mauriers have streaks in common, even the distant branches down to the third and fourth generation who no longer bear the name.

They hover between incurable optimism and profound despair. They laugh immoderately and cry without reason. The saving of money is not their strongest quality. They squander when and what they can, much as Louis-Mathurin did before any of them were born. They have a certain bitterness of tongue at times which echoes strangely in the air like the voice of Ellen Clarke.

One or two have been wanton, and the smile of Mary Anne passes across their tip-tilted features like a memory of what has been.

They are, generally speaking, easy to look at and easy to like. Their hearts are large, like their purses which contain so little, and their sense of humour is apt to be warped and tinged with satire.

They lie with grace and confidence, as Gyggy did before them, and are forgiven just as easily. They die before middle age, often rather painfully, and are soon forgotten. But they leave behind them a dim fragrance of their presence, like a whisper in the air.

Kicky was the wisest of them, the kindest and the best, and his story has already been told. And did his mother ever reconcile herself to his marriage, and look upon Emma with a calm, forgiving eye? She did more than this; she came over to London after their second child was born, and lived in rooms near them until her death in 1870. Kicky used to visit her every day. She had her little grumbles, of course, and found the children atrociously spoilt, especially Trixie, Kicky's first-born, and she thought Emma might manage her home better, paying as she did too much for groceries, and one thing and another. However, far be it from her to interfere: she could see that Mrs du Maurier was a very different person from inexperienced Miss Wightwick. She was glad to see Kicky getting on so well, but a married son is very different from a single one, and it was not her place to grumble if his home took up all his time.

'At our age, my dear Louise,' she wrote to her sister-in-law at Versailles, 'we cannot form new ties and we can only care about our own relations. There are few of us now remaining, and heaven knows when you and I shall ever meet again.' They never did, Louise, crippled entirely with her rheumatism and unable to write, had but one or two years to live, and passed away at Versailles in the sainted atmosphere of the convent she knew so well.

When Ellen died, rather suddenly, at the age of seventy-three, her son drew a picture of her as she lay asleep. The face is stern, even in repose, beneath the lace cap, and the Roman nose gives her the air of a warrior. It is a noble face, free from

311

pettiness and envy, and these qualities must have been surface ones, passing at death as though they had never been. She looks a true matriarch, and the mother of sons. There is no trace upon her features of that gay, inconsequent Mary Anne who gave her birth. No grain of likeness is between them, and her only inheritance was her sharp tongue.

Who was her father no one will ever know. It is easy to picture a man of firm principles, of intelligence, of rather narrow mind, and whose temper was not his easiest quality. As the servant said in those mud-flinging days of 1809, her father may have been a duke or a dustman. He was probably an honest tradesman of middle class, beguiled by Mary Anne into a moment's folly.

Ellen was buried beside Louis-Mathurin in the Abney Park Cemetery, and their tombstone was restored only the other day, having fallen into neglect since the last century.

What of the gentle Isobel? Did she ever find herself a husband? She did, at long last, but it was not Tom Armstrong, as might be supposed.

She married Clement Scott, the dramatic critic, and might have been happier had she stayed single. Their union was not a very smooth or even one, and little frowns of worry appeared on her face when her children were quite young. Perhaps she had left her heart behind in Düsseldorf, or maybe there was someone in her life that counted and could not be won, but, like all Victorian women, she hid her sorrows with a brave face. She had two sons and two daughters. The bad, irrepressible Gyggy left the Army in 1867 and married a French girl. He came to England and smilingly asked his brother to find him a job. Kicky, who had become very English by then and rather London society, was just the slightest bit abashed by this ex-corporal with the French accent, who wore the wrong kind of clothes and the most atrocious shoes, and wanted to know how many lords Kicky counted amongst his friends. Kicky lent him money, of course, and said there was a home for him in his house whenever he wanted one, and they talked about Paris and their boyhood with laughter and tears. And then Gyggy wandered from one situation to another, as many du Mauriers have done since, without any aim and with very little profit, his longest period of activity being some years of employment as a commercial traveller of sorts. His wife, Marie, presented him with two daughters and a son, and the son took a leaf out of his father's book and was a rebel from the start, running away from home while still in his teens and never returning. He is farming somewhere in the wilds of Canada to-day. Gyggy and Isobel died within a year of one another, and were buried together down at Saltash, in Cornwall.

As to the fair and frivolous Georgie, she did not come to a bad end, as her relations predicted. Nor did she make a home with the princes of Düsseldorf. She astonished all her friends and her family by 'finding the Lord', and joining – of all incredible institutions – the Salvation Army!

The golden-haired siren who had fluttered her lashes at Prussian royalty, and even made the gentle Kicky's heart beat a little faster, donned a poke bonnet and took a hymnal in her hand, and lifted her voice at street corners to the glory of God and Georgina Clarke. 'Are you saved?' she questioned the unwary passer-by, and the passer-by, rather than argue with so formidable an opponent, assented hastily and escaped her tenacious fingers. She outlived all her contemporaries, and her contemporaries' children, dying at ninety-five or some tremendous age, having survived the Great War without turning a hair. Her son Bobbie became rather a pompous individual, marrying late in life like his father before him.

The Clarkes to this day are proud of their Roman noses, and so are one or two scattered branches of the du Mauriers, but – alas for their illusions! – a slight research into the question of dates would enlighten them to the fact that ancestress Mary Anne did not meet His Royal Highness the Duke of York until the year 1803, when her son George was nine at least, and Ellen about six.

George was almost certainly a *bona fide* Clarke, but Ellen, with a little stretch of imagination, can be anyone.

So they pass out of memory and out of these pages, the figures of fifty, of a hundred years ago. Some of them were comic, and some a little tragic, and all of them had faults, but once they were living, breathing men and women like the rest of us, possessing the world that we possess to-day.

Whether immortality is true, or is a theory invented by man as a sop to his natural fear, none of us will ever know; but it is consoling and rather tender to imagine that when we die we leave something of ourselves, like the wake of a vessel, as a reminder that once we passed this way.

There are footprints in the sand, and the mark of a hand upon a wall. There are flowers pressed between the pages of a book, colourless and flat, to which a dim fragrance clings. There are letters, crumpled and yellow with age, but the message they bring stares up at the reader with vital, living force, as though they were penned yesterday. Ghosts there are in plenty – not phantoms with pale faces trailing their chains into eternity, not headless horrors creaking upon the boards of lonely houses, but the happy shadow-ghosts of what has been, no more fearful than the blurred photographs in the family album.

Whoever has loved much, felt deeply, trodden a certain path in happiness or pain, leaves an imprint of himself for evermore.

There are echoes for those who care to listen, and visions for him who dreams. There are scents that linger in the air, and whispers of the years that are gone. When the turmoil of the present day becomes like thunder in the ears, and the strain of modern life a burden too heavy to be borne, it is pleasant to shut out sound and sight and lose oneself in that silent shadow-world that marches a hand's breadth from our own.

There is a light rumble of painted wheels, and a carriage bowls past along the broad white road to Richmond. Mary Anne leans in her corner, her parasol protects her from the sun, and while my Lord Folkestone surveys her beneath heavy

314

lids, his chin upon his cane, she fires at him a torrent of abuse for his drunkenness at table the night before. She uses gutter language; the ears of the coachman are pink, for her voice has a carrying quality, but my Lord Folkestone does not care. He has never seen her look so handsome, her brown eyes flashing, and a loose curl escaping from her ridiculous bonnet.

He lets her run on, and then he attempts pacification – recounting some story he heard that morning at White's – and in a moment she has forgotten her anger; she wrinkles her tip-tilted nose, and the laugh that echoes down the Richmond road is exquisite in its pure vulgarity, the true, genuine gutter laugh of the ideal woman, slum-born, slum-bred, earth-bound to eternity. The yellow carriage vanishes in the distance in a cloud of dust, but the laughter lingers.

A sallow child waits for her mother's return at a bedroom window, her shoulders a little hunched, the mark of disapproval showing already upon her small plain face; and there is an air of shocked displeasure about that house to-day as it stands in Westbourne Place – doomed to destruction next year, no doubt, to make room for a monster block of flats – as though it would cover its riotous past with prim lace curtains and staid respectability.

Perhaps at midnight it relaxes, and anyone who listens very carefully may hear a splintering sound, for all the world like twenty wine-glasses shivering to fragments and falling upon a parquet floor.

In Paris, where to-day the newsboys scream *L'Intransigeant* at six o'clock and the trams and buses clang their way across the city, there was once a narrow cobbled street called the rue de la Lune. It is no longer recognisable as such, particularly in the rush hours of the day, but, maybe, in the very early hours, before they come to water the street, there is a hush upon the quarter, and a certain silence that is not so very different from a hundred years ago. Louise Busson patters down it on her way to early Mass, her smooth fair hair parted in the middle, her heart beating a little faster than usual in hopes there should be a letter from Godfrey Wallace on her return.

She looks young and immature, and very much as Isabella did thirty years later, though there is more gravity in her expression.

Round and round the Jardins du Roi paces a tall, square-shouldered figure with crazy blue eyes and flaming hair. It is Louis-Mathurin. He has not been to bed all night, but has been walking the streets since midnight on the track of a new invention. Sometimes he talks aloud to himself, and sometimes he frowns, and once – when he thinks he has solved his problem – he snaps his fingers in the air and laughs, and, throwing back his head, he sings from sheer exuberance of living, and because he is young and because the hundred francs in his pocket do not belong to him.

It is a little hard for these ghosts in modern Paris; their footways are destroyed and the houses that were theirs are now offices or shops.

Eugénie de Palmella cannot peep out of the windows of the *pension* in the rue Neuve St Étienne because the building no longer exists. Her descendants live to-day in Portugal among the great nobility, but it is extremely doubtful if they have ever heard of the du Maurier family, although Louise Busson was their great-grandmother's oldest friend.

The house in the rue de Passy cannot be traced either. Kicky tried to find it in 1887. They had built all over the enchanted garden, and in the Bois his beloved Mare d'Auteuil had become an artificial lake with horrible little rustic bridges and grotesque arches spoiling its natural symmetry. Even the school where Monsieur Froussard scolded Gyggy for his *caractère léger*, and Kicky tried so hard to be funny and failed, has blown itself into oblivion.

One day it would be nice to visit Malines, that sleepy town of churches, and walk the dull, straight roads that Kicky walked when his blindness first came upon him. And travel east to

Düsseldorf, to see what gaiety remains. There may be cafés there now where the frivolous Georgina chinked glasses with the German princes, and Isobel sat beside her, her nose just the tiniest bit out of joint.

It is to be hoped that Ellen did not leave too much of her worry and anxiety in the parlour of the lodgings where she lived, or other mothers, trailing out to gay Düsseldorf with their unmarried daughters, might catch something of the complaint, and, in a high fever of distress, find their horizon bounded by line after line of eligible young men, all prospective husbands, who in the furtive manner of their kind hover on the borderline of intimacy but never cross the threshold to be caught.

How badly Kicky behaved to the elder Miss Lewis is a question that cannot be answered. He swore his conscience was clear on the matter. And in a year or so it did not matter so much after all, because she married herself to one of the landed gentry and became mistress of a Welsh estate, which suited her much better than had she become the wife of an impecunious artist with one eye.

Houses and gardens can be destroyed, and cities become rearing things of horror compared with what they were, but the sea at least is unchanging, and the ghosts may wander upon it as they will. Kicky, and Kicky's descendants, hover in their characteristics between England and France, as do all hybrids who possess the blood of two countries in their veins, and the last picture in the scrapbook of memories is the one most often touched and looked upon.

The steamer is going to Boulogne, and in the bows of the vessel are two figures with their faces turned to France. It is Kicky and Emma starting out upon their honeymoon, with the future before them, and he is singing her one of his father's songs.

Virago

MARY ANNE

Daphne du Maurier

With an Introduction by Lisa Hilton

In Regency London, the only way for a woman to succeed is to beat men at their own game. So when Mary Anne Clarke seeks an escape from her squalid surroundings in Bowling Inn Alley, she ventures first into the scurrilous world of the pamphleteers. Her personal charms are such, however, that before long she comes to the notice of the Duke of York.

With her taste for luxury and power, Mary Anne, now a royal mistress, must aim higher. Her lofty connections allow her to establish a thriving trade in military commissions, provoking a scandal that rocks the government – and brings personal disgrace.

A vivid portrait of overweening ambition, Mary Anne is set during the Napoleonic Wars and based on du Maurier's own great-great-grandmother.

'With unfailing du Maurier skill, the author has coupled family interest with dramatic sense'   Elizabeth Bowen, *Tatler*

Virago

FRENCHMAN'S CREEK

Daphne du Maurier

With an Introduction by Julie Myerson

Lady Dona St Columb is beautiful, headstrong – and bored. Desperate to escape the pomp and ritual of the Restoration Court, she retreats to the hidden creeks and secret woods of the family estate at Navron, in Cornwall. Though renowned for her passionate engagement with life, privately she yearns for freedom, integrity and love – whatever the cost.

The peace Lady Dona craves, however, eludes her from the moment she stumbles across the mooring-place of a white-sailed ship that plunders the Cornish coast. And as she becomes embroiled in a plot to steal another ship from under the nose of the English authorities, she realises that her own heart is under seige from the French philosopher-pirate, Jean Aubrey . . .

'A storyteller of cunning and genius'   Sally Beauman

**You can order other Virago titles through our website: *www.virago.co.uk*
or by using the order form below**